The
TRADING
SYSTEMS
TOOLKIT

**How to Build,
Test and Apply
Money-Making
Stock and Futures
Trading Systems**

JOE KRUTSINGER

IRWIN
Professional Publishing®
Chicago • London • Singapore

ISBN 1-55738-534-3

Printed in the United States of America

BB

     6 7 8 9 0

CB/BJS

Disclaimer Regarding the Many Systems and Performance Results Illustrated in This Book

Hypothetical or simulated performance results have certain inherent limitations. Unlike an actual performance record, simulated results do not represent actual trading. Also, since the trades illustrated in this book have not been executed, the results may have under- or over-compensated for the impact, if any, of certain market factors, such as lack of liquidity. Simulated trading programs in general are also subject to the fact that they are designed with the benefit of hindsight. No representation is being made that any account will or is likely to achieve profits or losses similar to those shown. The use of stop orders does not guarantee limited loss. There is a risk of loss in futures trading.

Mr. Krutsinger is not advising or soliciting anyone to trade or use any system illustrated in this book. These are educational examples of the art of system writing and development that he wants to share with you. None of the information illustrated in these examples is to be construed as offers to buy or sell futures. Each of the hypothetical performances in the illustrations assumes one contract of the commodity traded and $55 per round turn for brokerage commission and slippage. None of the information illustrated purports to be a complete statement of all material facts relating to futures.

We gratefully acknowledge Omega Research, Inc., for permitting reproduction of the illustrated results produced by TradeStation™ software. Omega Research, Inc., is in no way associated with or responsible for these results.

ACKNOWLEDGMENTS

Technical Traders Guide to Computer Analysis of the Future Market
© Charles Lebeau & David W. Lucas, 1992

SystemWriter™ & TradeStation™
Omega Research, Inc.
9200 Sunset Drive, Miami, FL 33173
800-556-2022

Portana
Tom Berry
P.O. Box 433, Greensboro, NC 27404
919-687-0240

One Day at a Time
Frank Wilder
P.O. Box 128, McLeansvill, NC 27301
919-292-1402

Dedication

Everyone knows what happened yesterday.
Most of us have hopes for tomorrow.
We all must live today.

This book is dedicated to the one who has made my yesterdays memorable, my tomorrows hopeful, and today lively. My partner, my wife, Caren Lynne Krutsinger.

Table of Contents

TABLE OF CONTENTS

TABLE OF CONTENTS

Foreword

It's hardly fair.

Those of us who develop commodity trading systems have had a real monopoly on their development over the last few years. Joe Krutsinger has changed all that with the book you are about to read. Our monopoly has been broken . . . you will now be able to do what we do.

Let me tell you, our monopoly couldn't have been broken by a better person. I've watched Joe develop over the years as a trader and system developer and assure you he's already been through the walls of fire that you don't want to plunge through.

He will give you the benefit of his experience by teaching you the three most important aspects of understanding how the markets work. Certainly, it's not enough to just have a computer and some software to randomly generate numbers. Sadly, there are many people passing as system developers who do just that.

You will soon see that is not the case with Joe. Why? Because Joe has been through it all. As a broker he learned the mechanical functions of how the market operates, what orders you can use, why slippage occurs.

As a trader he's had big wins (ask him about the mansion he built with his first big hit) as well as some losses that acted as a learning experience.

Above and beyond all this, though, Joe has mastered the art of using a computer. Thus he's been able to synthesize trading with research. When I have problems writing systems, I call Joe. It's as simple as that. Now, you get to tap into his great knowledge: knowledge of the markets, knowledge of trading, and knowledge of how to research it all and build viable trading systems with a computer.

For 18 years I've trekked the highways of commodity trading system development. On that road I've been fortunate enough to meet some very bright people, and some very good people.

Joe Krutsinger, as you will soon see, is very bright. I hope your path crosses his on this road and you will discover he is also a very good man.

Larry Williams

Preface

*How many good books suffer neglect
through the inefficiency of their beginnings!*
— Edgar Allen Poe —

This book is not only for people who know how to write trading systems and just want to learn some different ideas, but for people who have never written a trading system. If you think system writing is too complicated for you, you are wrong. Writing trading systems is not difficult. Following trading systems, however, is difficult. Implementation is the *key* to all trading systems.

Trading systems normally only have three parts: where to get in, where to get out with a profit, and where to get out with a loss. The major key to remember is: Have a mission statement. Have an idea of what it is you are trying to accomplish with your trading system.

When you feel that you have a certain trading idea, the best way to write it is to take a blank piece of paper and write down exactly what it is you are trying to accomplish with this trading system and exactly step-by-step how you would like to do it. A good way to visualize this is to pretend you have a magic computer. All you have to do is tell the computer what you are trying to accomplish and what steps you would like to go through to get a certain result. Write that down on a piece of paper and you will be well ahead on your quest for your trading system.

Chapters 1 to 5 of this book are pretty easy: Do as I say. These chapters describe trading systems, and how you can go about devising your own systems.

Chapters 6 to 9 discuss several trading systems, their track records, their Portana, if available, which shows their quarterly profit and loss, their daily equity curve if available, and most importantly, the actual code used for either TradeStation or SystemWriter, so you can duplicate those results.

Remember, the trading systems in this book are not written as stand-alone trading systems for you to go out and put your money on. They are written as educational examples in the art of system writing to show you how you can take some of my code and some of your ideas and put them together to form your own trading systems—ones you are comfortable with, ones you know all the intricacies of, and ones you can actually follow. Without further ado, let's get started. . . .

Acknowledgments

Joel Robbins for his vision, Larry Williams for his encouragement, Ralph and Bill Cruz for their leadership in the field of system writing, and the hundreds of friends and clients who have attended my workshops over the years and encouraged my efforts.

Do Trading Systems Work?

Life can only be understood backwards;
but it must be lived forwards.
— Soren Kirkegaard —

Discretionary Trading versus Systematic Trading

Some traders use a trading system and some don't. That's pretty basic, and that is what this book is about: the traders who use systems. Trading systems, to my way of thinking, are futures, options, and stock trading design models. They are systematic ways to trade any of those markets.

The traders who do not use a trading system are *discretionary traders*. This kind of trader uses observation and instinct. A discretionary trader can look out the window and think, "Boy, it is hot and dry today. I think corn is going up. Let's buy some." Discretionary trading is also gathering information, reading the newspaper, listening to the radio, taking a look at your charts, and then saying, "It's time to buy bellies and wear diamonds. This thing is going up forever. That's all we've got to do. Bellies are cheaper than hogs. This hasn't happened in 35 years. I'm going to buy bellies, buy bellies, buy bellies." That's discretionary trading.

The one major disadvantage to discretionary trading is that you can never admit that you are wrong. If your market gets a little cheaper, that's great. "Hey! It's cheaper! Let's buy some more!" On the other hand, if your market goes up a little bit, you can say, "I didn't get enough. I'm going to buy some more." Eventually you'll get caught with this kind of trade, because you will have too many on at the wrong time. This is usually the fate of the discretionary trader.

The Systematic Approach

The advantage of systems trading is that it tries to take some of the emotion out of the market. Maybe you don't know this, but 90 percent of the futures traders quit a loser. Eighty to 90 percent of them will jump on the bandwagon of a new system and trade it until they get three losers in a row. They will change from system to system to system taking three losers in a row with each until they get discouraged and quit or lose their capital. Most good trading systems win only 40–50 percent of the time.

Statistically, most commodity traders quit after nine or ten trades, but few quit after nine or ten trades in the same system.

The Fundamentals

This is a simple book which covers a complex topic. I am attempting to teach you how to develop a trading system in a simple manner. There are going to be much more elaborate, more sophisticated things for you to do in the future. I hope you outgrow this basic book. However, for now, you need to learn the fundamentals. I believe this should be the first step when you start any new field of endeavor.

Ten Steps to Remember

A trading system design is a ten-step process:

1. **Know** which commodities you feel comfortable with and can afford to trade.

2. **Learn** all you can about these commodities, so you will know which indicators to look for.

3. **Design** a trading system around your knowledge, to please you.

4. **Test** your system for flaws before you trade realtime.

5. **Decide** when to get into the market (market entry).

6. **Decide** when to get out with a win.

7. **Decide** when to get out with a loss.

8. **Implement** your trading system.

9. **Fine tune** your trading system and continually evaluate your system.

10. **Be assured** that your system will fade over time, so you should constantly design a new system.

My First Trading System

To illustrate the first step, I want to tell you about my first trading system. I think you will get a kick out of it, because it was not technical. I had been in the commodities business for about three months, and I had two clients.

One was a corn hedger, whose idea of corn hedging was if you had a lot in the bin, you should buy more, because you couldn't have enough.

CHAPTER 1

Homer, my second client, was a speculator. That's a dirty word, I suppose, but Homer had $2,000 in 1976. He said, "Joe, I'll do anything you want to do, but when that $2,000 is gone, I'm gone."

Since I was determined to "make it" in the commodities business, I knew I was up against the odds. I also knew that I could not learn the entire business at once, so I decided to specialize.

I made up my mind to learn one commodity at a time. What should I study first? The financials? Meats? Grains? For my first venture I decided to learn everything I could about soybean meal.

My thinking was this: I was living in Des Moines, Iowa, and soybean meal would be attractive to anyone who grew soybeans. If a guy grew corn, I could talk to him about the substitute capabilities of soybean meal. Hog raisers would be interested in soybean meal. In short, soybean meal was a commodity I could talk about with almost everyone.

Someone would ask me, "What do you think about the sugar market, Joe?" and I'd say, "I don't know much about that, but let me tell you about soybean meal." That was my standard comeback.

After I learned everything I possibly could about soybean meal, I decided it was going to rise. The fundamentalists said it was, and what I had learned about charting said it was, so I devised a system. It was my very first one, and I am going to explain it to you:

I took all the money we had, which was $2,000, and bought two contracts of soybean meal. The margin was $1,000. I put a stop on each of them at $1,000 from where we bought them. If the stop was hit we would lose all the money.

It happened to work because the day after I bought these contracts, soybean meal went limit up. Quite frankly, I did not know too much about the commodities market at this time. However, I had learned everything I could about soybean meal, and I felt committed that meal was going up.

I knew that if I had excess money in the account I could buy more contracts. Meal went limit up and I saw that we had excess money in the account, so I decided to buy Homer more meal. Remember, I was a novice.

I did not know you could not trade a commodity when it is limit up. I kept calling the floor until I found a month that was not limit up, because in those days there were tax spreads. (There was always a back month that was trading a little bit.)

Most people did not even have the back months on their board. I just kept calling and saying, "Is there an October meal?" They said, "Yes, but it's almost limit up."

"Okay," I'd say. "Put in an order to buy one at the market. Is there a December meal?"

"Yeah."

"Well, buy one of those at the market."

I was diversifying!

(Have you ever heard the old saying that God takes care of fools and children? At this time I was very young.) The soybean meal kept running limit up every day, and we continued to buy more and more and more soybean meal in the back months. Eventually, back months became front months. In 11 weeks we had run up our $2,000 soybean meal account to over $93,000, and I had stops in every position.

Then it did something it sometimes does in Iowa; it rained. As the rain came down, soybean meal came down. It went limit, limit, and they knocked us out. When I cleared out all the orders we had $34,000 in cash left and no soybean meal position.

I called Homer and said, "We've had a very good run, but all I know is soybean meal and I think we should be out of it now. I'm having Chicago write you a check for $34,000. I hope we can do business again sometime."

Homer said, "Okay," and hung up. He never took my calls again, and later I discovered that he told everybody he ever met that Joe Krutsinger had lost him over $60,000 in the meal market!

The Contradiction of Systematic Trading

This was my first inkling of the contradiction of systematic trading. I thought I had done a great job. I had taken Homer from two grand to 34 grand in 11 weeks. Homer thought I had done a poor job because at one time we had $93,000. We were swinging for the fences.

So you might think that a logical next response to this story would be, "let's do what the star traders do." Let's use their systems. There are many more trading systems out there than there are star traders. Why? Because

5

star traders don't use systems. Think about all the people you know who have made and kept money in commodities. These are the star traders, and there are very few of them.

A star trader who comes to mind is a personal friend of mine. He took $10,000 in a trading contest to $1,100,000. I have not done it, and you have not done it. That is about as good as it gets in commodities.

But let me tell you the dark side of this story. He really took the $10,000 to $2,400,000, then $2,400,000 to $1,100,000. Do you understand the difference? A $1,300,000 drawdown is a big drawdown in anybody's book!

You have to be able to stand drawdown. Star traders can do it; most of us cannot, so we really should use a system.

Whether you go with a commercial system or a system you design yourself, it must take everything into account.

If you have not made a million dollars in trading; or if you have, but you still would like to control drawdown, read on.

2

Trading System Basics: Market Entry, Exit with Profit, Exit with Loss

Less is more.
— Robert Browning —

The Big Three Decisions

There are three building blocks in any system: market entry, exit with a profit, and exit with a loss. Identifying these and making decisions about them is a key element in a successful trading system. Anybody who tries to tell you there is much more to a system is kidding you. Before you trade, keep asking yourself: Where should I get into the market? Where should I get out with a profit? And where should I get out with a loss? You need to know the answer to all three of these questions before you trade. If you know the answer to only one or two, you do not have a complete trading system.

Market Entry

The key to system development is to combine long-term, intermediate-term, and short-term indicators in the best possible way. To determine the long-term trend, you need to measure weeks and months of price action. Moving averages and trendline analysis usually work pretty well for this purpose.

For intermediate signals, you have to look at the last few days of price action. Some of the more reliable indicators include DMI crossovers, channel breakouts, parabolic signals, trendline violations, point and figure studies, and pattern recognition methods.

If your long-term and intermediate indicators say it's time to get into the market, you then have to time your entry point. There are a variety of possible approaches—many of which I discuss later in the book. The key is to get in at a point that reduces the possibility of a countertrend move that will prematurely force you out of your position.

Timing the Exit

Although most traders focus their attention on entering the market, the key to profitable futures trading, in my mind, is knowing how to exit. Consider establishing a minimum acceptable profit level directly related to the amount being risked. If you risk $500, put in an objective of $1,000. This is your targeted exit. Closing out trades at a predetermined price objective is workable if you have a knack for picking targets with no regrets.

Why not use the highest price of the last 20 days as your price objective? If it reaches there, take your profit, step out, and let the market tell you when to get in again.

In review, we have taken a simple moving average concept which everybody knows, and said, "Here's a way to develop a constant stop *and* a constant price objective. I'll put my objective at the highest high of the last few days. I'll put my stop at the lowest low of the last few days, and I'll let the market be dynamic."

Compromise Exits

Some traders would trade two units—one with a close stop, and one with a far away stop. Not only does this require more capital, but you can suffer losses on both positions.

For one unit a trader should consider using an exit method with wide stops until the market is overbought or there is an unusually big run in his favor. Then he should tighten profit-taking stops. I personally like trailing stops at all times, and I will stay in the market until my stop or profit objective is hit.

Test Your Exit Proficiency

Most people concentrate on their entry signal, but your exit signal is important too. Make up a system that says, "If it's Monday, I'm going to buy at the market," then use different exit techniques to see which techniques work best with that system. Now freeze them, hold them to the side, and apply them to your favorite trading technique instead of just buying on Monday. This is a good way to test and find dynamic stops.

A Word about Stops

I love stops. Stops can get you out of losing trades, stops can get you out of winning trades, and stops can put you into a new trade. Some systems are stop and reversals where you are always either long or short.

Sometimes this makes me a little uncomfortable, but almost all of the big traders trade in the stop and reverse fashion. They are always either long or short. Many of us, especially in a whip-saw market, think that stop-reversal gets a little old because of the constant buying and selling.

Use long-term trends of weeks or months to determine the direction of the market. Use intermediate terms meaning the last few days and very short-term price action of yesterday or today to trigger the precise entry. This is the key to system development.

The Stop-Loss

I have written a little bit about some market entry techniques. Now I am going to examine the stop-loss. Remember the story of the three bears? One porridge was too cold, one porridge was too hot, and one porridge was just right!

A close stop is like hot porridge. It is a little too hot. It's a little too close. You may have small losses, modest total risk. Unfortunately though, you are stopped out of a lot of profitable trades, and you are stopped out often. Many people who start trading will start with very close stops because they think they are risking less money.

They trade frequently and lose their capital or they lose enough of it to lose confidence in their system. Then they trade with no stop at all. They go to a completely cold stop. They will think, "I won't trade with a stop for two or three days." Then they have a disaster, and they quit trading commodities.

There are a higher percentage of losing trades with close stops to gain an advantage of smaller average losses. One solution is to figure a re-entry method after you have been stopped out, but this can quite often chop you up. Increased activity leads to higher transaction costs and slippage.

Wide Stops

Wide stops, also called cold stops, often result in a high percentage of winning trades. I am certain you have seen systems that have won 75 percent to 80 percent of the time. Then all of a sudden they lose $3,000 on one contract, and the trader gives up. I have experience with this, and I want to explain what happens.

I had a system in realtime that had 42 consecutive winning trades. It blew up one of my commodity books. Those of you who are brokers know that when your book blows up it means your customers leave you, and you start over building a new book.

I had 156 individual clients, a lot for a commodities broker. Many of them had 42 consecutive winning trades, all in bonds. About 27 trades into this system clients would call me and say, "Joe, we have a problem."

I'd say, "What is it?"

And they would say, "The high of the day was 92.13, and you took us out at 92.07. What's wrong with the system?"

Or a guy would say, "You owe me some money."

I'd say, "Why is that?"

And he'd say, "You took us out at one o'clock today."

I'd say, "That's right. We had a profit and signal to exit with that profit."

Then he'd say, "Well, at 1:30 the president spoke and bonds went up 15 ticks. I figure you owe me another 15 ticks."

My most exciting call was the guy who said, "Joe, I just called the exchange and there is something you should know about bonds."

I said, "What's that?"

And he said, "You're trading one bond for every 6,000."

(Note: That was my matrix. As we made money and an account grew by $6,000, I would trade an additional contract. As we lost I would take contracts off. A $18,000 account would trade three contracts. A $24,000 account would trade four contracts.)

I said, "That's right."

Then he said, "I just talked to an exchange official and he said the current margin now is $2,000. I have a $20,000 account, so the exchange says you should be trading ten contracts!"

I had 156 phone calls of that type. Then all of a sudden we had a loss of ten ticks for a grand total of $312.50. That is a very small loss in bonds because bonds is a $100,000 instrument. To lose $312.50 trading a $100,000 instrument is not a big deal, but nevertheless, 25 percent of the clients quit. Obviously, the system was broken because we had 42 winners, and now we had a loser.

We had eight more winners, and then we had a big loser. It was $562.50. Why do I remember this number? At that time taking 20 percent of the profits was how I made my money. On that day another 25 percent of my clients quit, so it was a big losing day for me too.

Here is my record at that point: I had 52 trades with two losers, and 50 percent of my people were gone! I quit, and I traded for myself for a year and a half. So that's what can happen with wide stops. I had a high percentage of winning trades, my system controlled slippage and transaction fees, but it had a higher average loss per trade and a greater total risk.

The Ideal Stop

The ideal stop must be far enough outside the range of random price movements, yet close enough to control risks. You need to avoid short-term randomness. One way to do it is to place your stop one standard deviation from the entry. This is a simple way to go with moving averages. Most people know what moving averages are, and most traders use a moving average of the close.

If you are looking for an ideal simple stop why not say, "I'm going to take a moving average of the lows. If the price takes out the moving average of the lows, then I'm going to get out of my longs." That's a nice trailing stop that is dynamic with the market, and it is very simple to figure. Even the ideal stop-loss cannot guarantee limited loss. This is futures trading, and it is a grown-up's game.

3

How to Build and
Test a System

---

*Failure is, in a sense, the highway to success,
in as much as every discovery of what is false
leads us to seek earnestly after what is true.
— John Keats —*

Make a Plan

This Is Your Trading System

I believe in mission statements. We are going to identify the things that should be included in a good trading system, and then we are going to design one.

I want to emphasize that these are YOUR trading systems. What is good for me might not be good for you. Are you a short-term trader or a long-term trader? How much time do you want to spend today getting your trades ready for tomorrow? How much money can you afford to risk on a bad trading decision?

If you have a $10,000 to $15,000 account and a full-time job, then you probably want to look at a daily focus or a weekly focus, a focus you can use without interfering with your "real" job. You have probably heard the story about Jim, the guy who went to the bathroom with his Quotrek price receiver, so he could trade the stock indexes. Pretty soon Jim quit his job, so he could trade commodities full time.

He did pretty well. He made about $50,000 a year for 10 years trading the commodities market, but he used to make $60,000 a year at his job, and he had dental benefits, health insurance, and a pension. Now he has no dental benefits, no health insurance, no pension, and he has money at risk. I don't know about you, but I don't consider this a valid risk-taking decision.

When you pick a system you must decide what is right for you. Determine your temperament and preferences, your capital, your time restraints. Be sure to weigh each benefit against its cost. Most importantly, always assume there is a disadvantage to every benefit because there is.

Gathering Ideas from Commercial Systems

Looking into some of the better commercial systems can provide tangible evidence of successful systems and strategies to incorporate in your own system. If you want to look at the top ten commercial systems, you can look in *Futures* magazine. It features some systems that have been around for years.

Another good place to start is a book entitled *New Concepts in Commodities Trading* by Wells Wilder. This book was written in 1978. I will give you a little background on it. It has ten pretty good trading systems in it; three of them are still in the top 10 today, 16 years after the book's first publication! I suggest you take a look at that book. Look at Volatility systems. Look at Parabolic systems, and study these systems. You may say, "That's old stuff. I want new stuff," but do you really? These systems have been around for 16 years and have stood the test of time.

If you look at some of the well-known quotation equipment firms like Commodity Quote Graphics and Future Source, you will see that almost all of them have these systems built in. Why don't they include Joe's Jumpin' Index? Maybe it is because the systems they include have held up. They have a long track record.

LeBeau and Lucas have written an excellent trading textbook, *Computer Analysis of the Futures Market*, which should be included on everybody's shelf if a trader is seriously developing his or her own trading system.

Optimization

Optimization is finding the exact parameters that work the best. I will discuss briefly the Paul Revere system and Portana sheets here. (For a more detailed description, see Chapter 4.)

A Portana sheet looks like a SystemWriter sheet except for an added number, which is shown in Figure 3.1.

We're showing numbers starting at $20,000, making $221,000 worth of profit, and ending up with $241,000. Portana will let you analyze daily what your equity looks like (Figure 3.2).

Did you notice that there are two lines on this chart? With Paul Revere you buy at the highest high of the last six, sell at the lowest low of the last six, and you have a $1,000 stop. The bottom line is your total profit, not including your open trade equity. The squiggly line is the line including your open trade equity.

You can see what the dynamics are of a short-term system even though it is trading a long-term commodity. Would you agree that this is close to a 45-degree angle? Would you agree that it is a pretty healthy-looking equity curve?

Let me tell you a secret about systems. Most people will show you track records that are four or five years long. There is a reason. Let's take a look at that piece of the data and we can see (Figure 3.3). Gee! That looks great, but the drawdown was never over $4,000 or $5,000 during that period.

Figure 3.1—Paul Revere/Portana sheet

```
PAUL REVERE     03/03/75 to 12/31/92       C:\PA\
PRB(1)   2700
=============================================================
Total net profit     221,987.50   <  241,987.50>
Gross profit         461,762.50    Gross loss      -239,775.00

Total # of trades           423    Percent profitable       39%
Number winning trades       163    Number losing trades     260

Largest winning trade  14,712.50   Largest losing trade  -2,387.50
Average winning trade   2,832.90   Average losing trade   -922.22-
Ratio avg win/avg loss      3.07   Avg trade (win & loss)  524.79

Max consecutive winners       6    Max consecutive losers     7
Avg # bars in winners        20    Avg # bars in losers       5

Max drawdown         13,025.00     Avg # of contracts held    1
Profit factor             1.18     Max # of contracts held    1
Account size required 15,725.00    Return on account       1412%
=============================================================
```

Figure 3.2
Paul Revere/Portana

///\\\

Directory : C:\MAY   Printed on   : 06/10/93 11:55am

ENTRY SIGNAL

Signal Name   : Paul Revere   Developer   : Joe
Notes : CBO

Last Update : 06/10/93 11:47am
Long Entry Verified : YES
Short Entry Verified : YES

//////////////////////////////// LONG ENTRY \\\\\\\\\\\\\\\\\\\\\\\\\\\\\\\\\\\\\

{ Channel Breakout }

Buy tomorrow at @Highest(High,6) stop;

//////////////////////////////// SHORT ENTRY \\\\\\\\\\\\\\\\\\\\\\\\\\\\\\\\\\\\\

{ Channel Breakout}
Sell tomorrow at @Lowest(Low,6) stop;

//////////////////////////////// VARIABLE DESCRIPTION \\\\\\\\\\\\\\\\\\\\\\\\\\\\\\\\\\\\\

No variables used in entry signal.

//////////////////////////////// MODELS USING SIGNAL \\\\\\\\\\\\\\\\\\\\\\\\\\\\\\\\\\\\\

Model Name	Developer	Last Update
Joe's Paul Revere	Krutsinger	06/10/93 11:53am

\\\V//

Prepared using System Writer Plus Version 2.18 by Omega Research, Inc.

Figure 3.3—Portfolio Analyzer Graph for Paul Revere

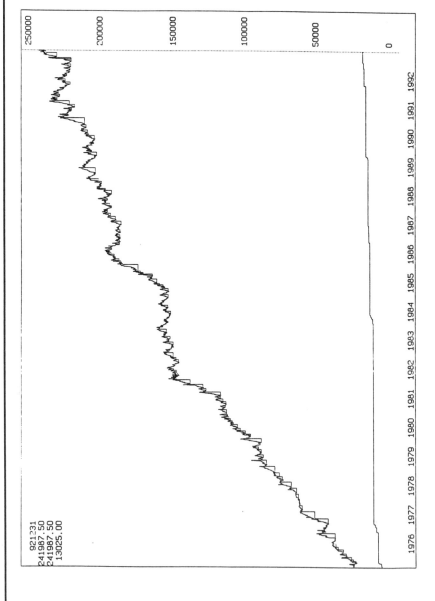

What you want to see is as long a track record as you possibly can over all the data you possibly can, so you can see how the system holds up when the market goes flat. Can you stand being flat, not making much money during this period? It is a long piece of time. From 1981 to 1985 we did not do too much in this system. It did not hurt us either, did it?

Portana

Again, Portana would give you this kind of report (Figure 3.4):

This report shows what the total equity is every year starting with $20,000 trading Paul Revere. What is the difference between $20,000 and $34,000? Is it a winner or a loser? It's a winner. $34,000 to $46,000? Winner. $46,000 to $63,000? Winner. $63,000 to $83,000? Winner. $83,000 to $102,000? Winner. $102,000 to $114,000? Winner. $114,000 to $149,000? Winner. $149,000 to $151,000? Winner. $151,000 to $153,000? Winner. $153,000 to $159,000? Winner. $159,000 to $193,000? Winner.

Can You Handle the Losers?

I have circled the losers. This is what I want you to do too. When you are researching something, forget the winners and focus on the losing periods. Can you handle them? Can you handle what's happened? Here is something that has won from 1975 to 1986. It had almost a $9,000 drawdown. The next year it won again.

Then it went from $184,000 to $191,000, $191,000 to $210,000, then $10,000 to $203,000, so we had about a $7,500 drawdown. Then it won $17,000. It won $3,000. It won about $18,000.

There were two losing years: one of about $7,500, one of about $9,000. Can you handle it? I do not know. You have to answer these questions yourself, but can you see how these tools will help you? Any trading system you have could be run through these pieces of software, and you can make these decisions.

Figure 3.4—Portana Report—Paul Revere

PORTFOLIO ANALYZER YEARLY REPORT for PAUL REVERE

DATE	OPEN EQUITY	CLOSED EQUITY	TOTAL EQUITY	MAX DRAWDOWN	% DD	% CHNG TOT EQ	NUM TRADE
750303	0.00	20000.00	20000.00	0.00	0.0	0.0	0
751231	306.25	33993.75	34300.00	2550.00	12.8	71.5	1
761231	8250.00	46768.75	55018.75	5662.50	21.2	60.4	1
771230	6150.00	63412.50	69562.50	5662.50	12.9	26.4	1
781229	6087.50	83500.00	89587.50	5662.50	8.7	28.8	
791231	750.00	102175.00	102925.00	5662.50	6.8	14.9	
801231	2775.00	114262.50	117037.50	5662.50	5.9	13.7	
811231	993.75	149893.75	150887.50	5662.50	4.4	28.9	
821231	743.75	151350.00	152093.75	5825.00	4.4	0.8	
831230	2025.00	153468.75	155493.75	8156.25	5.9	2.2	
841231	2562.50	159793.75	162356.25	8156.25	5.8	4.4	
851231	1025.00	193093.75	194118.75	8156.25	4.7	19.6	
861231	3468.75	184768.75	188237.50	9406.25	5.4	-3.0	
871231	2843.75	191875.00	194718.75	9406.25	5.3	3.4	
881230	100.00	210687.50	210787.50	9406.25	4.9	8.3	
891229	3000.00	203125.00	206125.00	10925.00	5.7	-2.2	
901231	150.00	220887.50	221037.50	10925.00	5.3	7.2	1
911231	4700.00	223812.50	228512.50	12175.00	5.7	3.4	1
921231	0.00	241987.50	241987.50	13025.00	5.9	5.9	0

Your System

I now want to move from the basics to the development of your own system. First of all, you should think about optimization, selection of the best size, and which markets you want to trade. I talked to you a little bit about finding liquidity. In most of the magazines around in stocks and commodities, you will see a liquidity table. It is shown in Figure 3.5.

Liquidity Table

A liquidity table shows the markets that have the most volume to the markets that have the least ranked.

I think if you trade one currency, one crude oil, one bond, and some kind of a stock index, you will have the markets covered as they are today.

Markets Change

Markets change. The grains get hot. The silver and gold can get hot. Over the last few years these particular markets had low volatility.

Developing a System in a Dormant Market

I am going to regress for a minute and tell you what I think is an interesting methodology to develop a system in a dormant market. If you have a market like corn and beans and nothing is happening, everybody will look at them, and devise little systems that make a little bit of money, but then the big market will come and they will be squashed.

Here is an idea. Go back in history and find a period of time when corn and beans did what you think they are going to do. Let's pretend you think that corn and beans are going to rally at some point. They are going to go higher than they are today.

Go back to a time period when corn and beans did rally, and develop systems using optimization to find which systems made the most money and kept the least amount of risk during those big high-flying times.

Figure 3.5—Liquidity Table

Trading Liquidity: Futures

Commodity Futures	Exchange	% Margin	Effective % Margin	Contracts to Trade for Equal Dollar Profit	Relative Contract Liquidity
Eurodollar	IMM	0.3	3.6	7	>>>>>>>>>>>>>>>>>>>>>>>>>>
Standard & Poor's 500	CME	6.3	10.5	1	····························
U.S. Treasury Bonds	CBT	1.7	5.1	3	··················
10 Yr. Treasury Notes	CBT	1.3	5.1	5	···········
Soybeans	CBT	2.6	5.1	7	··········
5 Yr. Treasury Notes	CBT	1.0	5.3	6	·········
Crude Oil	NYM	8.6	19.3	17	········
Silver	CMX	3.9	3.2	4	·······
Heating Oil #2	NYM	7.8	6.2	5	······
Japanese Yen	IMM	2.3	6.9	3	······
West German Mark	IMM	3.0	18.3	11	······
Gold	CMX	2.5	9.2	12	·····
Corn	CBT	3.8	8.7	24	·····
Coffee C	CSCE	7.3	5.4	4	····
Gasoline Unleaded	NYM	9.3	12.7	11	····
Cocoa	CSCE	7.0	7.0	10	····
Copper	CMX	6.3	6.7	7	···
Soybean Meal	CBT	2.4	5.1	12	···
Swiss Franc	IMM	3.3	15.8	8	···
British Pound	IMM	3.8	13.0	5	···
Sugar-World #11	CSCE	14.1	23.5	20	···
Municipal Bonds	CBT	1.2	4.1	5	···
Cattle-Feeder	CME	1.8	6.1	12	··
Soybean Oil	CBT	4.0	9.6	21	··
U.S. Treasury Bills	IMM	0.3	4.2	8	··
Wheat	CBT	6.1	13.5	19	··
Cattle-Live	CME	2.1	10.2	23	·
Cotton #2	CTN	4.8	13.8	13	·
NYSE Composite Index	NYFE	6.2	10.6	2	·
Canadian Dollar	IMM	1.2	11.6	16	·
Orange Juice	CTN	9.0	12.2	10	·
Platinum	NYM	7.4	11.8	18	·
Wheat	KC	6.9	14.3	18	·
Pork Bellies	CME	12.1	8.8	6	
Canola (Rapeseed U.S. $)	WPG	4.4	8.2	47	
Value Line Average	KC	6.0	10.3	1	
Major Market Index (Maxi)	CBT	12.5	22.6	3	
Hogs	CME	4.3	11.3	25	
Wheat	MPLS	6.8	14.0	18	
Soybeans	MCE	2.8	5.3	36	
U.S. Dollar Index	CTN	4.5	38.4	24	
CRB Futures Price Index	NYFE	4.0	16.3	10	
Silver	CBT	4.9	4.1	22	
Lumber	CME	23.2	64.9	10	
Palladium	NYM	8.0	23.7	29	

CBT Chicago Board of Trade
CME Chicago Mercantile Exchange
CMX Commodity Exchange, New York
CSCE Coffee, Sugar & Cocoa Exchange, New York
CTN New York Cotton Exchange
IMM International Monetary Market at CME, Chicago
KC Kansas City Board of Trade
MCE MidAmerica Commodity Exchange, Chicago
MPLS Minneapolis Grain Exchange
NYFE New York Futures Exchange (New York Stock Exchange)
NYM New York Mercantile Exchange
WPG Winnipeg Commodity Exchange

9309

Trading Liquidity: Futures is a reference chart for speculators. It compares markets according to their per-contract potential for profit and how easily contracts can be bought or sold (i.e. trading liquidity). Each is a proportional measure and is meaningful only when compared to others in the same column.

The number in the "Contracts to Trade for Equal Dollar Profit" column shows how many contracts of one commodity must be traded to obtain the same potential return as another commodity. Contracts to Trade = (Tick $ value) x (3-year Maximum Price Excursion).

"Relative Contract Liquidity" places commodities in descending order according to how easily all of their contracts can be traded. Commodities at the top of the list are easiest to buy and sell; commodities at the bottom of the list are the most difficult. "Relative Contract Liquidity" is the number of contracts to trade times total open interest times a volume factor, which is:

$$1 \text{ or } \exp\left(\frac{\ln(\text{volume})}{\ln(5000)}\right)^2$$

Freeze that system and apply it to the current data. Tune it until it does not lose any money over this period. It might not make anything, but it also will not lose much. Do you know what you have? You have a system in waiting.

Put your system in waiting on a TradeStation or a SystemWriter, look at it every day, and follow the signals. When the next corn move pops up again you will have math that is tuned to that kind of market. You will be ready to go. Most of the other participants will still be tuned to the little, small jiggles. Do you get the idea? It's an incredible concept, something you can use.

Ben Franklin's Decision Tree

It was rumored that Ben Franklin applied this decision tree to every decision he was going to make.

Here is the Ben Franklin decision tree applied to a trading system:

+ (BENEFIT)	– (DISADVANTAGE)
Time involved in the trade is short	You get bored easily
Capital required is small	You'll quit trading
The system may only trade one day per week	You'll want to trade more; maybe trade impulsively the other four days

You simply list each of the benefits in the plus column, and you list the disadvantages in the minus column. Then you weigh the pluses against the minuses and determine what the best decision for you will be.

The benefit of most systems I am going to show you is twofold. The time they take is short, and the capital they take is small. The disadvantage of some of these systems is that they only trade one day a week. What happens when you get bored and trade something else on the other four days a week? You lose your money and quit.

Simplify Your System

One of the best traders I know told me you do not have a system unless you can write all of the rules on the back of a very small envelope. I think this is true because the more pieces of code or letters you put into your code, the more likely you are to be form-fitting to the data. When I see somebody who has developed 15 or 20 pages of code that has only generated eight or nine trades, I suspect that the system will not hold up in the future.

Biasing Systems

Would you agree that the S&P markets in the last 30 years have been in an uptrend? If you agree with this, why take short trades? This is a concept called biasing systems; I think this will be the newest thing, but promoters will put another name on it.

It will be called "Patterned Artificial Intelligence" or "The Chaotic Candlestick." Here is how a bias system will work: You will fill out a questionnaire, and a computer will spit out what your biases are. This printout will tell you to run only one type of system from the longside, and another type of system from the shortside.

My Own Biases

Let me tell you why this will be good. I made a lot of money with clients in the 1980s in silver. For some reason, I don't want to ever be short silver. I just don't. I saw what it did. I saw how much money it made on the upside for people. When we are at three and four and five dollars an ounce, I don't want to be short silver; it is not for me. What is the worst thing that can happen to a silver bull or a gold bull? Is it to miss the move? No! To be short when the move is going up, that's the nightmare.

If you design a system and say, "Okay, if it gives me a long signal I'll buy it, but if it gives me a short signal, I'll just stand aside," look what you have done. If you have experienced a period of choppiness or a time when the market was going down, you have cut out half your trades and half your commission costs, and you've guaranteed that you will never be on the side of the market that you didn't want to be on! That is what a biased system will do for you.

Use Logic When Writing Your Systems

When you are writing your systems, think about your biases. If pork bellies are too cheap (if they are too low to be sold in your mind) then write a trading system that never sells pork bellies. Write your system to insure that if it gets a sell system you will exit long. It is quite a concept, because you can take an old-time trading system like a moving average system or a channel breakout and customize it to your biases and make it part of your trading system.

It is important to test a system in a number of ways before fully implementing it. Testing can reduce risk of loss and offer insight on how to use your system to its best ability. Can you get in and out quickly? The volume should be at least 5,000 contracts a day. The open interest should be over 20,000. What is the historical volume of the markets? Are there accurate fundamental and technical data?

I have been a guest speaker at the Board of Trade and the Chicago Mercantile Exchange. The Chicago Board of Trade members asked me to look at their new dollar contract. I designed a sample trading system for it. I showed them how to trade with and against the system, but I advised them not to trade systems in a contract until it gets up to 5,000 contracts daily. They said, "Can't we make an exception?" I said, "No. You have to have fish in fish-filled water to make it worthwhile to fish. You have to have liquidity."

You should wait for two to three delivery cycles of a new commodities market to make certain it is "going to go" before you jump in. The average daily volume doesn't mean a thing unless you study it for 10 days or more. You should also trade what the experts trade—bonds, currencies, crude oil, S&P, NYFE. If you have to trade these proven liquid markets with minis, that is okay. For short-term trades you must go with liquidity.

25

Many magazines have liquidity tables. The most liquid markets are listed at the top. The least liquid markets are at the bottom. You can find liquidity tables in the back of *Technical Analysis of Stocks and Commodities*. Look at the volume of open interest.

Identifying Trends

Are the markets trading upwards, downwards, or sideways? A lot of people "pooh-pooh" moving averages, but almost any indicator is based to some degree on moving averages. Stochastics, one of the most sophisticated indicators, is a high-level piece of math that measures the volatility of range based on a scale of 0 to 100.

That is what the K is. Do you know what the D is? It is simply a three period moving average of the K! Almost every indicator has a moving average built into it.

How Moving Averages Interface with Trends

One way to know trends is to know moving averages. Here is a rule of thumb: Look at today's price. Put your finger on it. Look at the price 20 days ago. Put your finger on it. Is today's price above or below the price 20 days ago?

If it is above, the trend is upward. If it is below, the trend is downward. If it is about the same, you are in a choppy "trendless" market. Stay out of a market when it is not trending. You should focus on simplicity and convenience while you are learning the commodities markets.

Respect the Direction of a Trend

If a trend is upward, consider using a buy only strategy until the trend changes. If a trend is downward, use a sell only strategy until the trend changes.

Other Directional Indicators

Trendlines, linear regression, parabolics, point and figure studies, and directional movement indices are all directional indicators. Most markets trend 30–35 percent of the time. This means 60–65 percent of the time trends are not in force.

Pyramiding

Finally, in testing your system, consider pyramiding, the process of *defining*. System trading lends itself to money management and risk management techniques. Discretionary trading does not. You can very easily take a spreadsheet, look at the amount of money you have and say, "Every time I make $10,000 in the market, I'll trade an additional contract. If I ever lose $10,000 in the market, I'll cut down one contract."

It is a very easy equation to do. You can pyramid up or pyramid down as your system is working or failing to work. The best reason to trade a system, is that you do not have to be a star trader to trade a system.

Testing Protocol

Let's talk about testing protocol.

Simple optimization is where you set up a SystemWriter or other device and test every moving average from 1 to 100 in steps of one. You will fine-tune the data and find the best one. Then you find the best stop, and you find this and find that. Pretty soon you will have a system for one set of circumstances. If your commodity trades exactly like this again, the system will work perfectly.

If This Pattern Comes Again, I'll Be Ready

A guy sent me a chart once with a buy/sell signal where he bought it at the very low, and sold it at the very high. I said, "Boy, that's great. That looks like 1983 silver." He said, "It is." I said, "It is 1992. How do we know what to do?" He said, "We don't, but if that pattern comes again, we are ready for it."

Well, you can't go to that "nth" of saying, this is what happened at the low, and this is what happened at the high, and I'm going to sit and wait for that. You have to be a little more broad-brushed than that.

What about Simple Forward Testing?

A system subject to simple testing and optimization without forward testing is doomed. I always suggest not testing the current data or the current year. Test the previous year. Do all of your "knicking around" on last year's data, then back test it and forward test it. If it holds up in both those tests, you have something. If it does not, you don't. That is the rule of thumb in testing.

What about Measuring Performance?

I will not get into the ratios, because I think the important ratios are fairly high level, and we are in System Writing 101, 102, and 103. The most important ratio to me is—how much money do you make versus how much drawdown do you have. Divide net profit by drawdown. If your solution number is not 10 or more, I would be suspicious. Ten or more usually indicates a great trading system.

How Do You Test for Specific Results?

Testing for specific results means designing a system to achieve predetermined sets of performance measures, percent winners, ratio of average wins to losers. Many people want systems that are right much of the time. Let me tell you how to do it. Use a $90 objective and a $2,000 stop with any system you want. Your objective will be hit very often, and your stop will not be hit very often. You will be correct a high percentage of the time. So what? This is overrated as a measure of success.

The Number of Trades in Your Test

The number of trades in your test sample must be over 30. If you do not have over 30 in your data, then keep testing using a different time frame. Look at the largest winning and losing trades. Discard both. Take away the largest winner and ask, "Does this system still hold up?"

You Must Learn How to Eliminate Systems

When you get a SystemWriter or TradeStation you will soon end up with more systems than money, and you will have to make an evaluation on which ones to trade, and which ones not to trade. These are the decisions I am trying to help you make.

Do Not Skip Big Losers

Do not skip big losers. A lot of people will say, "I never would have taken that great big trade in October of 1987, so I'm going to eliminate it." I have seen people eliminate it mathematically, and let me tell you how they do it.

The Concept of Setback

The concept of setback is in SystemWriter and TradeStation (or any testing software), and I want to warn you about it because there are people out there who are not scrupulous, believe it or not. If you have a 20-day moving average, what do you think the setback would be? 20. This means you cannot calculate a 20-day moving average unless you have 20 days of data. If you have 19 days of data it cannot be calculated.

Here is what the unscrupulous will do. They will start their track record in the middle of 1987, and they will say, "Look, I had the stock market crash in there." Then they put their setback to 100 or 200 days. The date still shows up in the trade summary as "Yes. They traded between here," but because the setback was set that way, there were no trades in that period.

This is the way they hide their big losers. So whenever you buy a system from somebody, ask them not only what data it was tested over, but what the setback was. Okay? Kind of interesting sidebar.

4

Selecting the Right System for You

What it lies in our power to do,
it lies in our power not to do.
— Aristotle —

How do you tailor a system to your own reward/comfort level? You should fit your system to your philosophy of how markets work, and incorporate your own trading psychology. This is the key to overcoming problems.

Examining Others' Approaches

By looking at my first SystemWriter experience, you can get an idea of how to incorporate traditional or other successful approaches into your own system.

The first time I worked on the system I am going to show you was in 1987 when I acquired my first SystemWriter. I was a speaker at one of the Futures Symposiums International in Las Vegas. I was an options guru, a speaker on the platform, and I was doing very well.

A young man came up to me. His name was Bill Cruz. He was an unknown at the time in the futures business. He is a very smart, good-looking, young, successful guy, in case you do not know.

He said, "Mr Krutsinger, I read your book, *The Commodities Cookbook*, and I saw that you had a trading system in there." (I had made the point in my book that it had taken me $300–$400 and three to four months to get the completed track record.) The trading system was: "If the close is above the 32-day moving average in silver, you are long. If it is not, you are short." (See Figures 4.1a, 4.1b, and 4.1c.)

Back in those days it was a great system because hardly anybody had this kind of equipment, and moving averages were terrific.

Bill took me over to a booth with no signs on it. There was an IBM computer. At this time I hated IBMs. I was a Macintosh guy. He said, "Let me show you something." Then he hit some buttons. About two and a half minutes later my exact track record came out for my silver system.

This track record had taken me lots of time and lots of money, because I had to find somebody who could program, somebody who had a computer, and somebody who had the data. In short, I had to hire three different people to write it for me.

Within minutes this guy had my entire silver system appear on a desk top by pushing a few buttons. I was impressed. It cost $3,000. The name of the system was SystemWriter.

I grabbed everybody I knew, and I knew everybody, and I said, "Come over here. You've got to buy this!"

They said, "What is it?"

Figure 4.1a

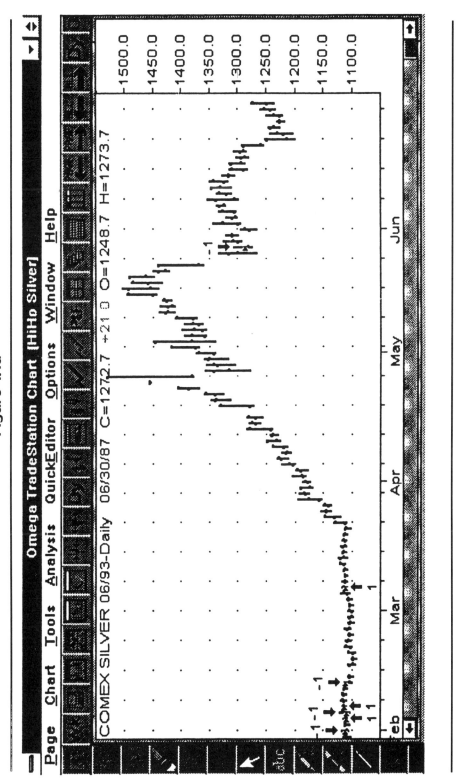

Figure 4.1b

//

SYSTEM

Name   : HiHo Silver
Notes   : Joe Krutsinger's 1982 Silver System

Last Update : 09/11/93 06:44pm
Printed on : 09/11/93 08:32pm
Verified   : YES

///////////////////////////////////// CODE \\\\\\\\\\\\\\\\\\\\\\\\\\\\

If C > @Average(C,32) then buy tomorrow at market;
If C < @Average(C,32) then sell tomorrow at market;

//

Prepared using Omega TradeStation Version 3.01 by Omega Research, Inc.

Figure 4.1c
Hi Ho Silver from Commodity Cookbook

```
HiHo Silver   COMEX SILVER 06/93-Daily    07/29/71 - 06/30/93
                    Performance Summary:  All Trades

Total net profit       $ 243480.00   Open position P/L      $    310.00
Gross profit           $ 502125.00   Gross loss             $-258645.00

Total # of trades             489    Percent profitable           24%
Number winning trades         117    Number losing trades         372

Largest winning trade  $ 107845.00   Largest losing trade   $  -7530.00
Average winning trade  $   4291.67   Average losing trade   $   -695.28
Ratio avg win/avg loss        6.17   Avg trade(win & loss)  $    497.91

Max consec. winners             3    Max consec. losers            29
Avg # bars in winners          29    Avg # bars in losers           6

Max intraday drawdown  $ -56945.00
Profit factor                 1.94   Max # contracts held           1
Account size required  $  59945.00   Return on account           406%
```
- -
```
                    Performance Summary:  Long Trades

Total net profit       $  91405.00   Open position P/L      $    310.00
Gross profit           $ 223325.00   Gross loss             $-131920.00

Total # of trades             244    Percent profitable           23%
Number winning trades          56    Number losing trades         188

Largest winning trade  $  82595.00   Largest losing trade   $  -5705.00
Average winning trade  $   3987.95   Average losing trade   $   -701.70
Ratio avg win/avg loss        5.68   Avg trade(win & loss)  $    374.61

Max consec. winners             6    Max consec. losers            27
Avg # bars in winners          26    Avg # bars in losers           5

Max intraday drawdown  $ -62015.00
Profit factor                 1.69   Max # contracts held           1
Account size required  $  65015.00   Return on account           141%
```
- -
```
                    Performance Summary:  Short Trades

Total net profit       $ 152075.00   Open position P/L      $      0.00
Gross profit           $ 278800.00   Gross loss             $-126725.00

Total # of trades             245    Percent profitable           25%
Number winning trades          61    Number losing trades         184

Largest winning trade  $ 107845.00   Largest losing trade   $  -7530.00
Average winning trade  $   4570.49   Average losing trade   $   -688.72
Ratio avg win/avg loss        6.64   Avg trade(win & loss)  $    620.71

Max consec. winners             4    Max consec. losers            16
Avg # bars in winners          32    Avg # bars in losers           6

Max intraday drawdown  $ -35915.00
Profit factor                 2.20   Max # contracts held           1
Account size required  $  38915.00   Return on account           391%
```

I said, "Just give this guy $3,000 and take one home. You're going to like it."

Bill sold seven of them that day; these were his first retail sales. Since he enjoyed meeting me, he gave me one free. I took it home, and I was appalled. First of all, I had to buy a new IBM computer because I did not have one.

After I hooked it up, I discovered that the manual was just a few Xeroxed pages. I pushed some buttons, and the screen said, "This test is going to take four and a half days." Four and a half days! I wondered what I had done wrong, but I did not know how to shut it down. I could not call Bill Cruz and ask him what had happened, because he thought I was a smart guy.

Bill was a lot less busy then than he is now. He called me three times a day and said, "Have you had a chance to look at it?" I kept saying, "I'm too busy to look at it now." Actually, I had let it run, and the thing was still running!

Much later I learned what I had done wrong. There were 50 indicators, and I had accidentally instructed the machine to consider all 50 indicators in every possible combination when I chose one-year British Pound data and put it on alternate.

Believe it or not, at the end of four and a half days, of the top 50 systems, all of them had a single component. Mathematically, how likely is that?

I am going to teach you this component at the end of this chapter. It has been at the base of most of my trading systems since that day, and I think it will be at the base of most of yours. Let's look and see if this component is any good. (See Figure 4.2a and 4.2b.)

My Paul Revere British Pound System

This chart shows the trading system from March 3, 1975 through December 31, 1992. It is figured with $50 commissions and $3,000 margins, and it is trading one contract of British Pound. This is a hypothetical, simulated 18-year track record.

Figure 4.2a
Paul Revere's British Pound System

```
/////////////////////////////////////////\\\\\\\\\\\\\\\\\\\\\\\\\\\\\\\\\
Directory : C:\WAY                          Printed on   : 06/10/93 12:05pm

                        PERFORMANCE SUMMARY

Model Name      : Joe's Paul Revere        Developer    : Krutsinger
Test Number     :        1 of        1
Notes : 1000 mm stop

Data            : BRITISH POUND       12/92
Calc Dates      : 03/03/75 - 12/31/92

Num. Conv. P. Value  Comm  Slippage  Margin  Format  Drive:\Path\FileName
-----------------------------------------------------------------------
  26   2  $  6.250  $ 50  $  0  $ 3,000  Omega   C:\20DATA\F008.DTA

/////////////////////////// ALL TRADES - Test 1 \\\\\\\\\\\\\\\\\\\\\\\\\\\

Total net profit        $221,987.50
Gross profit            $461,762.50   Gross loss               -239,775.00

Total # of trades           423       Percent profitable            38%
Number winning trades       163       Number losing trades          260

Largest winning trade   $14,712.50    Largest losing trade      $-2,387.50
Average winning trade    $2,832.90    Average losing trade      $ -922.21
Ratio avg win/avg loss       3.07     Avg trade (win & loss)      $524.79

Max consecutive winners      6        Max consecutive losers         7
Avg # bars in winners       19        Avg # bars in losers           4

Max closed-out drawdown $-12,875.00   Max intra-day drawdown   $-13,025.00
Profit factor                1.92     Max # of contracts held        1
Account size required   $16,025.00    Return on account          1,385%

                   Highlights - All trades
        Description              Date      Time      Amount
        ----------------------------------------------------------
        Largest Winning Trade    08/30/90   -   $    14,712.50
        Largest Losing Trade     09/24/90   -   $    -2,387.50
        Largest String of + Trades 09/16/85 -            6
        Largest String of - Trades 09/23/82 -            7
        Maximum Closed-Out Drawdown 08/07/92 -  $   -12,875.00
        Maximum Intra-Day Drawdown  08/14/92 -  $   -13,025.00

/////////////////////////// LONG TRADES - Test 1 \\\\\\\\\\\\\\\\\\\\\\\\\\\

Total net profit        $108,825.00
Gross profit            $231,437.50   Gross loss               -122,612.50

Total # of trades           213       Percent profitable            39%
Number winning trades        84       Number losing trades          129

Largest winning trade   $14,712.50    Largest losing trade      $-2,300.00
Average winning trade    $2,755.21    Average losing trade      $ -950.48
Ratio avg win/avg loss       2.89     Avg trade (win & loss)      $510.92

Max consecutive winners      7        Max consecutive losers  •       10
Avg # bars in winners       19        Avg # bars in losers           3
```

37

Figure 4.2b
Paul Revere's British Pound System

```
Max closed-out drawdown   $-17,431.25    Max intra-day drawdown    $-17,681.25
Profit factor                    1.88    Max # of contracts held            1
Account size required     $20,681.25     Return on account                526%
```

	Highlights - Long trades		
Description	Date	Time	Amount
Largest Winning Trade	08/30/90	-	$ 14,712.50
Largest Losing Trade	04/22/75	-	$ -2,300.00
Largest String of + Trades	02/03/78	-	7
Largest String of - Trades	06/26/89	-	10
Maximum Closed-Out Drawdown	02/28/85	-	$ -17,431.25
Maximum Intra-Day Drawdown	03/14/85	-	$ -17,681.25

```
/////////////////////////// SHORT TRADES  - Test 1 \\\\\\\\\\\\\\\\\\\\\\\\\\\\\

Total net profit          $113,162.50
Gross profit              $230,325.00    Gross loss              -117,162.50

Total # of trades                 210    Percent profitable               37%
Number winning trades              79    Number losing trades             131

Largest winning trade      $13,212.50    Largest losing trade     $-2,387.50
Average winning trade       $2,915.51    Average losing trade     $  -894.37
Ratio avg win/avg loss           3.25    Avg trade (win & loss)      $538.87

Max consecutive winners             5    Max consecutive losers            10
Avg # bars in winners              18    Avg # bars in losers               4

Max closed-out drawdown   $-18,162.50    Max intra-day drawdown    $-18,350.00
Profit factor                    1.96    Max # of contracts held            1
Account size required     $21,350.00     Return on account                530%
```

	Highlights - Short trades		
Description	Date	Time	Amount
Largest Winning Trade	09/29/92	-	$ 13,212.50
Largest Losing Trade	09/24/90	-	$ -2,387.50
Largest String of + Trades	02/27/85	-	5
Largest String of - Trades	08/22/79	-	10
Maximum Closed-Out Drawdown	09/08/92	-	$ -18,162.50
Maximum Intra-Day Drawdown	09/10/92	-	$ -18,350.00

```
\\\\\\\\\\\\\\\\\\\\\\\\\\\\\\\\\\\\\\\\\\\////////////////////////////////////
```

Prepared using System Writer Plus Version 2.18 by Omega Research, Inc.

It made $221,987.50. It did 423 trades, which is certainly a significant occurrence. Thirty-eight percent of the trades are correct. The largest winning trade is $14,712.50. The largest losing trade is $2,387.50. There are six winners in a row and seven losers in a row.

It holds winners 19 days on average. It holds losers four days on average. The biggest drawdown was $12,785.00 over the history of the contract.

Divide $12,785.00 into $221,987.50. The drawdown to equity ratio is about 17 to 1. A good system will be 10 to 1. In my opinion, this is a great trading system.

The Daddy-Go-to-Town Number

I have three daughters. They are all smart. I tried to teach them all I could about commodities. When one of my daughters was about six years old, she could understand everything on the SystemWriter sheet except one number. She could not understand the number for average trade.

She said, "Daddy, I understand what an average winning trade is, because that's the winners divided by this number. I understand what the average losing trade is, because that's the losers divided by that number, but I don't understand what that average trade number is."

I said, "Honey, that's the Daddy-go-to-town number."

She said, "What do you mean?"

I said, "Well, Daddy went to town 423 times since 1975, and every time Daddy went to town he came home with $524.79 in his pocket. Your decision, when you are trying to pick a trading system, is—should you send Daddy to town or not?"

She looked at me and said, "Daddy, go to town!"

What it all boils down to is this: What is the average trade? Is it over $150? Can it stand some slippage and commission? Is the ratio between total net profits and drawdown better than 10 to 1? This one is far better. It is a terrific trading system.

I will give you the rules. They are very difficult. The buy rule is: Buy tomorrow at the highest high of the last six days on a stop. The sell rule is:

39

Sell tomorrow at the lowest low of the last six days on a stop. Use a $1,000 money management stop after day of entry.

Let me tell you why Paul Revere is such a powerful system. First of all, let's look at moving average systems.

Those of us who have traded often have bought moving average crossovers where the close went above the crossover, and now we are long. Pretend you are trading soybeans or corn. All of a sudden the market tanks like that seen in Figure 4.3.

A Market That Tanks

The moving average is like this: We are long here. We got stopped out here, and we lose this piece of money.

A Channel Breakout System

A channel breakout system will be a little different. It will buy at the highest high of the last six. Then it will have a stop at the lowest low of the last six. Then it will reverse.

In a dynamic market where it runs away from indicators, a channel system will be vastly superior.

A Choppy Market

What about something that happens quite often—a choppy market? (See Figure 4.4.)

Indicators go flat in a choppy market, so you buy it here, sell it here, buy it here, and you sell it here. You chop up, pay commissions and slippage. Finally, hopefully, it breaks out and you make some money.

Figure 4.3—A Market That Tanks

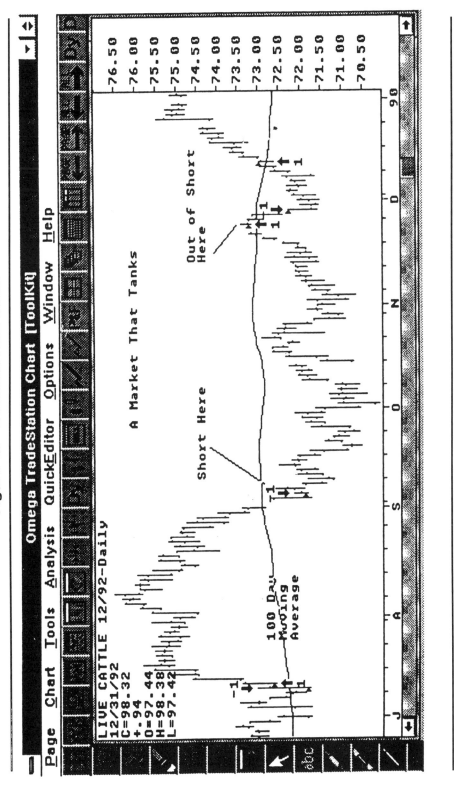

Figure 4.4—A Choppy Market

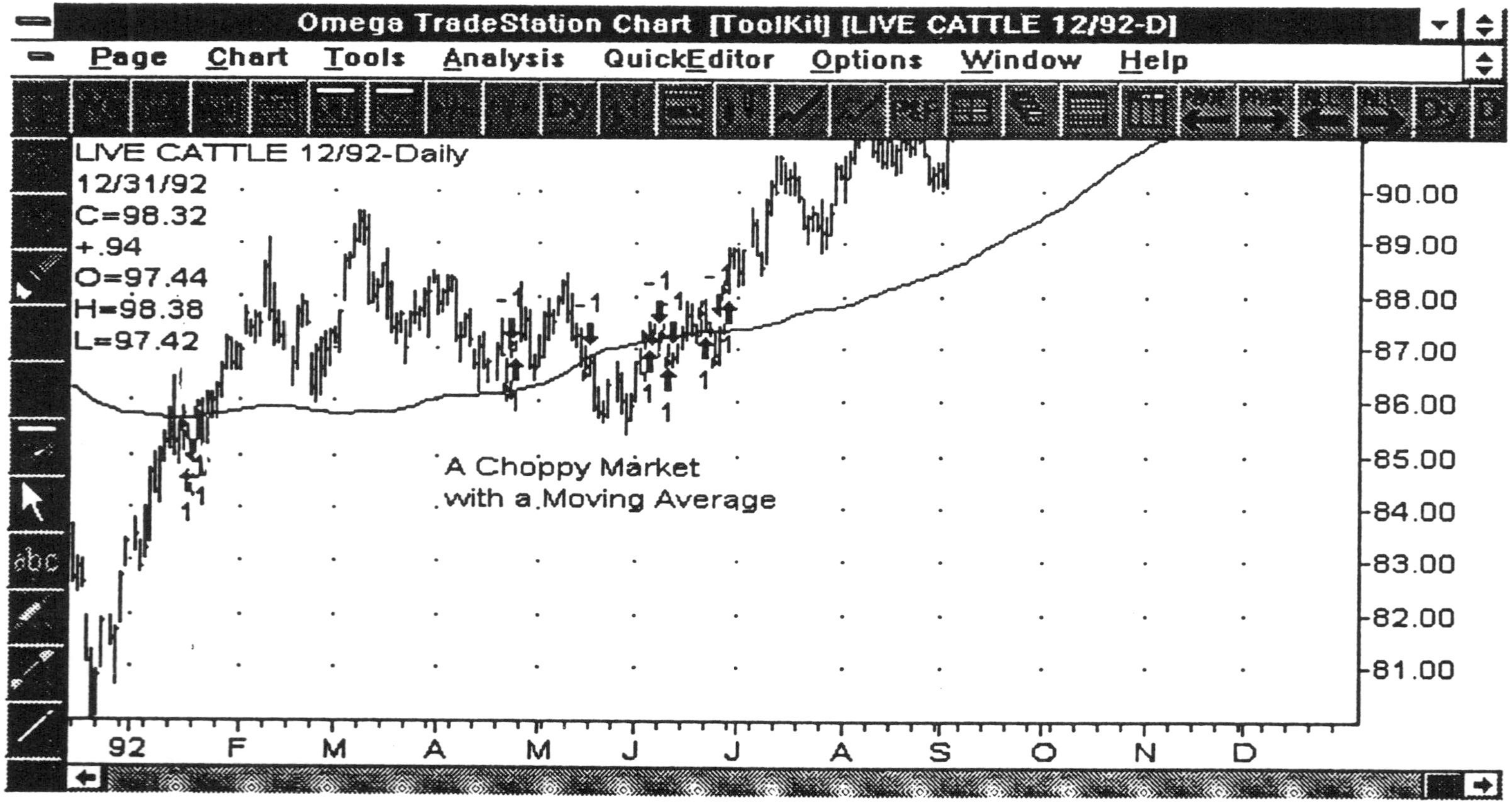
Omega TradeStation Chart [ToolKit] [LIVE CATTLE 12/92-D]
Page Chart Tools Analysis QuickEditor Options Window Help
LIVE CATTLE 12/92-Daily
12/31/92
C=98.32
+.94
O=97.44
H=98.38
L=97.42
A Choppy Market
with a Moving Average
90.00
89.00
88.00
87.00
86.00
85.00
84.00
83.00
82.00
81.00
92
F
M
A
M
J
J
A
S
O
N
D

Channel System

With a channel system—highest high, lowest low—you aren't going to be doing anything in these choppy markets. The only time period when an indicator-based system will be better than a channel-based system will be similar to the one in Figure 4.5.

You have seen this in some of the chart books. It is like a sine curve. It is a perfect market where the indicator buys it here, and sells it here. This has sold a lot of computers, by the way.

These are beautiful systems. With a channel system you will always buy a little higher and sell a little lower than that perfect system. Do you notice in all three types of markets the channel system makes a little money or stands aside? It is an interesting system.

What I am suggesting you do is take this idea and steal it from me to add to your own system. Let us pretend you are going to buy when Johnny's moving average is above Jimmy's moving average.

Instead of buying at the market, say if the 10-day moving average is above the 20 or whatever it is, then buy tomorrow at the highest high of the last two on the stop. That means the market will have to go in your direction to get you in. You combine the idea of the channel (which is a great stand-alone British Pound system) into your own work.

Exiting with a Loss

You can exit MOC (market on close). You can exit with a money management stop of $1,000, or you can exit with the lowest low or highest high of a couple of days. You can also exit so many bars since entry.

If you have a 20-day moving average and you are 12 days into the trade, don't you think that it is probably going to lose momentum coming into the next little cycle of the moving average? It does.

Here is one way to test a system like that. If you have a 20-day moving average, tell your system to arbitrarily get out after 11 days.

Let's say your 20-day moving average gets you in right here (see Figure 4.6).

Figure 4.5—A Channel System

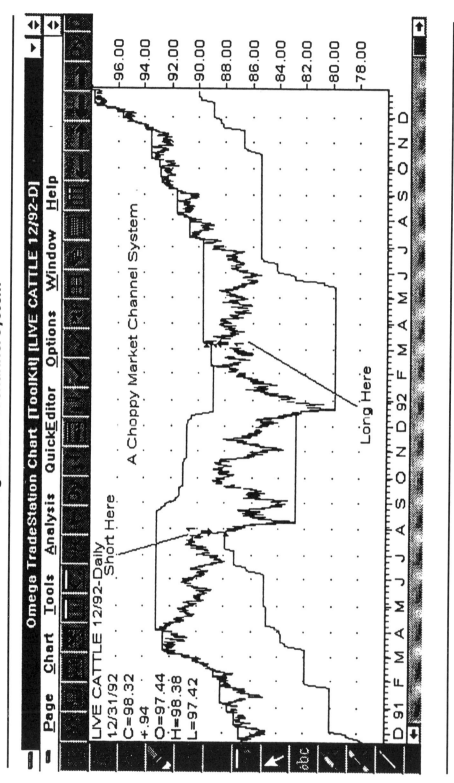

Figure 4.6—Exit after 11 Days

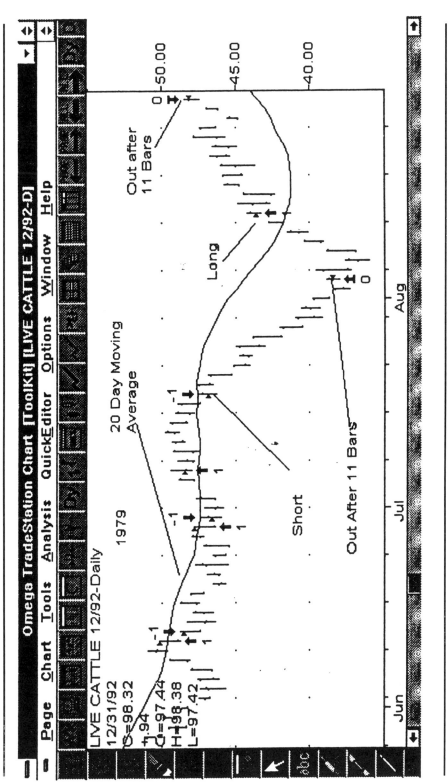

Count out until you get to 11. Eleven days will take you out over here, probably even before the crossover does.

By arbitrarily getting out at 11 days it not only resets your system, but makes your system put you in a new system if it should happen.

Exiting with a Profit

Possible exit with profit techniques: Exit market on close, exit after six bars in trade, exit with a profit objective (arbitrarily pick $1,000), or exit at resistance or support levels. If long, exit at the highest high of the last six days. If short, exit at the lowest low of the last six days.

Review

In review, I have taken a very old system that Richard Donchian developed in 1962 called Channel Breakout and shown you a number of ways to incorporate it into your own systems.

Look at the British Pound system. It is a traditional market that everybody trades with moving averages, because they say it is trending. You can trade this British Pound system without a computer, because all you need to know is the high and the low every day.

Record them on an Excel spreadsheet, and pick out the highest value and the lowest value. If the price today closes above the highest high of the last six, you are long. If it closes below the lowest low of the last six, you are short.

The next thing I ask you to do is take the channel system and incorporate it into your own trading system. Think of the dynamics of this. You decide your own way of getting in, but it makes the train go your way.

Let me explain this. If you are in Chicago wanting to travel to New York, isn't it a lot smarter to get on a train that is heading east than to get on a train that is heading west, hoping it will turn around? But everybody trades commodities getting on a westbound train, hoping it will go to

New York. Adding this concept to your own system should help you do very well.

Tailoring a System for Yourself

We are going to talk about tailoring a system to fit your temperament and personality. The *three* critical components are market entry (getting in with our chosen indicator), exiting with a profit, and exiting with a loss.

Remember how to evaluate a trading system? Maximum profits divided by net profit is a good rule to determine whether or not to go on. Some people say that it doesn't matter if a system is right 25 percent of the time or 80 percent of the time, it is the bottom line that counts.

They are lying to you. Anybody who gets a confirm day after day that shows loser after loser will eventually say, "This isn't for me." People who get winner after winner after winner statements, then all of a sudden get a statement with a very large loss on it, will also become disenchanted.

I am going to emphasize bet size a little bit more. Bet size is a gambling term. Some people would say it is not appropriate, but maybe it is. Commodity trading should be considered a game of chance.

This is a trading system called Joe's Paul Revere (Figure 4.7).

This is a track record from March 3, 1975 to December 31, 1992. The value of the British Pound is $6.25 a point. We have used a $50 commission, no slippage, and a $3,000 margin. It was tested using Omega continuous data. It made $221,000 plus.

It had 423 trades, 38 percent which were profitable. The average winning trade is $2,832.90. The average losing trade is $922. The average winning trade or the Daddy-go-to-town number is $524. The bigger that number, the better. The more trade instances over 30, the better.

Keep It Simple

The simpler the rules, the better. Now, remember, everything I am telling you is my opinion—the way I have developed systems. I have written

Figure 4.7—Joe's Paul Revere

```
PAUL REVERE      03/03/75 to 12/31/92      C:\PA\
PRB(1)    2700
=================================================================
Total net profit       221,987.50    <   241,987.50>
Gross profit           461,762.50    Gross loss        -239,775.00

Total # of trades          423       Percent profitable       39%
Number winning trades      163       Number losing trades     260

Largest winning trade  14,712.50     Largest losing trade  -2,387.50
Average winning trade   2,832.90     Average losing trade    -922.21
Ratio avg win/avg loss      3.07     Avg trade (win & loss)   524.79

Max consecutive winners      6       Max consecutive losers        7
Avg # bars in winners       20       Avg # bars in losers          5

Max drawdown           13,025.00     Avg # of contracts held       1
Profit factor               1.18     Max # of contracts held       1
Account size required  15,725.00     Return on account         1412%
=================================================================
```

about 520 systems for people all over the world. This does not mean I am the best, but I am probably one of the quickest.

I hope that you take the work I give you and make it much better, make it your own. This is my goal for giving you these rules. Remember, when I say something is better or worse, it is my opinion. If you believe something else, that is fine.

Bet Size and Evaluating Your System

Let's talk about bet size, whether you win or lose. Pretend we are in Las Vegas. I know most of you have never gone to Las Vegas, but in Las Vegas there is a game called roulette. Half the numbers are black, and half are red. There is a 0 and a double 0, but we will pretend they are commission, and ignore them.

To play roulette you put money on the table and bet black. If it comes up black, they give you back your dollar and another dollar besides. If it comes up red, they take your dollar away, and hope that you have more money in your pocket.

If a roulette wheel is perfectly balanced with no 0s or double 0s, you should win 50 percent of the time and lose 50 percent of the time. The house wins because the roulette wheel does have a 0 and double 0, and you don't stay around after you have a string of losses. This is called gambling. The bet size in this case is $1. The win or the loss in this case is $1.

Another Way to Evaluate Your System

Look at Paul Revere as a gambling deal. Pretend we have a crooked wheel because this system is only right 38 percent of the time. That means that 62 percent of the time they are going to take your money. They are going to take $922 when you lose.

To make it easy, pretend that when you lose, you lose 92 cents, but when you win you are going to win $2.80. This means that the ratio of win to loss is 3.07 to 1. For every dollar you lose in this game, you are going to win $3. Would you play this game? Of course you would. This is another way to evaluate a trading system.

It Is a Game of Chance

Pretend it is a game of chance. Forget it is a commodity. Forget it has any economic value at all. It is a game of chance, and you evaluate it using the percentage of times you win, the amount of money they give you if you win, and the amount of money they take away if you lose.

Paul Revere—the Trading Rules

We will now reiterate the trading rules of this system, so you understand. The trading rules are: Buy at the highest high of the last six days on a stop, and sell at the lowest low of the last six days on a stop. There is a $1,000 risk management stop in case someone shoots at somebody and you want to get out. These rules are all there is to this system.

Paul Revere—Balance

Let's talk about balance. The long side of this system made $108,000, had 213 trades, and it was correct 39 percent of the time over this 18-year period. If you took only the long side, the average trade size or Daddy-go-to-town number is $510.

Here is what the short side of that system looks like: Hypothetically, it made $113,162.50 with 210 trades. It was correct 37 percent of the time, and the Daddy-go-to-town number was 538.87. If you make $108,000 on the longs and $113,000 on the shorts, and you have 213 trades on the longs and 210 trades on the shorts, this is what is called balance.

Hedging Currencies

Who would only trade the long side of a currency market? How about a bank? It would have to be someone who actually has a currency risk. This is how you could hedge currencies.

First, you would find a good system. When the system gave you a good buy signal and you needed to be long in your futures position, you would take the buy signal. When it gave you a sell signal you would liquidate. By doing this you would develop hedging programs for yourselves out of your own trading systems.

Paul Revere—Summation

Paul Revere should hold up because it has a long history, it is not a complicated system, and the rules are very easy. Here is how you would write it in computer language: Buy tomorrow at the highest high of the last six periods on a stop, and sell tomorrow on the lowest low of the last six periods on a stop. You can trade this as a system by itself or add it to your current currency system.

An Overview of Four Software Systems

I think it is important to see some of the tools that are available in the industry, and to see how you might want to use them to develop your system. All of the companies discussed below have either demonstration disks or something else so you can get a better hands-on feel for the software. Maybe you did not know some of these products exist. I hope I will enlighten you.

SystemWriter is a system development tool. It can be used when you come up with an idea, and you want to see the best moving average, the best indicator, the best stop. Use it when you want to really dig into research, and come up with what you think is *your* Holy Grail.

TradeStation is used after you discover your Holy Grail. When you want to be able to implement your new system you type it onto TradeStation. Then when it beeps, you do what it says.

One of the reasons I went with Robbins Trading was to help them train a staff who would implement the systems. Clients had systems, but they were not trading them, so I helped develop a staff who could read the software, listen to it beep, and put in the order.

What do you suppose happened? They put in the trades. They do not wait to see how it is going to open or think, "It's Tuesday. I don't want to do it because there may be a cattle report." They just follow the systems, listen to the beeps, and implement the trades.

Implementation is the key to commodity trading. No matter what your system is, make your plan, then follow your plan. It is very simple.

Portana

Portana is a wonderful product that will allow you to take your research from SystemWriter, lay it together, and see what happens if you do all these things at once using real money. It shows you what has happened historically.

One Day at a Time

One Day at a Time is more of a teaching tool that will let you look at old data and ask, "What would I have done in this situation?" You can then move it up one day at a time until you see what it actually did.

It is a great teaching tool not only for technical traders, but for people who want to look at the fundamentals of a market. They remember back to 1987. They remember back to 1975. They can pull up the data, show that piece of data, and see what they would have done.

Tools Do Not Make the Builder

These are the tools, but let me tell you about tools. My father was a master mechanic. People would bring their cars on flatbed trucks from hundreds of miles around to my dad's house. He would take the car off the truck, drive it around, and tell them how to fix it. This was before Sun Technologies would let you analyze what was wrong with a car.

Dad could get a hammer at K-Mart and build a car. I could get a set of S & K tools, and still not be able to change a tire. Tools do not make the builder, but it is much easier to take a screw loose with a screwdriver than it is with a hammer. You can do them both, but it is easier on the screw and the person if you have the right tool.

I would suggest, if you're going to invest the time and the effort in commodity trading, to get some tools even if they are lower level ones. My dad, as good a mechanic as he was, would not have taken nuts off with his bare hands. He used the lugwrench. I suggest you use some of these products which are available.

Look at One Night Stand Trading System. You are supposed to buy at the highest high of so many days on a Friday. You will not do it, because the market is making a new high on a Friday. This high is higher than it has been for eight days, so you decide to wait and try to buy it cheaper.

Psychologically, you do not want to carry it over the weekend. You will watch this trade, and you will watch it and you will watch it. In the last five years you would have watched it 463 times. It is very difficult to implement your own system.

The Software Tools You May Need

TradeStation

TradeStation, SystemWriter, One Day at a Time, and Portana are popular software tools you can use to develop your own trading system.

The first product we are going to discuss is TradeStation. It is the most complicated of the four software systems, the most sophisticated, and the most expensive. The trading system we are going to use applying Trade-Station is: "If today is Friday, then buy tomorrow at the market." As you can see in Figure 4.8, this is pretty much how the system is written.

The system is called Buy Monday, and the system is written, "If day of week is 5 (in other words, if today is Friday), then buy tomorrow at the market." This is done in the section of TradeStation marked Quick Editor.

Most software programs on the market today have no Quick Editor. They are simply charting packages that let you look at a chart and decide, "Oh, I'd like to buy it here, and I'd like to sell it here."

Both SystemWriter and TradeStation will let you write your strategy, test it on the data, and see what hypothetically would have or could have happened. We are going to go into the analysis section of TradeStation to turn on that system we wrote called Buy Monday. We will check our stops, then we will say, "The first test we will do is with no stops at all, but we will close all trades at end of day."

For costs, I've put down $55 commissions and a $3,000 margin, although we are trading it intraday, so there really is no margin consideration except for whatever your firm charges for a daytrade. (Refer to Figure 4.8.)

This is a test over daily bars historical from 1988 through 1992. It covers five years of every day of the S&P 500 futures. (See Figure 4.9.)

See all this activity? Since it is a buy only system, it is buying only on Mondays, and then getting out on the close. It tells you where you got in with the green arrows and the green flags. It tells you where you got out with the white squat bars. White squat bars with a zero means that you are flat. Green means that you are in the market.

Using TradeStation

I am going to tell TradeStation to show me a performance summary very similar to what we saw for the British Pound system. How long do you think it will take it to do a 10-year study on this chart? Less than one second (see Figures 4.10 and 4.11).

Figure 4.8—Buy Monday

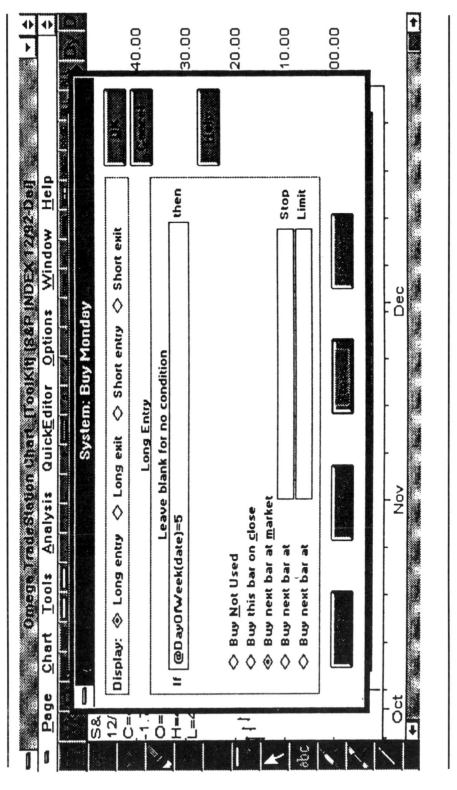

Figure 4.9—Chart for Buy Monday

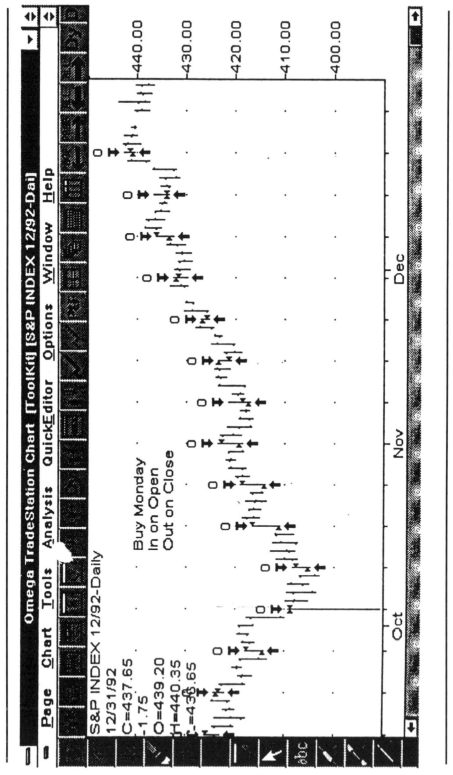

Figure 4.10
Performance Summary of Buy Monday

```
Buy Monday   S&P INDEX 12/92-Daily     01/04/88 - 12/31/92
                    Performance Summary:  All Trades

Total net profit        $   77225.00   Open position P/L      $       0.00
Gross profit            $  177800.00   Gross loss             $-100575.00

Total # of trades            251       Percent profitable           56%
Number winning trades        140       Number losing trades         111

Largest winning trade   $   10275.00   Largest losing trade   $   -5350.00
Average winning trade   $    1270.00   Average losing trade   $    -906.08
Ratio avg win/avg loss         1.40    Avg trade(win & loss)  $     307.67

Max consec. winners          11        Max consec. losers             7
Avg # bars in winners         0        Avg # bars in losers           0

Max intraday drawdown   $  -13200.00
Profit factor                 1.77     Max # contracts held           1
Account size required   $   16200.00   Return on account            477%

  — · ·  — ·  — ·  —  — ·  — · —  — ·  — ·  —  — · ·  — · —  — ·  — · —

                    Performance Summary:  Long Trades

Total net profit        $   77225.00   Open position P/L      $       0.00
Gross profit            $  177800.00   Gross loss             $-100575.00

Total # of trades            251       Percent profitable           56%
Number winning trades        140       Number losing trades         111

Largest winning trade   $   10275.00   Largest losing trade   $   -5350.00
Average winning trade   $    1270.00   Average losing trade   $    -906.08
Ratio avg win/avg loss         1.40    Avg trade(win & loss)  $     307.67

Max consec. winners          11        Max consec. losers             7
Avg # bars in winners         0        Avg # bars in losers           0

Max intraday drawdown   $  -13200.00
Profit factor                 1.77     Max # contracts held           1
Account size required   $   16200.00   Return on account            477%

  — · ·  — ·  — ·  —  — ·  — · —  — ·  — ·  —  — · ·  — · —  — ·  — · —

                    Performance Summary:  Short Trades

Total net profit        $       0.00   Open position P/L      $       0.00
Gross profit            $       0.00   Gross loss             $       0.00

Total # of trades              0       Percent profitable            0%
Number winning trades          0       Number losing trades           0

Largest winning trade   $       0.00   Largest losing trade   $       0.00
Average winning trade   $       0.00   Average losing trade   $       0.00
Ratio avg win/avg loss       100.00    Avg trade(win & loss)  $       0.00

Max consec. winners           0        Max consec. losers             0
Avg # bars in winners         0        Avg # bars in losers           0

Max intraday drawdown   $       0.00
Profit factor                100.00    Max # contracts held           0
Account size required   $       0.00   Return on account             0%
```

CHAPTER 4

Figure 4.11
Buy Monday

```
////////////////////////////////////////\\\\\\\\\\\\\\\\\\\\\\\\\\\\\\\\\\\\\\
Directory : F:\KK                              Printed on   : 10/03/93 12:30pm

                               ENTRY SIGNAL

Signal Name      : Monday                   Developer     : KRUTSINGER
Notes :

Last Update : 09/06/93 02:55pm
Long  Entry Verified : YES
Short Entry Verified : NO

//////////////////////////////// LONG ENTRY \\\\\\\\\\\\\\\\\\\\\\\\\\\\\\\




If @DayOfWeek(0)=5 then buy tomorrow at market
with ExitOnCloseOfEntryBar=True;


//////////////////////////////// SHORT ENTRY \\\\\\\\\\\\\\\\\\\\\\\\\\\\\\\


//////////////////////////// VARIABLE DESCRIPTION \\\\\\\\\\\\\\\\\\\\\\\\\\\\

No variables used in entry signal.

//////////////////////////// MODELS USING SIGNAL \\\\\\\\\\\\\\\\\\\\\\\\\\\\\

Model Name                   Developer         Last Update
-------------------------------------------------------------------------
Monday Buy                   KRUTSINGER         10/03/93 12:29pm

\\\\\\\\\\\\\\\\\\\\\\\\\\\\\\\\\\\\\\\\\\\\////////////////////////////////////

Prepared using System Writer Plus Version 2.18 by Omega Research, Inc.
```

58

TradeStation is a very smart program. Whenever I pull up a chart, it will automatically figure the next step that is normally taken.

It is showing me longs only. It made approximately $77,000, had 253 trades, and was 56% right. The average winner is $1,268. The average loser is $906. The average trade is $305. The drawdown is approximately $13,000 over this period. This is testing from January 4, 1988 to December 31, 1992, five years of doing nothing but buying on Mondays and getting out on the close with no stops. I think it is a pretty interesting program.

If you divide the $13,000 drawdown into the $77,000 net profit, you get a six to one ratio. This is not as good as some of our other systems, but remember, the less words you put into a trading system, the better system it is. This is about as simple as it can get.

Now, I'm going to make a little change in the program. I'm going to put in a $1,000 stop. (See Figure 4.12.)

Our largest losing trade before was $5,000. Now, theoretically, our largest losing trade should be $1,000 plus commission. The software is going through the system, doing five years of work. Seconds later, the new trades are here. (See Figure 4.13.)

Here is the system trade by trade, and here is the profit and loss. Buy Monday made $61,000 and had an $11,000 drawdown. That is about a five to one ratio. Now our losing trade is $1,050, and the system is right about 50 percent of the time.

If this were a gambling wheel that was right 50 percent of the time, it's a straight wheel. The average winner is $1,327. The average loser is $833, and you win half the time. Would you play this game in Las Vegas? You would have to wait in a long line first.

The Benefit of TradeStation Software

The major benefit of TradeStation is that it will take your idea no matter how complicated, apply it to the data, and beep at you (tell you what is happening) in the future. This is a very powerful helper. You do not have to sit and stare at the screen to see what is happening. TradeStation watches for you. TradeStation is a windows product developed by Omega Research.

Figure 4.12—Stop Setting, Show How to Do This

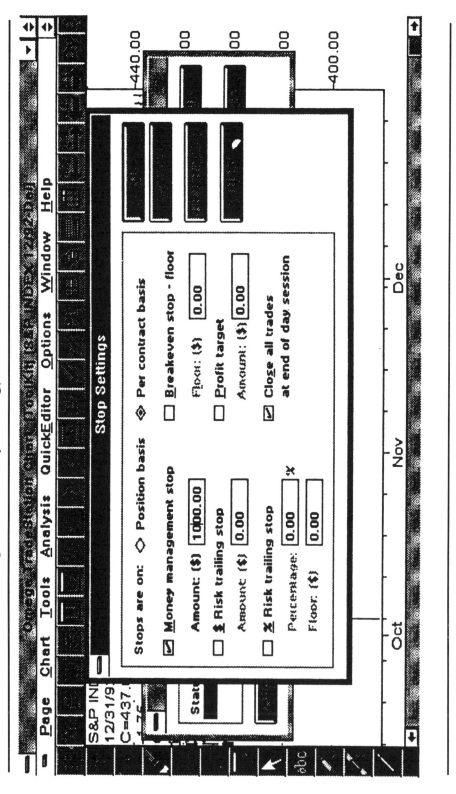

Figure 4.13
Performance Summary for Buy Monday

```
Buy Monday   S&P INDEX 12/92-Daily   01/04/88 - 12/31/92

                    Performance Summary:  All Trades

Total net profit     $  61485.00  Open position P/L   $       0.00
Gross profit         $ 167295.00  Gross loss          $-105810.00

Total # of trades          253    Percent profitable       50%
Number winning trades      126    Number losing trades     127

Largest winning trade $ 10270.00  Largest losing trade $  -1055.00
Average winning trade $  1327.74  Average losing trade $   -833.15
Ratio avg win/avg loss      1.59  Avg trade(win & loss) $   243.02

Max consec. winners         11    Max consec. losers         7
Avg # bars in winners        0    Avg # bars in losers       0

Max intraday drawdown $ -11395.00
Profit factor               1.58  Max # contracts held       1
Account size required $  14395.00 Return on account        427%
```
— ·· — ·· — ·· — ·· — ·· — ·· — ·· — ·· — ·· — ·· — ·· — ·· — ·· — ·· — ·· —
```
                    Performance Summary:  Long Trades

Total net profit     $  61485.00  Open position P/L   $       0.00
Gross profit         $ 167295.00  Gross loss          $-105810.00

Total # of trades          253    Percent profitable       50%
Number winning trades      126    Number losing trades     127

Largest winning trade $ 10270.00  Largest losing trade ₃  -1055.00
Average winning trade $  1327.74  Average losing trade $   -833.15
Ratio avg win/avg loss      1.59  Avg trade(win & loss) $   243.02

Max consec. winners         11    Max consec. losers         7
Avg # bars in winners        0    Avg # bars in losers       0

Max intraday drawdown $ -11395.00
Profit factor               1.58  Max # contracts held       1
Account size required $  14395.00 Return on account        427%
```
— ·· — ·· — ·· — ·· — ·· — ·· — ·· — ·· — ·· — ·· — ·· — ·· — ·· — ·· — ·· —
```
                    Performance Summary:  Short Trades

Total net profit     $      0.00  Open position P/L   $       0.00
Gross profit         $      0.00  Gross loss          $       0.00

Total # of trades            0    Percent profitable        0%
Number winning trades        0    Number losing trades       0

Largest winning trade $     0.00  Largest losing trade $      0.00
Average winning trade $     0.00  Average losing trade $      0.00
Ratio avg win/avg loss    100.00  Avg trade(win & loss) $      0.00

Max consec. winners          0    Max consec. losers         0
Avg # bars in winners        0    Avg # bars in losers       0

Max intraday drawdown $     0.00
Profit factor             100.00  Max # contracts held       0
Account size required $      0.00 Return on account         0%
```

CHAPTER 4

SystemWriter

The best product I know to develop a trading system is an older product called SystemWriter. SystemWriter is a DOS product written originally in 1987 by Omega Research.

The Benefits of SystemWriter

We can actually attach different trading ideas, different stops, different exits, on an alternate basis, and let SystemWriter find what the best stop or the best combination of systems would be in the past. This is a very powerful program.

This is how I use my SystemWriter. At night before I leave my office I set up a bunch of elaborate tests, turn the machine on and the screen off, and let it run all night long. When I come back in the morning I have the results of my trading research.

I take that research and fine-tune it on my TradeStation, which is plugged into live data working on current markets. By using System-Writer this way I can do the research of four or five different people at once. (See Figures 4.14a–4.14e.)

One Night Stand

Here is a system called One Night Stand. We have entries, exits, and stops. We have an entry system which I call Easy Moving Average, which is not even a moving average! It has an exit rule to get out at the very next opening, and we have no stops turned on.

To show you how to edit this model, I'm going to use the data on one commodity and run a quick test on one market. Using British Pound, I will now do a five-year test on the SystemWriter. I want to tell you the rules of One Night Stand, so you can get a feel for this system.

One Night Stand buys the highest high of the last four days if the 10-day moving average is above the 40-day moving average, and the program sells the lowest low of the last eight days if the 10-day moving average is lower than the 40-day moving average. We only trade it on a

Figure 4.14a—One Night Stand

```
                                    SYSTEM

Name    : One Night Stand
Notes :

Last Update : 04/27/93 09:29am
Printed on  : 06/10/93 02:14pm
Verified    : YES

//////////////////////////////// CODE \\\\\\\\\\\\\\\\\\\\\\\\\\\\\\\\\\

If Average(C,10)[1] > Average(C,40)[1] and
   DayOfweek(date)=4 then buy tomorrow at
Highest(H,4) stop;

If Average(C,10)[1] < Average(C,40)[1] and
   DayOfweek(date)=4 then Sell tomorrow at
Lowest(L,8) stop;

If barssinceentry> 0 then exitlong at market;
If barssinceentry> 0 then exitShort at market;
If DayOfWeek(date)=5 then
ExitShort at market;
If DayOfWeek(date)=5 then
ExitLong at market;
```

Figure 4.14b—One Night Stand

```
ONE NIGHT STAND 01/04/88 to 12/31/92   C:\PA\
BP1(1)    2700  DM1(1)    2700  SF1(1)    2700  JY1(1)    2700  CL1(1)    2700
DX1(1)    2700
=============================================================================
Total net profit        115,257.50  <     135,257.50>
Gross profit            163,106.25     Gross loss              -47,848.75

Total # of trades              445     Percent profitable             65%
Number winning trades          291     Number losing trades          154

Largest winning trade     3,095.00     Largest losing trade       -2,267
Average winning trade       560.50     Average losing trade         -310
Ratio avg win/avg loss        1.80     Avg trade (win & loss)        259

Max consecutive winners         20     Max consecutive losers          9
Avg # bars in winners            1     Avg # bars in losers            1

Max drawdown              5,700.00     Avg # of contracts held         3
Profit factor                 1.18     Max # of contracts held         6
Account size required    21,900.00     Return on account            526%
=============================================================================
```

Figure 4.14c—One Night Stand

PORTFOLIO ANALYZER YEARLY REPORT for ONE NIGHT STAND

DATE	OPEN EQUITY	CLOSED EQUITY	TOTAL EQUITY	MAX DRAWDOWN	% DD	% CHNG TOT EQ	NUM TRADE
880104	0.00	20000.00	20000.00	0.00	0.0	0.0	0
881230	180.00	33297.50	33477.50	5687.50	28.4	67.4	1
891229	0.00	48740.00	48740.00	5700.00	17.1	45.6	0
901231	0.00	77167.50	77167.50	5700.00	10.0	58.3	0
911231	0.00	115022.50	115022.50	5700.00	6.0	49.1	0
921231	0.00	135257.50	135257.50	5700.00	4.9	17.6	0

Figure 4.14d—One Night Stand

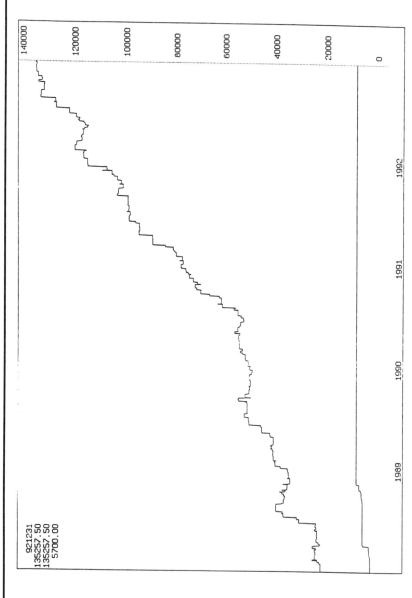

Figure 4.14e—One Night Stand

DATE	OPEN EQUITY	CLOSED EQUITY	TOTAL EQUITY	MAX DRAWDOWN	% DD	% TOT EQ CHNG	NUM TRADE
	PORTFOLIO	ANALYZER	QUARTLY REPORT for	ONE NIGHT	STAND		
880104	0.00	20000.00	20000.00	0.00	0.0	0.0	0
880331	0.00	23282.50	23282.50	605.00	3.0	16.4	0
880630	0.00	28747.50	28747.50	3153.75	15.8	23.5	0
880930	380.00	34390.00	34770.00	3627.50	18.1	20.9	1
881230	180.00	33297.50	33477.50	5687.50	28.4	-3.7	1
890331	-985.00	40142.50	39157.50	5687.50	28.2	17.0	1
890630	0.00	49230.00	49230.00	5687.50	19.5	25.7	
890929	-840.00	50507.50	49667.50	5687.50	17.1	0.9	1
891229	0.00	48740.00	48740.00	5700.00	17.1	-1.9	
900330	0.00	52860.00	52860.00	5700.00	17.1	8.5	
900629	280.00	51240.00	51520.00	5700.00	16.4	-2.5	
900928	0.00	68965.00	68965.00	5700.00	11.6	33.9	
901231	0.00	77167.50	77167.50	5700.00	10.0	11.9	
910329	0.00	89007.50	89007.50	5700.00	8.3	15.3	
910628	-292.50	98500.00	98207.50	5700.00	7.3	10.3	
910930	0.00	102575.00	102575.00	5700.00	6.8	4.4	
911231	0.00	115022.50	115022.50	5700.00	6.0	12.1	
920331	0.00	117295.00	117295.00	5700.00	5.7	2.0	
920630	0.00	122057.50	122057.50	5700.00	5.6	4.1	0
920930	0.00	131992.50	131992.50	5700.00	5.0	8.1	0
921231	0.00	135257.50	135257.50	5700.00	4.9	2.5	0

Friday, and we get out on Monday's opening! The idea behind this system is that currencies tend to breakout on the weekend, and people are afraid to take breakouts over the weekends. They are afraid of world events, they are afraid of the news.

Whatever people are afraid to do is probably what you should do. Basically, you are paying the margin, and taking the risk over the weekend.

This test is done for the five-year period. (See Figure 4.15.)

One Night Stand's Track Record

It made $32,000. It was right 69 percent of the time, and there were 82 trades in five years. The average trade of a winner was $790. The average trade of a loser was $506. And the Daddy-go-to-town number was $394. It had a $2,600 drawdown. There were 20 consecutive winners, and four consecutive losers. (See Figure 4.16.)

Here are the longs. It is a balanced system. The long side made $15,000 with 49 trades. The short side made $16,000 with 33 trades. Even though the British Pound in the last five years has been fairly directional, here is a system that only carries positions over the weekend when no one else will carry them.

Portana

The next program is a product called Portana, by Tom Berry Software. The idea here is to take output from SystemWriter Plus and say, "I like these systems, but what if I want to handle a bunch of them at a time? What if I want to handle the Swiss Franc, the British Pound, the Deutsche Mark, simultaneously? What will that do?"

With Portana we will import some files, and we will go down to where it says British Pound 1, which is One Night Stand, Japanese Yen 1, Deutsche Mark 1, and Swiss Franc 1. We will make sure we do not have anything else, because Portana is very powerful. You can add one hundred different systems simultaneously!

I am going to have these four commodities—the BP, the JY, the SF, and the DM. I previously ran these on SystemWriter, and just dumped them

Figure 4.15
Performance Summary of British Pound

```
Max closed-out drawdown   $-2,145.00    Max intra-day drawdown    $-2,145.00
Profit factor                   3.24    Max # of contracts held            1
Account size required     $5,145.00     Return on account               304%
```

```
                      Highlights - Long trades
        Description                Date      Time      Amount
        --------------------------------------------------------------
        Largest Winning Trade      12/23/91   -    $    2,232.50
        Largest Losing Trade       10/07/91   -    $   -1,167.50
        Largest String of + Trades 09/09/91   -            14
        Largest String of - Trades 12/18/89   -             3
        Maximum Closed-Out Drawdown 12/18/89  -    $   -2,145.00
        Maximum Intra-Day Drawdown 12/18/89   -    $   -2,145.00
```

///////////////////////// SHORT TRADES - Test 1 \\\\\\\\\\\\\\\\\\\\\\\\\

```
Total net profit         $20,928.75
Gross profit             $26,111.25     Gross loss              $-5,182.50

Total # of trades               33     Percent profitable            72%
Number winning trades           24     Number losing trades            9

Largest winning trade    $3,020.00     Largest losing trade    $-2,267.50
Average winning trade    $1,087.97     Average losing trade    $ -575.83
Ratio avg win/avg loss        1.88     Avg trade (win & loss)    $634.20

Max consecutive winners         12     Max consecutive losers          3
Avg # bars in winners            1     Avg # bars in losers            1

Max closed-out drawdown   $-2,535.00   Max intra-day drawdown    $-2,535.00
Profit factor                   5.03   Max # of contracts held            1
Account size required     $5,535.00    Return on account               378%
```

```
                      Highlights - Short trades
        Description                Date      Time      Amount
        --------------------------------------------------------------
        Largest Winning Trade      06/27/88   -    $    3,020.00
        Largest Losing Trade       09/06/88   -    $   -2,267.50
        Largest String of + Trades 02/24/92   -            12
        Largest String of - Trades 06/20/88   -             3
        Maximum Closed-Out Drawdown 09/19/88  -    $   -2,535.00
        Maximum Intra-Day Drawdown 09/19/88   -    $   -2,535.00
```

\\//////////////////////////////////

```
Prepared using System Writer Plus Version 2.18 by Omega Research, Inc.
```

Figure 4.16
British Pound Long Trades

```
//////////////////////////////////////////\\\\\\\\\\\\\\\\\\\\\\\\\\\\\\\\\\\\\\
Directory : F:\KK                          Printed on   : 10/03/93 11:25am

                        PERFORMANCE SUMMARY

Model Name      : One Night Stand        Developer   : Krutsinger
Test Number     :     1 of       1
Notes : Combo Of MA and Channel Breakout, in on Fri.     -Out on Mon.

Data            : BRITISH POUND    06/93
Calc Dates      : 01/01/88 - 12/31/92

Num. Conv. P. Value  Comm Slippage Margin  Format  Drive:\Path\FileName
------------------------------------------------------------------------
  26   2  $  6.250  $ 55  $  0  $ 3,000  Omega   F:\20DATA06\F008.DTA

/////////////////////////// ALL TRADES  - Test 1 \\\\\\\\\\\\\\\\\\\\\\\\\\

Total net profit        $36,615.00
Gross profit            $48,798.75    Gross loss           $-12,183.75

Total # of trades            82       Percent profitable         71%
Number winning trades        59       Number losing trades        23

Largest winning trade   $3,020.00     Largest losing trade   $-2,267.50
Average winning trade     $827.10     Average losing trade   $ -529.73
Ratio avg win/avg loss      1.56      Avg trade (win & loss)   $446.52

Max consecutive winners      20       Max consecutive losers       4
Avg # bars in winners         1       Avg # bars in losers         1

Max closed-out drawdown $-2,625.00    Max intra-day drawdown $-2,887.50
Profit factor               4.00      Max # of contracts held      1
Account size required   $5,887.50     Return on account          621%

                Highlights - All trades
      Description              Date      Time      Amount
      -----------------------------------------------------------
      Largest Winning Trade    06/27/88   -   $   3,020.00
      Largest Losing Trade     09/06/88   -   $  -2,267.50
      Largest String of + Trades 09/09/91 -        20
      Largest String of - Trades 06/20/88 -         4
      Maximum Closed-Out Drawdown 05/11/92 - $  -2,625.00
      Maximum Intra-Day Drawdown 05/15/92  - $  -2,887.50

/////////////////////////// LONG TRADES  - Test 1 \\\\\\\\\\\\\\\\\\\\\\\\\\

Total net profit        $15,686.25
Gross profit            $22,687.50    Gross loss            $-7,001.25

Total # of trades            49       Percent profitable         71%
Number winning trades        35       Number losing trades        14

Largest winning trade   $2,232.50     Largest losing trade   $-1,167.50
Average winning trade     $648.21     Average losing trade   $ -500.09
Ratio avg win/avg loss      1.29      Avg trade (win & loss)   $320.13

Max consecutive winners      14       Max consecutive losers       3
Avg # bars in winners         1       Avg # bars in losers         1
```

on a file. Portana will read the SystemWriter file directly, so I don't have to re-run them. (See Figure 4.17.)

Portana processes five years of trading on all of these commodities, laying them together, and showing us how they would come out. This is a very powerful tool.

One Night Stand

One Night Stand only trades over the weekend. The Buy Monday system (S&P) only trades Mondays. So, theoretically, since the currencies open before the S&P, you never have both those positions on simultaneously. You could have one account trade both of these, but you would like to see what the implications would be of putting them together. (See Figure 4.18.)

This shows what happens when all of those four commodities are trading the One Night Stand simultaneously. It looks very similar to the British Pound trading alone. It is right 68 percent of the time, and it makes $97,000. The drawdown is $5,900, and there were 20 winners in a row. This is very powerful.

Benefit of Portana

Here is the most powerful feature of Portana: You can get reports that will show you monthly, daily, and quarterly where you would be. I am going to show you a graph now which is incredible. This is the daily equity graph. It shows you what would happen if you traded all four currencies simultaneously. Then it shows you day by day what your equity would be, and what your maximum drawdown would be. (See Figure 4.19.)

The bottom line is your maximum drawdown, which is $5,900. The only line is $97,000, which is your profits. You can look at it day by day by day and see your equity curve. The closer to a 45-degree angle your equity curve is, the better your system is. What you want to look at when you are analyzing systems, is the times of drawdown. Figure 4.19 shows the places where periods of drawdown occur. Can you stand those? Then you may have a winning piece of strategy.

Figure 4.17—Portfolio Analyzer—Portana

PORTFOLIO ANALYZER YEARLY REPORT for ONE NIGHT STAND

DATE	OPEN EQUITY	CLOSED EQUITY	TOTAL EQUITY	MAX DRAWDOWN	% DD	% CHNG TOT EQ	NUM TRADE
880104	0.00	50000.00	50000.00	0.00	0.0	0.0	0
881230	0.00	59317.50	59317.50	5912.50	11.8	18.6	0
891229	0.00	73425.00	73425.00	5912.50	11.8	23.8	0
901231	0.00	94432.50	94432.50	5912.50	11.8	28.6	0
911231	0.00	127822.50	127822.50	5912.50	7.6	35.4	0
921231	0.00	147037.50	147037.50	5912.50	6.1	15.0	0

Figure 4.18—One Night Stand

```
ONE NIGHT STAND 01/04/88 to 12/31/92      C:\PA\
BP1(1)   2700 DM1(1)   2700 SF1(1)   2700 JY1(1)   2700
=========================================================================
Total net profit        97,037.50   <   147,037.50>
Gross profit           131,586.25   Gross loss         -34,548.75

Total # of trades             285   Percent profitable         68%
Number winning trades         194   Number losing trades        91

Largest winning trade    3,070.00   Largest losing trade  -2,267.50
Average winning trade      678.28   Average losing trade    -379.66
Ratio avg win/avg loss       1.79   Avg trade (win & loss)   340.48

Max consecutive winners        20   Max consecutive losers       5
Avg # bars in winners           1   Avg # bars in losers         1

Max drawdown             5,912.50   Avg # of contracts held      2
Profit factor                1.22   Max # of contracts held      4
Account size required   16,712.50   Return on account         581%
=========================================================================
```

Figure 4.19—Portfolio Analyzer for Test

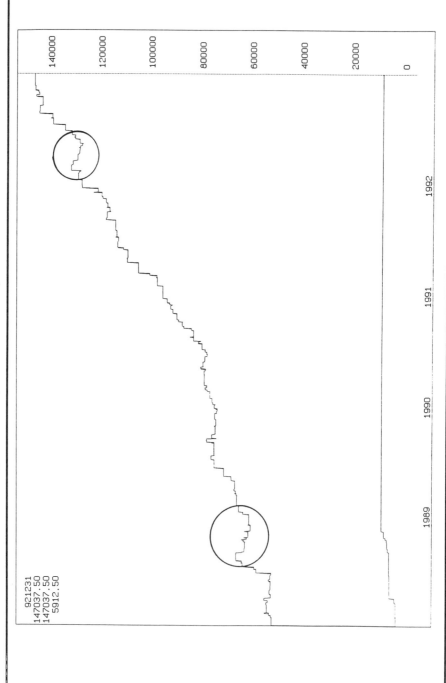

One Day at a Time

The last piece of software I want you to see is a product called One Day at a Time; it is more a trading tool. It is a product written by Wells Wilder which came into use as a game. As you actually look at the markets it will hold off on some of the bars that are there, and show you just a few of the bars at a time. Your goal is to make trading decisions based on what you see. It is a beautiful charting package. I just want you to see how easy it is to use. (See Figure 4.20.)

There is a chart of the S&P in a daily mode through December 1992 on daily bars. I have elected to see the moon phases. It shows me when there is a full moon and when there is a half moon. If I wanted to see candlestick charts I would touch the J key for Japanese Yen, and then hit candlestick charts. (See Figure 4.21.)

If I wanted to do one of Wells Wilder's models which is called an Adam Projection (a very high level piece of math that projects where it thinks the market is going to go in the next few bars), I would hit the letter A and One Day at a Time would project where that piece of math would put the market in the next few days. (See Figure 4.22.)

If I wanted to see weekly charts, I'd just hit the W, and One Day at a Time would change all that data to weekly data (Figure 4.23).

If I wanted to see monthly charts, I would hit the W one more time (Figure 4.24).

My machine, by the way, is a 386-20, which is very low tech now. Three years ago it was state-of-the-art. So it's a little slower than the one on your desk. Here we have monthly bars of the S&P back through 1984 in candlestick format with an Adam Projection, and I never use more than one finger. One Day at a Time is a very good system for someone who is trying to learn the markets and learn how to manipulate data.

Implementation

The power of using your system or any system rests in your implementation. The key is not in the writing or the testing of a system, it is in imple-

Figure 4.20—Chart of S&P Daily Mode

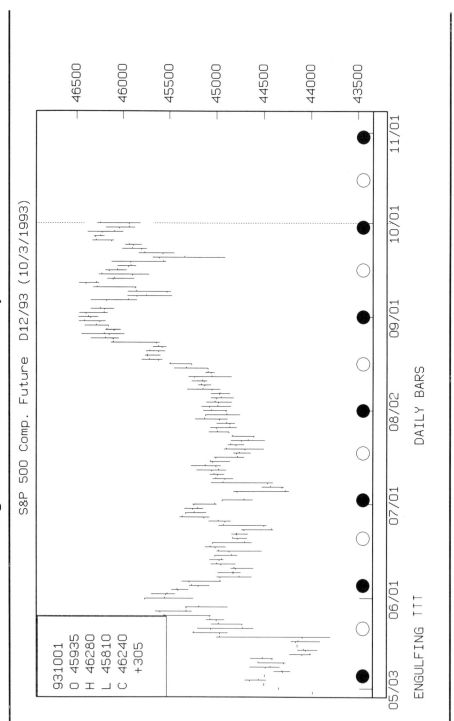

S&P 500 Comp. Future D12/93 (10/3/1993)

931001
O 45935
H 46280
L 45810
C 46240
+305

Figure 4.21—Candlestick Charts

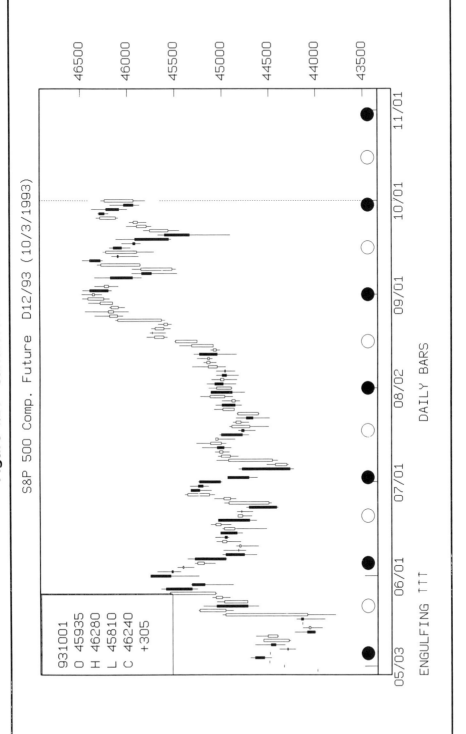

S&P 500 Comp. Future D12/93 (10/3/1993)

931001
O 45935
H 46280
L 45810
C 46240
  +305

ENGULFING ↑↑↑   DAILY BARS

Figure 4.22

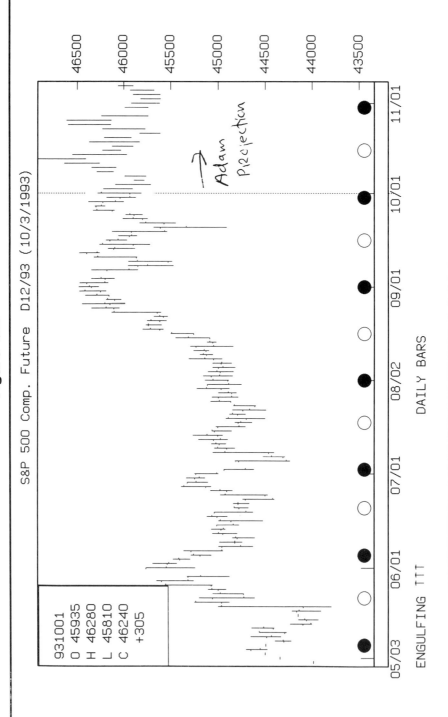

Figure 4.23

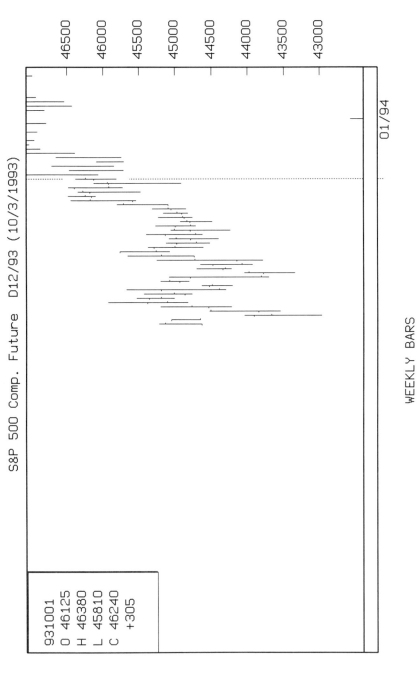

S&P 500 Comp. Future   D12/93 (10/3/1993)

931001
O 46125
H 46380
L 45810
C 46240
  +305

46500
46000
45500
45000
44500
44000
43500
43000

01/94

WEEKLY BARS

Figure 4.24

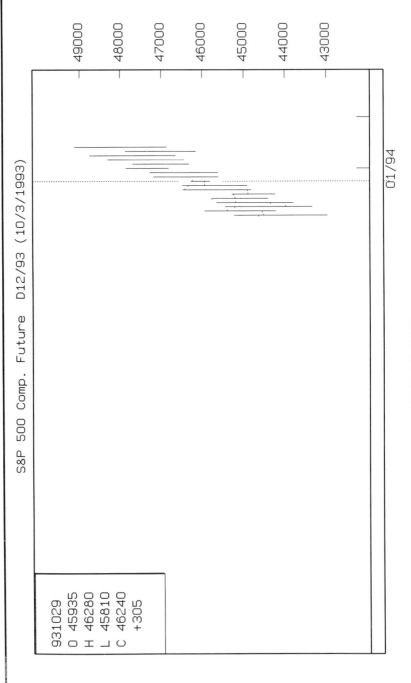

S&P 500 Comp. Future D12/93 (10/3/1993)

931029
O 45935
H 46280
L 45810
C 46240
+305

49000
48000
47000
46000
45000
44000
43000

01/94

MONTHLY BARS

menting it every day. You will forget to run your numbers if you are trading a third-party system or you will look at a trade and say, "I do not want to do that. There is a report coming out next Tuesday, and I do not want to be in that position," or you will say, "It's been too choppy lately. I don't want to trade the dollar index." *You* will defeat your own system.

You can get the best system I develop, the best system you develop, the best system Wells Wilder develops, but if you don't follow the rules explicitly the way they were written and tested, you do not have a system.

Plan Your Strategy, Then Follow Your Plan

Take, for example, the Buy Monday plan, discussed earlier in this chapter. Here is the entry rule. If it is Monday, buy it. I will repeat that. If it is Monday, buy it. Here is the exit rule. Get out on the close on Monday. We are trading S&P, and we will buy it every Monday. We will put in a $500 stop, and we will get out on Monday's close.

I have given this same system in many seminars around the country. People invariably call me up and say, "I tried your system and it didn't work." I say, "Oh, really?" (By the way, it only works half the time, so it is not illogical that this would happen.) I will ask the client, "How did you do it?"

"Well, last Tuesday I bought it, and then I got out and I lost money."

"Last Tuesday!" I would reiterate. "But the system says to buy on Monday. It is a very simple S&P system. You put in a $500 stop, and you get out on the close. Why didn't you buy it on Monday?"

"We weren't open Monday."

The point is: It doesn't matter how simple a system is. If you do not implement it correctly, then you really do not have a system. I think this is an extreme example, but if someone can foul up a system like this, think about what they can do with three or four pages of Fortran or C Programming.

5

System Ingredients

The ingredients in your system stew are indicators. How many you use is entirely up to you, but just as spices in chili, keep it simple.

Technical Indicators

There are trend-following indicators, momentum indicators, volume indicators, and time-sensitive indicators. I will illustrate how to use systems using all of these in Chapter 9, as we get into more elaborate systems. Right now, let's think about indicators. Many books have been published showing the various momentum indicators, oscillators, and moving averages. I will refer you to those texts if you want to know the difference between an RSI and stochastic, the difference between an MACD oscillator and a moving average. That is beyond the scope of this book. You will have various indicators which you will personally like. I am going to show you how to take whatever indicator you like and drop it into code and make it into a trading system. The way I am going to show you how to do that is to actually show you trading systems.

I am going to show a simple reversal system which is the way I feel you should write *your* first trading system. What this means is: If you are not long, you should be short, and vice versa. You are always in the market. (See Figure 5.1a and Figure 5.1b.)

This is a one-year test of British Pound done on a TradeStation. It is done on 180-minute data. It was from the period of August 1, 1990 through July 31, 1991. There were 56 trades. It was correct 46 percent of the time. There was $1,700 on the winners, $999 on the losers. No stop. You were always long or short. $55 commission. This is not a great system because $8,200 is the drawdown to make $15,000, and the net profits to drawdown ratio is not even two to one.

Think with me a minute. S&P margins are currently about $15,000. British Pound margins are less than $3,000, so that means you can trade five of these for one S&P. If I was showing you a S&P track record that was five times 15 ($75,000 in one year), you would get a little excited.

It is an interesting system. I will show you the rules in a minute. I am going to go through and show you these different segments using reversals. You are always long or short. This is the first year. This is a five-month segment following that first year. Do you notice it is about the same percent right, and about the same dollar per trade? These are the important numbers.

Forty-two percent right, $374. This is a full year. This is a straight reversal. Now, this is over the March data, and it is losing its momentum. It did not work. This is over the June data. It is back to about where it was in the right column, but it has lost its momentum.

Figure 5.1a
Joe's Gap

```
Joe's Gap  BP E91-180 min    08/01/90 - 07/31/91
                    Performance Summary:  All Trades

Total net profit        $   15257.50   Open position P/L      $     -25.00
Gross profit            $   45232.50   Gross loss             $  -29975.00

Total # of trades              56      Percent profitable            46%
Number winning trades          26      Number losing trades          30

Largest winning trade   $    5545.00   Largest losing trade   $   -2430.00
Average winning trade   $    1739.71   Average losing trade   $    -999.17
Ratio avg win/avg loss          1.74   Avg trade(win & loss)  $     272.46

Max consec. winners             3      Max consec. losers             5
Avg # bars in winners          17      Avg # bars in losers          10

Max intraday drawdown   $   -8275.00
Profit factor                   1.51   Max # contracts held           1
Account size required   $    8275.00   Return on account            184%
```
- -
```
                    Performance Summary:  Long Trades

Total net profit        $    4847.50   Open position P/L      $     -25.00
Gross profit            $   20615.00   Gross loss             $  -15767.50

Total # of trades              28      Percent profitable            43%
Number winning trades          12      Number losing trades          16

Largest winning trade   $    5170.00   Largest losing trade   $   -2430.00
Average winning trade   $    1717.92   Average losing trade   $    -985.47
Ratio avg win/avg loss          1.74   Avg trade(win & loss)  $     173.13

Max consec. winners             3      Max consec. losers             5
Avg # bars in winners          19      Avg # bars in losers          10

Max intraday drawdown   $   -8625.00
Profit factor                   1.31   Max # contracts held           1
Account size required   $    8625.00   Return on account             56%
```
- -
```
                    Performance Summary:  Short Trades

Total net profit        $   10410.00   Open position P/L      $       0.00
Gross profit            $   24617.50   Gross loss             $  -14207.50

Total # of trades              28      Percent profitable            50%
Number winning trades          14      Number losing trades          14

Largest winning trade   $    5545.00   Largest losing trade   $   -2355.00
Average winning trade   $    1758.39   Average losing trade   $   -1014.82
Ratio avg win/avg loss          1.73   Avg trade(win & loss)  $     371.79

Max consec. winners             6      Max consec. losers             4
Avg # bars in winners          15      Avg # bars in losers           9

Max intraday drawdown   $   -5547.50
Profit factor                   1.73   Max # contracts held           1
Account size required   $    5547.50   Return on account            188%
```

Figure 5.1b
Joe's Gap

```
Joe's Gap   BP E91-180 min    08/01/90 - 07/31/91
                   Performance Summary:  All Trades

Total net profit      $   13422.50   Open position P/L     $       0.00
Gross profit          $   25057.50   Gross loss            $  -11635.00

Total # of trades             113    Percent profitable           63%
Number winning trades          71    Number losing trades          42

Largest winning trade $    1320.00   Largest losing trade  $    -680.00
Average winning trade $     352.92   Average losing trade  $    -277.02
Ratio avg win/avg loss       1.27    Avg trade(win & loss) $     118.78

Max consec. winners             7    Max consec. losers             4
Avg # bars in winners           1    Avg # bars in losers           1

Max intraday drawdown $   -1450.00
Profit factor                2.15    Max # contracts held           1
Account size required $    1450.00   Return on account           926%
- - .. - -- - .. - -- - .. - -- - .. - -- - .. - -- - .. - -
                   Performance Summary:  Long Trades

Total net profit      $    6425.00   Open position P/L     $       0.00
Gross profit          $   12775.00   Gross loss            $   -6350.00

Total # of trades              55    Percent profitable           64%
Number winning trades          35    Number losing trades          20

Largest winning trade $    1320.00   Largest losing trade  $    -680.00
Average winning trade $     365.00   Average losing trade  $    -317.50
Ratio avg win/avg loss       1.15    Avg trade(win & loss) $     116.82

Max consec. winners             6    Max consec. losers             5
Avg # bars in winners           1    Avg # bars in losers           1

Max intraday drawdown $   -1607.50
Profit factor                2.01    Max # contracts held           1
Account size required $    1607.50   Return on account           400%
- - .. - -- - .. - -- - .. - -- - .. - -- - .. - -- - .. - -
                   Performance Summary:  Short Trades

Total net profit      $    6997.50   Open position P/L     $       0.00
Gross profit          $   12282.50   Gross loss            $   -5285.00

Total # of trades              58    Percent profitable           62%
Number winning trades          36    Number losing trades          22

Largest winning trade $    1195.00   Largest losing trade  $    -680.00
Average winning trade $     341.18   Average losing trade  $    -240.23
Ratio avg win/avg loss       1.42    Avg trade(win & loss) $     120.65

Max consec. winners             8    Max consec. losers             4
Avg # bars in winners           1    Avg # bars in losers           1

Max intraday drawdown $   -1792.50
Profit factor                2.32    Max # contracts held           1
Account size required $    1792.50   Return on account           390%
```

Showing You Methodology

This is what I suggest you do:

1. Devise a system.

2. Make it a stop and reversal system.

3. Say, "Okay, now I want to try it with a money management stop, and I want to get out on the close, day of entry."

4. Make it a daytrading system.

I will run through these same sheets. Now we are talking about something. Look at the first period. It was 63 percent right, it made $13,000 with a $1,400 drawdown. Now we are closer to the 10 to 1 we were talking about as a daytrading system—the exact same entry technique.

The next period is 52 percent right, made $3,800. It is about a two to one system, but better than this segment without this stop and objective.

In the third period it made $2,100, 51 percent right. Nothing there really to brag about. I am showing you methodology. This is the first three months of this year. Nothing there. Then this is the current—about the same.

The last test I am going to show you is a 625 stop, which is a full point in British Pound, no magic there, nothing optimized, and a reversal. Now remember, the first system I had was pure reversal—long or short. The second system was a 625 stop or get out on the close. The third system is the same entry technique with a 625 stop or a stop and reverse.

Let's look at this in Figure 5.2.

Write these numbers down: $17,000 the first year. $6,800 the next five months. $22,000 the next year. Now you're going to have some subtracting to do. A negative $1,100 and a negative $175—you've got open loss. About $1,300 negative and a negative $3,000, so about a $4,300 negative from the positive—$4,100 and change. This is trading one contract of BP for a little less than 36 months through tick data, and you have a $41,000 gain trading one contract. Now, I am going to give this system to you, and

Figure 5.2

```
Joe's Gap  BP E91-180 min   08/01/90 - 07/31/91
                  Performance Summary:  All Trades

Total net profit      $  17005.00  Open position P/L     $    287.50
Gross profit          $  44652.50  Gross loss            $ -27647.50

Total # of trades           64     Percent profitable         42%
Number winning trades       27     Number losing trades       37

Largest winning trade $   6320.00  Largest losing trade  $  -1555.00
Average winning trade $   1653.80  Average losing trade  $   -747.23
Ratio avg win/avg loss      2.21   Avg trade(win & loss) $    265.70

Max consec. winners          3     Max consec. losers          6
Avg # bars in winners       15     Avg # bars in losers        5

Max intraday drawdown $  -4765.00
Profit factor               1.62   Max # contracts held        1
Account size required $   4765.00  Return on account         357%
--------------------------------------------------------------------
                  Performance Summary:  Long Trades

Total net profit      $   8415.00  Open position P/L     $    287.50
Gross profit          $  22097.50  Gross loss            $ -13682.50

Total # of trades           32     Percent profitable         41%
Number winning trades       13     Number losing trades       19

Largest winning trade $   6320.00  Largest losing trade  $  -1555.00
Average winning trade $   1699.81  Average losing trade  $   -720.13
Ratio avg win/avg loss      2.36   Avg trade(win & loss) $    262.97

Max consec. winners          3     Max consec. losers          5
Avg # bars in winners       18     Avg # bars in losers        5

Max intraday drawdown $  -5022.50
Profit factor               1.62   Max # contracts held        1
Account size required $   5022.50  Return on account         168%
--------------------------------------------------------------------
                  Performance Summary:  Short Trades

Total net profit      $   8590.00  Open position P/L     $      0.00
Gross profit          $  22555.00  Gross loss            $ -13965.00

Total # of trades           32     Percent profitable         44%
Number winning trades       14     Number losing trades       18

Largest winning trade $   3907.50  Largest losing trade  $  -1505.00
Average winning trade $   1611.07  Average losing trade  $   -775.83
Ratio avg win/avg loss      2.08   Avg trade(win & loss) $    268.44

Max consec. winners          6     Max consec. losers          4
Avg # bars in winners       12     Avg # bars in losers        4

Max intraday drawdown $  -3992.50
Profit factor               1.62   Max # contracts held        1
Account size required $   3992.50  Return on account         215%
```

hopefully you can make it better. But this is a pretty good system. (See Figure 5.3.)

When You Are Analyzing, Do Things in Baby Steps

Only analyze one line at a time. If the high is less than L1, then sell tomorrow at market. What does that mean? If the high is less than the low of yesterday, then sell tomorrow at market.

The buy side is: If L is above H1 (if the low is more than the high of yesterday), then buy tomorrow at the market. I had a rule I was going to test, but I didn't bother. This rule says: *If bar since entry greater than 12, then exit long at market. If bar since entry greater than 12, then exit short at market.* I have placed French brackets around it. In computer language when you put French brackets around something, you can leave it there, but the machine won't read it. That will be my next idea to test.

A Scientific Method—Trading Logic Nobody Teaches You

Let's review what my scientific method is. I first come up with an idea. I think, "when markets gap, if the gap holds, it will continue in that direction." Okay? So what I am saying is, on a three-hour bar, if that is the last three hours and this is the current three hours, this low has not gone down to that high if it is see-through, then on the next bar, I want to buy.

Here is the sell. If this high is below that low and it holds there for three hours on the next bar, I want to sell. This is all there is to this. It is a gap. Let me tell you why it works. This is part of SystemWriter that nobody will teach you, and I want to teach it to you. Everybody will teach you the match part, but use your brain and think logically. *Why* does this thing happen?

Figure 5.3
Computer Code

```
////////////////////////////////////////////\\\\\\\\\\\\\\\\\\\\\\\\\\\\\\\\\\\\\\\\\\\:
                                        SYSTEM

Name        : Joe's Gap
Notes :

Last Update : 10/03/93 11:06am
Printed on  : 10/03/93 11:06am
Verified    : YES

//////////////////////////////////////// CODE \\\\\\\\\\\\\\\\\\\\\\\\\\\\\\\\\\\\\\\\\

{System: Joe's Gap
Notes : Written as a 60 min. daytrade system in 1991

[ 2] MaxBarsBack
  [*] Generate Realtime Orders
Entry Options :
  [* ] Do not allow multiple entries in same direction
  [ ] Allow multiple entries in same direction
      by different entry signals
  [ ] Allow multiple entries in same direction
      by same and different entry signals( up to 20 contracts)

  [* ] Money Management Stop
      Amount: ($) [625.00]
  [ ] Close all trades at end of day

 Copyright 1993, Krutsinger & Krutsinger, Inc. 1-800-767-2508,
 PO Box 822, Centerville, Iowa 52544

Provided as an educational example in the art of system writing
}

If H < L[1] then Sell tomorrow at market;
If L > H[1] then Buy  tomorrow at market;


{ Here's a currency model that's simple enough to execute without a computer,
The thinking behind this model is that most currency trading happens while US
traders sleep. If a gap occurs and is not filled, there is a tendency to trend in the
direection of the gap. The model adds positions on additional gaps in the same
direction and is always in the market. A $55 commission per contract has been
deducted.


Prepared using Omega Tick Data and Omega TradeStation
Version 3.01 by Omega Research,Inc.}
```

```
//////////////////////////////////////////\\\\\\\\\\\\\\\\\\\\\\\\\\\\\\\\\\\\\\\\\\\\\
Prepared using Omega TradeStation Version 3.01 by Omega Research, Inc.
```

Here is why. Pretend that you are short coming into this day. Those are the last three-hour bars for the last couple of days. Pretend that a position-trading guy is short, and he sees this happen. All of a sudden the market opens against his position. What does he do the very first time this happens? Nothing because the trend is down. It is reacting against the trend a little bit.

However, as the day wears on and he sees the gap is not filled, he will start re-evaluating positions and he will start taking off positions, and the market—as long as this gap isn't filled these last three hours—will tend to close in this direction.

I can prove it because I have shown you with over three years of tick data that it works over 50 percent of the time and pulls out $42,000—$41,500 actually, simulated, so this idea holds up.

How Did I Come Up with Three-Hour Bars?

Nobody trades three-hour bars, but I do. At one time I was living in Las Vegas. We were on west coast time, and I hated coming in at 5:20 in the morning, so I was looking for systems that would let me come in at 8:20 in the morning. I kept making my bar size bigger so I wouldn't have to be there until my first bar was formed. The first bar was formed at 8:20, and I would see the market and I would make my decision.

Your Secret Weapon: Thinking and Planning

I want to take a sidebar here and talk to you about how you will come up with your ideas. It is one thing for me to say, "Here is what I did." I am going to tell you a real secret—you can come up with great ideas too, probably better than mine. All you have to do is think. What you have to do is get up one hour earlier in the morning or go to bed one hour later at night.

Forget about everything else. Take a yellow pad, and think about one thing. Focus all of your attention on this one thing. Maybe you want to focus on how to trade pork bellies, how you have seen them traded in the

91

past, or how you would like to trade them. Write down all the things that a good trader in pork bellies would do—what reports he would read, what charts he would study, everything.

Some of you in marketing know that when you find a guy who buys something in the mail, and he buys a lot of it constantly, you want to focus on that guy and find out these types of things: Where did that guy come from? How old is he? Where does he live? So you can find more guys like him.

You need to use the same concept with trading. When you find a technique that works, something that holds, focus on that technique and see not only what you can learn from it, but how you can replicate it.

How often have you set aside an hour for thinking and sat down with a pad and pencil? This is what the great traders and the great system developers do. They sit down and think, "What happened today in the market today that was unusual? How could I have made money from it?" Try this. You are bound to come up with all kinds of trading ideas.

Implementing Your Trading System

How can you put your newly designed trading system to work? This is one thing you could do. You could combine Paul Revere with Joe's Gap and say, "I only want to take Paul Revere trades that have worked using Joe's Gap system." You see how you could do that? You could put the power of something you have learned over tick data and put the power of something you have learned over a massive amount of daily data and just take big trades, trades that are destined for greatness.

6

Sophisticated and Unusual Systems

The reasonable man adapts himself to the world:
the unreasonable man persists in trying to adapt
the world to himself. Therefore all progress
depends on the unreasonable man.
— George Bernard Shaw —

Before I get into the sophisticated systems, remember the building blocks of a trading system are: (1) market entry, (2) exiting with a profit, and (3) exiting with a loss.

Now we are going to look at building sophisticated trading systems, unveiling several trading systems which include technical tools; look at some trading rules; talk about testing your trading systems for profitability, percentage of winners and losers, average profit and loss and maximum drawdown; and evaluate both daytrading and longer term systems. Before we go too much further, let's take a look at systems themselves and decide what components we should have in those systems.

Trend-Following Systems

Momentum Indicators

You can look at momentum indicators. The simplest momentum indicator is to take a 10-day moving average and a 40-day moving average and subtract the two to see how the momentum has lost or gained. I want to show you an example of a momentum indicator. It's not very sophisticated, but I think you'll get a real kick out of it. (See Figure 6.1.)

Joe's Oil Well

This system is called Joe's Oil Well. It covers a piece of daily data from June 13, 1983 through January 31, 1991. I have no stop or exit rule. This is a stop and reverse system. (Remember, a stop and reverse system is when you are always long or short in the market, never out.) It has a 50-day setback with a 50-day commission. Remember how I said, "always find out from a system developer what the setback is." There is no slippage figure. There are no stops.

It carries positions overnight. We are looking at a margin of $3,000. Let's look at the gain on this product. We have a $53,000 gain over the whole period. We have 52 trades over that period. Forty-two percent are right. The average winner is $3,400. The average loser is $735. The average trade or the Daddy-go-to-town number is $1,020 after commissions.

You hold winners 64 days, and you hold losers 16 days. The drawdown is $6,800. If you take $6,800 into $53,000 our ratio is a little over 8 to 1. According to the criteria we have developed so far, this is a good trading

Figure 6.1—Joe's Oil Well—Daily Crude Oil

Joe's Oil Wells -Daily Crude Oil

Data from 6/13/83-1/31/91 with no stop, no exit rules, 50 days set back and $50 commission, no slippage figured, toggle no stops on day of entry. This system carries positions over night.

```
/////////////////////////////////////////\\\\\\\\\\\\\\\\\\\
Directory : C:\SMP                          Printed on    : 11/04/91 11:36r

                        PERFORMANCE SUMMARY

Model Name    : Joe's Oil Wells           Developer    : Krutsinger
Test Number   :     1 of     1
Notes : More Info? Call 1-800-767-2508, Joe Krutsinger's 24 Hour Voice Mail

Data     : CRUDE OIL NYMEX   01/91
Calc Dates  : 06/13/83 - 01/31/91

Num. Conv. P. Value Comm  Slippage Margin Format  Drive:\Path\FileName
------------------------------------------------------------------
 188   2  $ 10.000  $ 50   $ 0   $ 3,000 Omega   C:\SMPDATA\F037.DTA

//////////////////////////// ALL TRADES  - Test 1 \\\\\\\\\\\\\\\\\\\\\\\\\\\\

Total net profit      $53,050.00     Gross loss           $-22,070.00
Gross profit          $75,120.00

Total # of trades          52        Percent profitable         42%
Number winning trades      22        Number losing trades        30

Largest winning trade   $18,360.00   Largest losing trade    $-2,880.00
Average winning trade    $3,414.55   Average losing trade      $-735.67
Ratio avg win/avg loss       4.64    Avg trade (win & loss)   $1,020.19

Max consecutive winners     4        Max consecutive losers        6
Avg # bars in winners      64        Avg # bars in losers         16

Max closed-out drawdown $-6,850.00   Max intra-day drawdown  $-7,140.00
Profit factor              3.40      Max # of contracts held       1
Account size required   $10,140.00   Return on account          523%

                     Highlights - All trades
Description                  Date       Time      Amount
---------------------------------------------------------------
Largest Winning Trade      10/30/90     --    $  18,360.00
Largest Losing Trade       08/07/86     --    $  -2,880.00
Largest String of + Trades 01/17/91     --            4
Largest String of - Trades 12/15/86     --            6
Maximum Closed-Out Drawdown 12/15/86    --    $  -6,850.00
Maximum Intra-Day Drawdown  12/17/86    --    $  -7,140.00
```

Entry Signal Rules:

If @Average(Close,10) > @Average(Close,40) then buy tomorrow Market on Open;

If @Average(Close,10) < @Average(Close,40) then sell tomorrow Market on Open;

Logic:

Why do I think the system appears to work?

The crude oil market is very trend sensitive. Most traders try very hard to make complex formulas to determine when to be in the market, try the oil well method–(always in the market!)

Lesson?

This is an example of using the most basic moving average crossover, always in the market. Simple systems can work, can't they!

system. It has a big average trade. It has more than 30 trade instances. It has a good ratio. It is a very good trading system.

I think you will get a kick out of the rules. Here they are: If the 10-day moving average is above the 40-day moving average you are long. If it is not, you are not. That is it. It is a true momentum system. If the 10 is above the 40, you are long. If it is not, you are short.

What is the logic? Why does this system appear to work? The crude oil market is very trend-sensitive. It is a very liquid market. Most traders try very hard to make a complex formula to determine when to be in the market, but the oil market approach really lends itself to oil producers.

If you think about it—if you leased oil land and put a drill out there, every time oil went up a dollar or down a dollar, you would not pull your drill out of the ground and go home. This program tells you to either be long or short all the time. You can take a look at it and tell how it did over the Iraqi war, and so forth. It came through like a champ. It is the basic momentum system.

Joe's Volume and Minute S&P System

Remember, these are hypothetical examples run on simulated data to show an illustration. I'm going to teach you how to use some of this code and put it into your own systems. I'm not saying these are systems for you to trade. We're going to be talking about volume. This system I call Joe's Vol. (See Figure 6.2.)

This is tick data for only five months—August 1, 1990 through December 31, 1990, but it is five-minute tick data. Let's think about that. If it is an eight-hour day and it is 12 five-minute bars, that is 60 time periods in an hour. You have 12 bars in an hour. You have eight hours in a day. So you are looking at 90 bars a day. Every day you analyze is like looking at 90 daily bars. A five-month track record which is 150 days is the same as 150 times 92, which means that we are talking about a very long track record on daily bars.

When somebody shows you a shorter track record on five-minute bars, remember, they almost have to show you a shorter track record. You can

96

Figure 6.2—Joe's Volume and Minute S&P System

Entry Signal Rules:

If Time > 1500 and V >45
then Sell at Low[1] stop;

If Time > 1500 and V >45
then Buy at High[1] stop;

Note:
Time is New York and
V represents total tick volume for the bar

Logic:

Why do I think the system appears to work?
At 3:00 New York time, currency and bond futures
markets close and all trader's eyes turn to the S&P.
Increased activity (?Tick Volume) and a breakout of the
recent highs or lows can lead to a substantial move in
the direction of the breakout. If 75% "losing" trades
bothers you, try a stop that is wider than $150. More
and more traders try to even up for the day and stop
fighting the newly established trend moving the
market towards the close ever more dramatically.

Lesson?

This is an example of using Time and Volume in a
signal, both are rare, try them.

Joe's Vol -5 Minute S&P 500

Tick data from 8/01/90-12/31/90 with a $150 stop,
exit Market on Close is checked, 10 bars set back and
$30 commission , no slippage figured.
This system can carry a position over night.

Performance Summary: All Trades

Total net profit	$	7145.00	Open position P/L	$ 0.00
Gross profit	$	9305.00	Gross loss	$ -2160.00
Total # of trades		16	Percent profitable	25%
Number winning trades		4	Number losing trades	12
Largest winning trade	$	3795.00	Largest losing trade	$ -180.00
Average winning trade	$	2326.25	Average losing trade	$ -180.00
Ratio avg win/avg loss		12.92	Avg trade(win & loss)	$ 446.56
Max consecutive winners		3	Max consecutive losers	7
Avg # bars in winners		78	Avg # bars in losers	8
Max intraday drawdown	$	-1260.00		
Profit factor		4.31	Max # contracts held	1
Account size required	$	1260.00	Return on account	567%

Notes:

analyze only so many datapoints. This one only has 16 trades, so it does not meet our rule of having enough trades to reach a conclusion. But I think you will find the math interesting. It made $714. It uses a $150 stop in the S&P. This is a close stop, too close actually. This is one of the reasons this system is only right 25 percent of the time—because the stop is placed too close.

One of the tricks I do when I develop a system is: I try to break it. I try to put a stop too close. I try to find the fatal flaw, if you will. One hundred fifty dollars is about as close a stop as you would ever use.

The average winner is $2,300. The average loser is $180. There has been a $2,100 drawdown. The ratio is very good. Ready for the rules? If time is greater than 1500 in New York, and the tick volume is greater than 45, then buy at the highest high of the last bar on a stop. If time is greater than 1500 in New York and tick volume is greater than 45, then sell at the lowest low of the last bar on a stop. Whichever one of those hits first, use a $150 stop and get out on the close. This is the system. The logic is the important thing. First, whenever I write about time, I write in New York time because I travel all over the world, and I never remember where I was when I wrote a system. Second, when we talk about tick volume, if 45 ticks have taken place in a five-minute span, then we will take action. 1500 New York time is 2:00 in Chicago. What happens at 2:00 in Chicago? Bonds close. Currencies close. Do you know what this means to the S&P? A whole bunch of new players. People who have played all day in these other markets have an hour and a half to trade, and they trade S&P.

Stops

If you can stand 75 percent of your trades being losing trades, then use the $150 stop. If you cannot stand 75 percent of your trades being losing trades, then make the stop wider. This is the way to clean that out. This is an example of using both time and volume in a signal, and both of them are very rare. Hardly anybody trades this way, which is probably why this particular piece of code works so well.

Joe's Texas Two Step

This one is complicated. I haven't shown you anything complicated yet, but here goes—this is Joe's Texas Two Step (Figure 6.3).

Here is what you can do with indicators. This is tick data from August 1, 1990 through July 31, 1991. We are using a $500 stop, a 17-bar setback, and a $30 commission. Look at the profits—this is for one year of data. $32,000 plus $267 and the drawdown is $5,900, so our ratio is 5 to 1.

Not the best, but this is a system trading British Pound. The British Pound market is less than $3,000. The average trade is $138. The average winner is 2.38 times the average loser. It is right 40 percent of the time.

Look at the math on this. This piece of math is the key to all of you indicator traders. Read only the buy side because it is a little elaborate. How do we get a 14-period RSI? It is the RSI that comes in the can. By the way, if you want to know indicator lengths, if you take the length of the average indicator and divide it by half, this is a good point for an indicator length. This is the way you came up with 20-day and 10-day moving averages. They were half the size of the main cycle.

Wells Wilder, who came up with the RSI, believed in the 28-day moon cycles, so a lot of the indicators based on that work are 14 days, half the lunar cycle.

Pretend we are not going to test for any cycle lengths. We are going to take what is in the books. The one in the book is a 14-period RSI. Here is where it gets tricky.

"If the 14-period RSI is above the 3-period moving average of the RSI, and if the RSI of yesterday was below the moving average of yesterday . . ." Although this is elaborate, what we have done is a crossover of the RSI. If this is all true, then buy at the market. If this is false, sell at the market.

Let me tell you why this is such a cool code for you. Using any and every indicator you can think of—DMI, channel index, ADX, all you have to do is change the word RSI to your favorite indicator, and now you have a trading system. This is great. This means if you have a favorite indicator, you can drop it in what I call the shell code, and you have a trading system to revamp.

Figure 6.3—Joe's Texas Two Step

Joe's Texas Two Step -
180 Minute British Pound
Tick data from 8/01/90-7/31/91 with a $500 stop,
17 bars set back and $30 commission no slippage
figured. This system carries positions over night.

Performance Summary: All Trades

Total net profit	$ 32625.00	Open position P/L	$ 262.50
Gross profit	$ 91122.50	Gross loss	$ -58497.50
Total # of trades	235	Percent profitable	40%
Number winning trades	93	Number losing trades	142
Largest winning trade	$ 5895.00	Largest losing trade	$ -2117.50
Average winning trade	$ 979.81	Average losing trade	$ -411.95
Ratio avg win/avg loss	2.38	Avg trade(win & loss)	138.83
Max consecutive winners	7	Max consecutive losers	8
Avg # bars in winners	4	Avg # bars in losers	2
Max intraday drawdown	$ -5910.00		
Profit factor	1.56	Max # contracts held	1
Account size required	$ 5910.00	Return on account	552%

Notes:

Entry Signal Rules:

If @RSI(c,14) > @Average(@RSI(C,14),3)
and @RSI(c,14)[1] < @Average(@RSI(C,14),3)[1]
then buy at market;

If @RSI(c,14) < @Average(@RSI(C,14),3)
and @RSI(c,14)[1] > @Average(@RSI(C,14),3)[1]
then sell at market;

Logic:

Why do I think the system appears to work?

Unlike most crossover systems, Joe's Texas Two Step
requires a NEW signal in the opposite direction if it is
stopped out with a loss! This technique might help a lot
of trend following systems. By using a moving average
of the RSI as the trade indicator, you can slow down or
smooth a ragged system. This is the basic logic of "slow"
stochastic.

Lesson?

This is an example of using a function of a
function,(Two steps) and an unusual size bar,
(3 hours), try both of these ideas!

Why does this system appear to work? Unlike most crossover systems, Joe's Texas Two Step requires a new signal in the opposite direction if it is stopped out with a loss. This technique might help a lot of trend-following systems. By using a moving average of the RSI as the trade indicator, you slow down or smooth a ragged system.

This is the base premise of slow stochastic in the first place—taking a moving average of an indicator to slow it down. This is an example of using a function of a function, which are two steps, an unusual sized bar—a 3-hour bar—and putting them together. It is a very interesting code.

Stock Systems

I am going to talk about stock systems. I am not a stock expert, and I do not mean to sound like one. However, I want to show you how you can take some of the things you are learning here and apply them to stock trading. The basic premise behind the stock market is buying and holding.

I took a TradeStation and generated IBM data weekly back through 1962. I said to myself, "The first day I get the data I am going to buy 1,000 shares of IBM stock and I am going to hold them and never do anything with them." (See Figure 6.4.) Over that period of time I would have had a $12,000 drawdown, and I would have had $25,000 made on 1,000 shares of stock.

Parabolic

What can we do to beat that? I am going to show you a system called Parabolic, a known system written by Wells Wilder in 1978. It has been publicized since that time, so it is certainly not brand new. It does not work on every stock, but I think it works well on IBM. I want to show you on a weekly chart what this does (see Figure 6.5).

This system made $138,000 plus $1,375 currently on those 1,000 shares, and it traded 126 times. All I am saying is, if you are above the parabolic you are long the stock, and if you are below the parabolic you are short the stops. That is it. No fancy stops. Nothing sophisticated at all.

CHAPTER 6

Figure 6.4
Buy and Hold—IBM Weekly

```
Buy and Hold  IBM-Weekly    01/05/62 - 03/19/93      18
                    Performance Summary:  All Trades

Total net profit      $      0.00   Open position P/L      $   25766.00
Gross profit          $      0.00   Gross loss             $       0.00

Total # of trades            0      Percent profitable             0%
Number winning trades        0      Number losing trades           0

Largest winning trade $      0.00   Largest losing trade   $       0.00
Average winning trade $      0.00   Average losing trade   $       0.00
Ratio avg win/avg loss    100.00    Avg trade(win & loss)  $       0.00

Max consec. winners          0      Max consec. losers             0
Avg # bars in winners        0      Avg # bars in losers           0

Max intraday drawdown $ -12859.00
Profit factor             100.00    Max # contracts held        1000
Account size required $  62859.00   Return on account              0%
-- -- -- -- -- -- -- -- -- -- -- -- -- -- -- -- -- -- -- -- --
                    Performance Summary:  Long Trades

Total net profit      $      0.00   Open position P/L      $   25766.00
Gross profit          $      0.00   Gross loss             $       0.00

Total # of trades            0      Percent profitable             0%
Number winning trades        0      Number losing trades           0

Largest winning trade $      0.00   Largest losing trade   $       0.00
Average winning trade $      0.00   Average losing trade   $       0.00
Ratio avg win/avg loss    100.00    Avg trade(win & loss)  $       0.00

Max consec. winners          0      Max consec. losers             0
Avg # bars in winners        0      Avg # bars in losers           0

Max intraday drawdown $ -12859.00
Profit factor             100.00    Max # contracts held        1000
Account size required $  62859.00   Return on account              0%
-- -- -- -- -- -- -- -- -- -- -- -- -- -- -- -- -- -- -- -- --
                    Performance Summary:  Short Trades

Total net profit      $      0.00   Open position P/L      $       0.00
Gross profit          $      0.00   Gross loss             $       0.00

Total # of trades            0      Percent profitable             0%
Number winning trades        0      Number losing trades           0

Largest winning trade $      0.00   Largest losing trade   $       0.00
Average winning trade $      0.00   Average losing trade   $       0.00
Ratio avg win/avg loss    100.00    Avg trade(win & loss)  $       0.00

Max consec. winners          0      Max consec. losers             0
Avg # bars in winners        0      Avg # bars in losers           0

Max intraday drawdown $      0.00
Profit factor             100.00    Max # contracts held           0
Account size required $      0.00   Return on account              0%
```

Figure 6.5
Parabolic IBM Chart

```
Parabolic  IBM-Weekly    01/05/62 - 03/19/93          19
                         Performance Summary:  All Trades

Total net profit        $ 138185.00   Open position P/L      $    1375.00
Gross profit            $ 489895.00   Gross loss             $-351710.00

Total # of trades            126      Percent profitable            43%
Number winning trades         54      Number losing trades           72

Largest winning trade   $  40849.00   Largest losing trade   $ -14134.00
Average winning trade   $   9072.13   Average losing trade   $  -4884.86
Ratio avg win/avg loss         1.86   Avg trade(win & loss)  $   1096.71

Max consec. winners            5      Max consec. losers             6
Avg # bars in winners         18      Avg # bars in losers           8

Max intraday drawdown   $ -43532.00
Profit factor                  1.39   Max # contracts held        1000
Account size required   $  93532.00   Return on account           148%
- - - - - - - - - - - - - - - - - - - - - - - - - - - - - - - - - - - - - -
                         Performance Summary:  Long Trades

Total net profit        $  85382.00   Open position P/L      $   1375.00
Gross profit            $ 266184.00   Gross loss             $-180802.00

Total # of trades             63      Percent profitable            44%
Number winning trades         28      Number losing trades           35

Largest winning trade   $  26875.00   Largest losing trade   $ -13327.00
Average winning trade   $   9506.57   Average losing trade   $  -5165.77
Ratio avg win/avg loss         1.84   Avg trade(win & loss)  $   1355.27

Max consec. winners            3      Max consec. losers             5
Avg # bars in winners         19      Avg # bars in losers           9

Max intraday drawdown   $ -35810.00
Profit factor                  1.47   Max # contracts held        1000
Account size required   $  85810.00   Return on account           100%
- - - - - - - - - - - - - - - - - - - - - - - - - - - - - - - - - - - - - -
                         Performance Summary:  Short Trades

Total net profit        $  52803.00   Open position P/L      $       0.00
Gross profit            $ 223711.00   Gross loss             $-170908.00

Total # of trades             63      Percent profitable            41%
Number winning trades         26      Number losing trades           37

Largest winning trade   $  40849.00   Largest losing trade   $ -14134.00
Average winning trade   $   8604.27   Average losing trade   $  -4619.14
Ratio avg win/avg loss         1.86   Avg trade(win & loss)  $    838.14

Max consec. winners            4      Max consec. losers             5
Avg # bars in winners         18      Avg # bars in losers           7

Max intraday drawdown   $ -52388.00
Profit factor                  1.31   Max # contracts held        1000
Account size required   $ 102388.00   Return on account            52%
```

If you only want to do something complicated with the same concept, and if you want to do your homework only once a month, here is the exact same concept on the exact same data—monthly (see Figure 6.6).

The drawdowns are about the same. This system makes $85,000 and has an open profit of $47,000. Now you have $130,000, which means you made almost the same amount of money, but do you notice now how many fewer trades you have? There are only 23 trades over the whole 30-year period.

Maybe when you are trading stocks you will want to look at your key stock. If the current price is above the parabolic, you may want to be a little longer. If it is below, maybe you will not want to have so many long trades. It looks interesting when you compare it to buy and hold when buy and hold makes $25,000.

Here is a chart from TradeStation which shows buying and selling 1,000 shares using the parabolic on the monthly (see Figure 6.7). If you had purchased 1,000 shares at about $60 per share, sold it out above $110, bought it again at about $110, held it up to about $135 and so on, your current trade would be short from about $100 a share. The last time I looked at IBM it was closer to $50 than it was to $100.

Those of you who don't know parabolic—you can buy the Wells Wilder book.

As you can see, the code for Parabolic gets fairly involved. (See Figures 6.8a and 6.8b.) All this code does is compute the level for the parabolic number. The actual trading system to trade parabolic says nothing more than, "If the market position is not long, then buy at the parabolic on a stop. If the market position is long, sell at the parabolic on a stop."

Parabolic was originally developed when they were sending torpedoes out of submarines. As a torpedo goes out of a submarine tube, it starts to float off its course. Maybe you are shooting at another ship and all of a sudden, the torpedo waves off in the other direction. A torpedo gunner uses parabolic mathematics to adjust his aim to hit the ship.

We are taking a very sophisticated piece of math and saying, "You don't have to know how to engineer a Corvette to drive a Corvette. You just have to have confidence that General Motors knows how to engineer a Corvette, so you can drive a Corvette." You do not have to know the ins

Figure 6.6
Parabolic IBM Monthly

```
Parabolic   IBM-Monthly    01/31/62 - 03/31/93      20
                           Performance Summary:  All Trades

Total net profit          $   85633.00    Open position P/L       $   47500.00
Gross profit              $  183671.00    Gross loss              $  -98038.00

Total # of trades                 23      Percent profitable            39%
Number winning trades              9      Number losing trades           14

Largest winning trade     $   53049.00    Largest losing trade    $  -20976.00
Average winning trade     $   20407.89    Average losing trade    $   -7002.71
Ratio avg win/avg loss           2.91     Avg trade(win & loss)   $    3723.17

Max consec. winners                3      Max consec. losers              5
Avg # bars in winners             21      Avg # bars in losers            8

Max intraday drawdown     $  -43337.00
Profit factor                    1.87     Max # contracts held         1000
Account size required     $   93337.00    Return on account             92%
- -  - - - - - - - - - - - - -  - - - - - - - - - - - - - - - - - - - - - - -
                           Performance Summary:   Long Trades

Total net profit          $   76434.00    Open position P/L       $       0.00
Gross profit              $  131929.00    Gross loss              $  -55495.00

Total # of trades                 12      Percent profitable            50%
Number winning trades              6      Number losing trades            6

Largest winning trade     $   53049.00    Largest losing trade    $  -20976.00
Average winning trade     $   21988.17    Average losing trade    $   -9249.17
Ratio avg win/avg loss           2.38     Avg trade(win & loss)   $    6369.50

Max consec. winners                3      Max consec. losers              2
Avg # bars in winners             21      Avg # bars in losers            8

Max intraday drawdown     $  -37468.00
Profit factor                    2.38     Max # contracts held         1000
Account size required     $   87468.00    Return on account             87%
- -  - - - - - - - - - - - - -  - - - - - - - - - - - - - - - - - - - - - - -
                           Performance Summary:   Short Trades

Total net profit          $    9199.00    Open position P/L       $   47500.00
Gross profit              $   51742.00    Gross loss              $  -42543.00

Total # of trades                 11      Percent profitable            27%
Number winning trades              3      Number losing trades            8

Largest winning trade     $   33324.00    Largest losing trade    $  -10364.00
Average winning trade     $   17247.33    Average losing trade    $   -5317.88
Ratio avg win/avg loss           3.24     Avg trade(win & loss)   $     836.27

Max consec. winners                1      Max consec. losers              4
Avg # bars in winners             23      Avg # bars in losers            8

Max intraday drawdown     $  -29628.00
Profit factor                    1.22     Max # contracts held         1000
Account size required     $   79628.00    Return on account             12%
```

Figure 6.7—TradeStation IBM

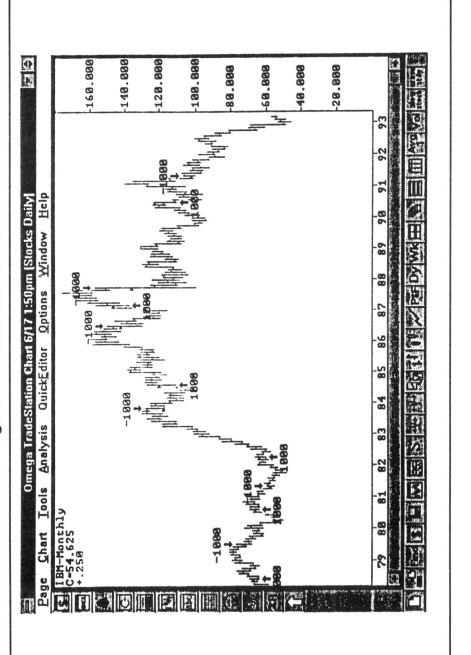

Figure 6.8a
The Code for Parabolic Insert

```
//////////////////////////////////////////////\\\\\\\\\\\\\\\\\\\\\\\\\\\\\\\\\\\\\\\\\\\\\
                            BULIT-IN FUNCTION

Name       : Parabolic
Notes :

Last Update : 01/27/93 08:26pm
Printed on  : 06/17/93 01:32pm
Verified    : YES

////////////////////////////////////////////// CODE \\\\\\\\\\\\\\\\\\\\\\\\\\\\\\\\\\\\\\\\\\\

Vars: Position(-1),SAR(Close),AF(0.02),Hi(High),Lo(Low);

IF CurrentBar = 1 Then
  Position = 1
Else if CurrentBar >1 then Begin
  IF High > Hi Then
    Hi = High;
  IF Low < Lo Then
    Lo = Low;
  IF Position = 1 Then Begin
    IF Low <= Parabolic[1] Then
      Position = -1; {Reverse position}
  End
  Else Begin
    IF High >= Parabolic[1] Then
      Position = 1; {Reverse position}
  End;
End;
IF Position = 1 Then Begin
  IF Position[1] <> 1 Then Begin
    SAR = Lo;
    AF = 0.02;
    Lo = Low;
    Hi = High;
  End
  Else Begin
    SAR = SAR[1]+AF*( Hi-SAR[1]);
    IF Hi > Hi[1] And AF < 0.2 Then
      AF = AF+0.02;
  End;
  IF SAR > Low Then
    SAR = Low;
  IF SAR > Low[1] Then
    SAR = Low[1];
End
Else Begin
  IF  Position[1] <> -1 Then Begin
    SAR = Hi;
    AF = 0.02;
    Lo = Low;
    Hi = High;
  End
  Else Begin
    SAR = SAR[1]+AF*(Lo-SAR[1]);
    IF Lo < Lo[1] And AF < 0.2 Then
      AF = AF+0.02;
  End;
  IF SAR < High Then
    SAR = High;
  IF SAR < High[1] Then
    SAR = High[1];
End;
Parabolic = SAR;


//////////////////////////////////////////////\\\\\\\\\\\\\\\\\\\\\\\\\\\\\\\\\\\\\\\\\\\\\\

Prepared using Omega TradeStation Version 3.01 by Omega Research, Inc.
```

Figure 6.8b—Code for Parabolic Insert

```
/////////////////////////////////////////////////////////////////////////////

                          SYSTEM

Name      : Parabolic
Notes :

Last Update : 10/14/92  07:02pm
Printed on  : 06/17/93  01:31pm
Verified    : YES

//////////////////////////////// CODE \\\\\\\\\\\\\\\\\\\\\\\\\\\\\\\\\\\\\

IF CurrentBar = 1 or MarketPosition <> 1 Then Buy Parabolic Stop;
IF CurrentBar > 1 and MarketPosition = 1 Then Sell Parabolic Stop;
```

and outs of all the math, of all the fancy stuff—the parabolics, the DMIs, the ADXs. Take my shell code, for instance, and play around with it.

This Is a Ten

This Is a Ten is based on 10-minute bars in the S&P and we have a $500 stop, and we exit MOC (see Figure 6.9).

This Is a Ten made $16,205 in 49 trades in a one-year period. It was right 43 percent of the time. I do not like this ratio, but I want to look at it in other time segments. This Is a Ten had as much as an $8,100 drawdown, but it also made $16,000 in this period.

The next period covered is five months (Figure 6.10). This system is working better now. It made $17,000 with only a $2,600 drawdown. It is right 52 percent of the time, and the average trade is $829 dollars. This Is a Ten suddenly looks interesting.

This next period of time covers a full year (see Figure 6.11). This Is a Ten made $12,000 in 49 trades. It is right 51 percent of the time, and it drew down by $3,400 ($246 a trade).

This period of time did not perform well. (See Figure 6.12.) This is the first quarter of this year, but it only lost $490. It is still right 50 percent of the time. This is over more current data. This is the most current data I have available. The most drawdown it ever had was that $8,000 at the very first on the oldest data.

Evaluating Your Test

If when you evaluate your test you discover that your test is worse in the oldest data, this is great! This means the system is getting better! If the percent right is hanging in there at 50 to 54 percent, and the average trade is hanging in there at a big number, that is good too.

The drawdown ratio on any one test is not that reliable, but if you look at the summation of the test it will give you a good indication of the kind of drawdowns you can expect.

CHAPTER 6

Figure 6.9
This Is a Ten

This Is A 10 ! SP E91-10 min   08/01/90 - 07/31/91   25

Performance Summary: All Trades

Total net profit	$ 16205.00	Open position P/L	$	0.00
Gross profit	$ 30770.00	Gross loss	$	-14565.00
Total # of trades	49	Percent profitable		43%
Number winning trades	21	Number losing trades		28
Largest winning trade	$ 4470.00	Largest losing trade	$	-555.00
Average winning trade	$ 1465.24	Average losing trade	$	-520.18
Ratio avg win/avg loss	2.82	Avg trade(win & loss)	$	330.71
Max consec. winners	4	Max consec. losers		12
Avg # bars in winners	33	Avg # bars in losers		11
Max intraday drawdown	$ -8110.00			
Profit factor	2.11	Max # contracts held		1
Account size required	$ 11110.00	Return on account		146%

Performance Summary: Long Trades

Total net profit	$ 16205.00	Open position P/L	$	0.00
Gross profit	$ 30770.00	Gross loss	$	-14565.00
Total # of trades	49	Percent profitable		43%
Number winning trades	21	Number losing trades		28
Largest winning trade	$ 4470.00	Largest losing trade	$	-555.00
Average winning trade	$ 1465.24	Average losing trade	$	-520.18
Ratio avg win/avg loss	2.82	Avg trade(win & loss)	$	330.71
Max consec. winners	4	Max consec. losers		12
Avg # bars in winners	33	Avg # bars in losers		11
Max intraday drawdown	$ -8110.00			
Profit factor	2.11	Max # contracts held		1
Account size required	$ 11110.00	Return on account		146%

Performance Summary: Short Trades

Total net profit	$ 0.00	Open position P/L	$	0.00
Gross profit	$ 0.00	Gross loss	$	0.00
Total # of trades	0	Percent profitable		0%
Number winning trades	0	Number losing trades		0
Largest winning trade	$ 0.00	Largest losing trade	$	0.00
Average winning trade	$ 0.00	Average losing trade	$	0.00
Ratio avg win/avg loss	100.00	Avg trade(win & loss)	$	0.00
Max consec. winners	0	Max consec. losers		0
Avg # bars in winners	0	Avg # bars in losers		0
Max intraday drawdown	$ 0.00			
Profit factor	100.00	Max # contracts held		0
Account size required	$ 0.00	Return on account		0%

Figure 6.10
This Is a Ten

```
This Is A 10 !  SP E92-10 min   08/01/91 - 12/31/91        26

                 Performance Summary:  All Trades

Total net profit      $  17410.00   Open position P/L   $      0.00
Gross profit          $  22960.00   Gross loss          $  -5550.00

Total # of trades           21      Percent profitable        52%
Number winning trades       11      Number losing trades       10

Largest winning trade $   4870.00   Largest losing trade $   -555.00
Average winning trade $   2087.27   Average losing trade $   -555.00
Ratio avg win/avg loss      3.76    Avg trade(win & loss) $   829.05

Max consec. winners          3      Max consec. losers          4
Avg # bars in winners       33      Avg # bars in losers       11

Max intraday drawdown $  -2620.00
Profit factor               4.14    Max # contracts held        1
Account size required $   5620.00   Return on account         310%
- - . . - — . — — . — — . — - — . . — — . . — . — — . . — . — — . . — . —

                 Performance Summary:  Long Trades

Total net profit      $  17410.00   Open position P/L   $      0.00
Gross profit          $  22960.00   Gross loss          $  -5550.00

Total # of trades           21      Percent profitable        52%
Number winning trades       11      Number losing trades       10

Largest winning trade $   4870.00   Largest losing trade $   -555.00
Average winning trade $   2087.27   Average losing trade $   -555.00
Ratio avg win/avg loss      3.76    Avg trade(win & loss) $   829.05

Max consec. winners          3      Max consec. losers          4
Avg # bars in winners       33      Avg # bars in losers       11

Max intraday drawdown $  -2620.00
Profit factor               4.14    Max # contracts held        1
Account size required $   5620.00   Return on account         310%
- - . . - — . — — . — — . — - — . . — — . . — . — — . . — . — — . . — . —

                 Performance Summary:  Short Trades

Total net profit      $      0.00   Open position P/L   $      0.00
Gross profit          $      0.00   Gross loss          $      0.00

Total # of trades            0      Percent profitable         0%
Number winning trades        0      Number losing trades        0

Largest winning trade $      0.00   Largest losing trade $      0.00
Average winning trade $      0.00   Average losing trade $      0.00
Ratio avg win/avg loss    100.00    Avg trade(win & loss) $      0.00

Max consec. winners          0      Max consec. losers          0
Avg # bars in winners        0      Avg # bars in losers        0

Max intraday drawdown $      0.00
Profit factor             100.00    Max # contracts held        0
Account size required $      0.00   Return on account          0%
```

Figure 6.11
This Is a Ten

This Is A 10 !   SP E92-10 min   01/02/92 - 12/31/92   27

Performance Summary: All Trades

Total net profit	$ 12055.00	Open position P/L	$	0.00
Gross profit	$ 23350.00	Gross loss	$	-11295.00
Total # of trades	49	Percent profitable		51%
Number winning trades	25	Number losing trades		24
Largest winning trade	$ 6595.00	Largest losing trade	$	-555.00
Average winning trade	$ 934.00	Average losing trade	$	-470.63
Ratio avg win/avg loss	1.98	Avg trade(win & loss)	$	246.02
Max consec. winners	5	Max consec. losers		5
Avg # bars in winners	33	Avg # bars in losers		13
Max intraday drawdown	$ -3445.00			
Profit factor	2.07	Max # contracts held		1
Account size required	$ 6445.00	Return on account		187%

Performance Summary: Long Trades

Total net profit	$ 12055.00	Open position P/L	$	0.00
Gross profit	$ 23350.00	Gross loss	$	-11295.00
Total # of trades	49	Percent profitable		51%
Number winning trades	25	Number losing trades		24
Largest winning trade	$ 6595.00	Largest losing trade	$	-555.00
Average winning trade	$ 934.00	Average losing trade	$	-470.63
Ratio avg win/avg loss	1.98	Avg trade(win & loss)	$	246.02
Max consec. winners	5	Max consec. losers		5
Avg # bars in winners	33	Avg # bars in losers		13
Max intraday drawdown	$ -3445.00			
Profit factor	2.07	Max # contracts held		1
Account size required	$ 6445.00	Return on account		187%

Performance Summary: Short Trades

Total net profit	$ 0.00	Open position P/L	$	0.00
Gross profit	$ 0.00	Gross loss	$	0.00
Total # of trades	0	Percent profitable		0%
Number winning trades	0	Number losing trades		0
Largest winning trade	$ 0.00	Largest losing trade	$	0.00
Average winning trade	$ 0.00	Average losing trade	$	0.00
Ratio avg win/avg loss	100.00	Avg trade(win & loss)	$	0.00
Max consec. winners	0	Max consec. losers		0
Avg # bars in winners	0	Avg # bars in losers		0
Max intraday drawdown	$ 0.00			
Profit factor	100.00	Max # contracts held		0
Account size required	$ 0.00	Return on account		0%

Figure 6.12
490 Sheet

```
...IS IS A 10 :  SP3H-10 min    01/04/93 - 03/03/93        28
```

Performance Summary: All Trades

Total net profit	$	-490.00	Open position P/L	$ 0.00
Gross profit	$	1730.00	Gross loss	$ -2220.00
Total # of trades		8	Percent profitable	50%
Number winning trades		4	Number losing trades	4
Largest winning trade	$	970.00	Largest losing trade	$ -555.00
Average winning trade	$	432.50	Average losing trade	$ -555.00
Ratio avg win/avg loss		0.78	Avg trade(win & loss)	$ -61.25
Max consec. winners		4	Max consec. losers	3
Avg # bars in winners		33	Avg # bars in losers	14
Max intraday drawdown	$	-1665.00		
Profit factor		0.78	Max # contracts held	1
Account size required	$	4610.00	Return on account	-11%

Performance Summary: Long Trades

Total net profit	$	-490.00	Open position P/L	$ 0.00
Gross profit	$	1730.00	Gross loss	$ -2220.00
Total # of trades		8	Percent profitable	50%
Number winning trades		4	Number losing trades	4
Largest winning trade	$	970.00	Largest losing trade	$ -555.00
Average winning trade	$	432.50	Average losing trade	$ -555.00
Ratio avg win/avg loss		0.78	Avg trade(win & loss)	$ -61.25
Max consec. winners		4	Max consec. losers	3
Avg # bars in winners		33	Avg # bars in losers	14
Max intraday drawdown	$	-1610.00		
Profit factor		0.78	Max # contracts held	1
Account size required	$	4610.00	Return on account	-11%

Performance Summary: Short Trades

Total net profit	$	0.00	Open position P/L	$ 0.00
Gross profit	$	0.00	Gross loss	$ 0.00
Total # of trades		0	Percent profitable	0%
Number winning trades		0	Number losing trades	0
Largest winning trade	$	0.00	Largest losing trade	$ 0.00
Average winning trade	$	0.00	Average losing trade	$ 0.00
Ratio avg win/avg loss		100.00	Avg trade(win & loss)	$ 0.00
Max consec. winners		0	Max consec. losers	0
Avg # bars in winners		0	Avg # bars in losers	0
Max intraday drawdown	$	0.00		
Profit factor		100.00	Max # contracts held	0
Account size required	$	0.00	Return on account	0%

Look at the Buy Monday chart (Figure 6.13). Did you notice there are 49 trades here? Did you notice that in every full year there are 49 trades? This system only trades on Mondays that the markets are open. You can be off work four days a week because you do not trade this system four days a week. It is a very interesting system. This chart shows trades for every Monday from August 1, 1990 through June 10, 1992.

I think this is an important point (see Figure 6.14). We have $64,485 in 60 months, and we have about five years of data, and there are 49 trades a year. So we take 245 into $61,485. This means $251 is our average Daddy-go-to-town number. I do not know about you but a five-year track record trading the S&P with no overnight exposure, a $1,000 stop, and only trading on Mondays looks like a pretty good trading system.

I am going to give you the rules for this one, and this is, I believe, the best trading system I'm giving you, so make sure you understand it. (See Figure 6.15.) It shows the trade by trades since March 8th, and you can see it does get stopped out, it does lose. It is not a cure-all system. It once had $7,600 worth of profit. When I ran this print it was at $5,400. Let me tell you about writing computer code. There are two schools of thought.

The Correct School of Thought

One is the right school of thought, which I do not subscribe to. Sam Tennis, who is one of the original innovators, the guy who wrote System-Writer Plus, is a great computer programmer. Through Omega, he will write code for you at $45 per hour. Sam can do anything. He may be backed up and take a couple of months to get something done, but it will be right and it will be exactly what you tell him to do. If you tell him to have the computer beep every time a D comes across on a newswire, he will have your computer do that. This is different from asking a computer if your system makes money.

SOPHISTICATED AND UNUSUAL SYSTEMS

Figure 6.13
Buy Monday

```
//////////////////////////////////////////\\\\\\\\\\\\\\\\\\\\\\\\\\\\\\\\\\\\\
Directory : F:\KK                          Printed on   : 10/03/93 12:29pm
                        PERFORMANCE SUMMARY

Model Name     : Monday Buy            Developer    : KRUTSINGER
Test Number    :      1 of      1
Notes :

Data           : S&P INDEX        06/93
Calc Dates     : 01/01/88 - 12/31/92

 Num. Conv. P. Value  Comm  Slippage  Margin  Format  Drive:\Path\FileName
 ------------------------------------------------------------------------
  149   2  $  5.000  $ 55   $  0   $ 3,000  Omega   F:\20DATA06\F002.DTA

/////////////////////////// ALL TRADES  - Test 1 \\\\\\\\\\\\\\\\\\\\\\\\\

Total net profit          $61,485.00
Gross profit              $167,295.00   Gross loss              -105,810.00

Total # of trades            253        Percent profitable            49%
Number winning trades        126        Number losing trades          127

Largest winning trade   $10,270.00      Largest losing trade    $-1,055.00
Average winning trade   $1,327.74       Average losing trade    $ -833.15
Ratio avg win/avg loss       1.59       Avg trade (win & loss)    $243.02

Max consecutive winners       11        Max consecutive losers          7
Avg # bars in winners          0        Avg # bars in losers            0

Max closed-out drawdown $-10,990.00     Max intra-day drawdown  $-10,990.00
Profit factor                1.58       Max # of contracts held         1
Account size required   $13,990.00      Return on account            439%

                    Highlights - All trades
       Description                 Date     Time      Amount
       ------------------------------------------------------------
       Largest Winning Trade      10/16/89    -    $   10,270.00
       Largest Losing Trade       11/30/92    -    $   -1,055.00
       Largest String of + Trades 04/25/88    -         11
       Largest String of - Trades 02/06/89    -          7
       Maximum Closed-Out Drawdown 07/24/89   -    $  -10,990.00
       Maximum Intra-Day Drawdown  07/24/89   -    $  -10,990.00

/////////////////////////// LONG TRADES  - Test 1 \\\\\\\\\\\\\\\\\\\\\\\\\

Total net profit          $61,485.00
Gross profit              $167,295.00   Gross loss              -105,810.00

Total # of trades            253        Percent profitable            49%
Number winning trades        126        Number losing trades          127

Largest winning trade   $10,270.00      Largest losing trade    $-1,055.00
Average winning trade   $1,327.74       Average losing trade    $ -833.15
Ratio avg win/avg loss       1.59       Avg trade (win & loss)    $243.02

Max consecutive winners       11        Max consecutive losers          7
Avg # bars in winners          0        Avg # bars in losers            0
```

Figure 6.14
Hand Written Numbers

```
Max closed-out drawdown  $-10,990.00   Max intra-day drawdown   $-10,990.00
Profit factor                   1.58   Max # of contracts held            1
Account size required     $13,990.00   Return on account                439%

                    Highlights - Long trades
          Description                    Date      Time      Amount
          -----------------------------------------------------------------
          Largest Winning Trade        10/16/89     -   $    10,27 .00
          Largest Losing Trade         11/30/92     -   $    -1,055.00
          Largest String of + Trades   04/25/88     -               11
          Largest String of - Trades   02/06/89     -                7
          Maximum Closed-Out Drawdown  07/24/89     -   $   -10,990.00
          Maximum Intra-Day Drawdown   07/24/89     -   $   -10,990.00

//////////////////////////// SHORT TRADES  - Test 1 \\\\\\\\\\\\\\\\\\\\\\\  \\

Total net profit            $0.00
Gross profit                $0.00   Gross loss                      $0.00

Total # of trades               0   Percent profitable                0%
Number winning trades           0   Number losing trades               0

Largest winning trade       $0.00   Largest losing trade           $0.00
Average winning trade       $0.00   Average losing trade           $0.00
Ratio avg win/avg loss       0.00   Avg trade (win & loss)         $0.00

Max consecutive winners         0   Max consecutive losers             0
Avg # bars in winners           0   Avg # bars in losers               0

Max closed-out drawdown     $0.00   Max intra-day drawdown         $0.00
Profit factor                0.00   Max # of contracts held            0
Account size required       $0.00   Return on account                 0%

                    Highlights - Short trades
          Description                    Date      Time      Amount
          -----------------------------------------------------------------
          Largest Winning Trade                     -   $       0.00
          Largest Losing Trade                      -   $       0.00
          Largest String of + Trades                -               0
          Largest String of - Trades                -               0
          Maximum Closed-Out Drawdown                   $       0.00
          Maximum Intra-Day Drawdown                    $       0.00

\\\\\\\\\\\\\\\\\\\\\\\\\\\\\\\\\\\\\\\\\\\\//////////////////////////////////
```

Prepared using System Writer Plus Version 2.18 by Omega Research, Inc.

Figure 6.15—Trade by Trade Current

This Is A 10 ! SP3M-10 min   03/04/93 - 06/10/93   31

Date	Time	Type	Cnts	Price	Signal Name	Entry P/L	Cumulative
03/08/93	10:52am	Buy	1	448.80			
03/08/93	4:15pm	LExit	1	456.70	End of Day Ex	$ 3895.00	$ 3895.00
03/15/93	11:22am	Buy	1	450.60			
03/15/93	4:15pm	LExit	1	452.40	End of Day Ex	$ 845.00	$ 4740.00
03/22/93	10:52am	Buy	1	447.00			
03/22/93	4:15pm	LExit	1	449.00	End of Day Ex	$ 945.00	$ 5685.00
03/29/93	10:42am	Buy	1	451.45			
03/29/93	4:15pm	LExit	1	451.60	End of Day Ex	$ 20.00	$ 5705.00
04/05/93	10:42am	Buy	1	442.25			
04/05/93	4:15pm	LExit	1	442.85	End of Day Ex	$ 245.00	$ 5950.00
04/12/93	10:42am	Buy	1	447.15			
04/12/93	4:15pm	LExit	1	448.35	End of Day Ex	$ 545.00	$ 6495.00
04/19/93	11:22am	Buy	1	447.05			
04/19/93	4:15pm	LExit	1	446.65	End of Day Ex	$ -255.00	$ 6240.00
04/26/93	10:42am	Buy	1	437.55			
04/26/93	11:52am	LExit	1	436.55	Money Mngmt S	$ -555.00	$ 5685.00
05/03/93	10:42am	Buy	1	438.25			
05/03/93	4:15pm	LExit	1	442.30	End of Day Ex	$ 1970.00	$ 7655.00
05/10/93	10:52am	Buy	1	445.30			
05/10/93	2:22pm	LExit	1	444.30	Money Mngmt S	$ -555.00	$ 7100.00
05/17/93	11:12am	Buy	1	439.60			
05/17/93	12:12pm	LExit	1	438.60	Money Mngmt S	$ -555.00	$ 6545.00
05/24/93	10:42am	Buy	1	447.20			
05/24/93	3:02pm	LExit	1	446.20	Money Mngmt S	$ -555.00	$ 5990.00
06/07/93	11:12am	Buy	1	449.80			
06/07/93	1:42pm	LExit	1	448.80	Money Mngmt S	$ -555.00	$ 5435.00

My School of Thought

This is what I do: You give me an idea, and I will get it back to you very quickly and say, "I think it works," or "It doesn't work." Then I proceed to show you why. I will fine-tune it and try to make some money with it. I do my best to try to show you how to make money with the code. What you come out with in the end may not be anything you started with, but it will be close.

I do quick and dirty programming. I charge $100 bucks an hour. I can turn anything around in 10 days, and it is going to cost you $400 to get anything done. These are the differences in the two schools of thought. One is programming which is iron-clad code, and the other is "let's make some money in the market."

This Is a Ten

When I write code I give you a lot of stuff. Remember how I told you about French brackets? The stuff between French brackets does not mean anything. It is just there. This is all the code there is to This Is a Ten. (See Figure 6.16.)

It is a short-term contract which trades one contract only. It buys on Monday. It is based on 10-minute bars that end in two. It is perfect for Future Link. Future Link is a product, by the way, that gets a snapshot of the market every 10 minutes. It starts at 9:32 in the morning New York time, so it has a perfect 10-minute bar. This system could be run on this because it is based on a 10-minute bar.

We are not allowing multiple entries. In other words, once we are in the market for the day, we are finished. After you get a signal to be in, you put in your $500 stop, get out on the close, and go play golf. This is it. Do not look at the market. Do not fool with it. It closes all trades at the end of the day.

Here is the meat: If day of week date equals one, and this is through 10-minute data, and the time is greater than 10:31 in New York, and trades today's date equals 0 (which means you have not traded anything yet),

118

Figure 6.16—This Is a Ten's Code

```
/////////////////////////////////////////////////////////////////////////////////////////

                                     SYSTEM

Name     : This Is A 10 !
Notes    :

Last Update : 06/10/93  07:30pm
Printed on  : 06/10/93  07:30pm
Verified    : YES

///////////////////////////////////////// CODE \\\\\\\\\\\\\\\\\\\\\\\\\\\\\\\\\\\\\\\\\\\\\

(
System: This Is A 10 !
Notes : Short term system with one contract only
                    Buys on Monay, based on 10 min
                    bars that end in 2. Perfect for FutureLink.


[ 2] MaxBarsBack
   [*] Generate Realtime Orders
Entry Options :
   [*] Do not allow multiple entries in same direction
   [ ] Allow multiple entries in same direction
       by different entry signals
   [ ] Allow multiple entries in same direction
       by same and different entry signals

   [ ] Money Management Stop
       Amount: ($) [ $500 ]
   [*] Close all trades at end of day


Copyright June 1993 by Joe Krutsinger, Krutsinger & Krutsinger, Inc.
All rights reserved.  No portion may be reproduced in
any form without the permission of the publishers.
)
```

```
If Day of Week (date) = 1 and Time > 1031
and Trades Today (date) = 0
then Buy at highest (C,3) stop;
```

then buy at the highest close of the last three bars on a stop. This is all there is to this.

What I am telling you is, "After the first hour of trading in New York on a 10-minute basis, buy at the highest close that we have had" (in other words, buy a little breakout on a Monday). This is all there is, and it lets you do this with a $500 stop. This is high powered code because the fewer letters you put on a piece of paper, the less form-fit it is.

A Quick Review

If you are trading Paul Revere, you do not need a computer. Paul Revere can be done with a spreadsheet, and I told you how to do that. If you are trading Joe's Gap you will have to call three hours after the market opens and ask your broker, "Is there an opening gap or not?" If there is, you will trade. You do not need any equipment for either of these two trading systems.

One Day at a Time can be done with a spreadsheet using moving averages in one column, and the highest high in another column. You would only have to do that with One Night Stand.

Even though This Is a Ten is a daytrade program, here is how you can do it with a spreadsheet: Put your times down in Eastern time. (See Figure 6.17.)

Now put your closing price and call your broker. (If you prefer, you can get a Future Link for $90 and every 10 minutes it will give you the price.) Put the price on the spreadsheet, and then you can easily see the highest close of the last three bars.

I instructed my program to tell me every time it would have told me to buy. Remember, I only take the first trade, and I am using a $500 stop getting out on the close. You can play with this and see where multiple buys will help you.

This system does not buy weaknesses, and it waits in the day until strength comes back in the market. Whenever weakness appears, it will not give me any buys. It is a buy-strength program, and it is sophisticated.

Figure 6.17
This Is a Ten

Monday	It's A 10!		
Time-EST	c		
932	345.25		
942	345.50		
952	346.00	346.00	
1002	[346.25]	346.25	Buy!
1012	346.00	346.25	
1022	347.20	347.20	Buy!
1032	347.00	347.20	
1042	347.10	347.20	
1052	347.60	347.60	Buy!
1102	347.80	347.80	Buy!
1112	347.90	347.90	Buy!
1122	348.00	348.00	Buy!
1132	348.50	348.50	Buy!
1142	349.00	349.00	Buy!
1152	348.50	349.00	
1202	348.00	349.00	
1212	347.00	348.50	
1222	347.50	348.00	
1232	347.60	347.60	
1242	347.55	347.60	
1252	347.40	347.60	
1302	348.00	348.00	Buy!
1312	348.50	348.50	Buy!
1322	348.35	348.50	
1332	349.00	349.00	Buy!
1342	349.10	349.10	Buy!
1352	348.70	349.10	
1402	348.20	349.10	
1412	348.35	348.70	
1422	349.00	349.00	Buy!
1432	349.10	349.10	Buy!
1442	349.00	349.10	
1452	349.25	349.25	Buy!
1502	349.30	349.30	Buy!
1512	349.50	349.50	Buy!
1522	350.00	350.00	Buy!
1532	351.00	351.00	Buy!
1542	350.25	351.00	
1552	351.00	351.00	
1602	351.25	351.25	Buy!
1612	352.00	352.00	Buy!
1615	351.00	352.00	

121

CHAPTER 6

Spreadsheet Software

If you do not have a spreadsheet you can go to a placed called Electronic Boutique, and get a software system called SwiftCalc. It costs around $9.95, and it runs on any computer—even a Commodore. Do not think because you do not have all the high-powered equipment you cannot get started tracking some of these things.

A little matrix is shown in Figure 6.18. The figure shows the time and the prices. This is the Excel formula that you will have to write on your spreadsheet to get the results that I obtained. I have done everything but do the trade for you on this one. I think you will agree with me that This Is a Ten.

Review

In reviewing, I have shown you how to take a technique known as Parabolic, and apply it to weekly and monthly stock market data. Look at what we have accomplished. Instead of buying and hold and making $26,000, you have now made $140,000 over the same data.

Then I said, "Okay, I am taking you off monthly data, and I am running you over to 10-minute data. I am letting you do it with equipment that costs $90 a month, so now you can daytrade too."

I have also given you a system with a five-year simulated record and shown you all the rules and how to do it. These are what I call unconventional systems.

Now, think with me about what you could accomplish in your own system. After you have written a system and you think you have it "right," stop and take a breath and say these next words: "If day of week date equals one, then—do anything else I was going to do." Then do it for days two, three, four, and five.

You will do five little tests to see if your system is day of week sensitive. It will be because people eat at certain times, certain days. This means that people leave the pit at certain times, certain days. Certain re-

122

Figure 6.18
Matrix

Monday	It's A 10!		
Time-EST	c		
932	345.25		
942	345.5		
952	346	=MAX(B4:B6)	
1002	346.25	=MAX(B5:B7)	=IF(B7>C6,"Buy!"," ")
1012	346	=MAX(B6:B8)	=IF(B8>C7,"Buy!"," ")
1022	347.2	=MAX(B7:B9)	=IF(B9>C8,"Buy!"," ")
1032	347	=MAX(B8:B10)	=IF(B10>C9,"Buy!"," ")
1042	347.1	=MAX(B9:B11)	=IF(B11>C10,"Buy!"," ")
1052	347.6	=MAX(B10:B12)	=IF(B12>C11,"Buy!"," ")
1102	347.8	=MAX(B11:B13)	=IF(B13>C12,"Buy!"," ")
1112	347.9	=MAX(B12:B14)	=IF(B14>C13,"Buy!"," ")
1122	348	=MAX(B13:B15)	=IF(B15>C14,"Buy!"," ")
1132	348.5	=MAX(B14:B16)	=IF(B16>C15,"Buy!"," ")
1142	349	=MAX(B15:B17)	=IF(B17>C16,"Buy!"," ")
1152	348.5	=MAX(B16:B18)	=IF(B18>C17,"Buy!"," ")
1202	348	=MAX(B17:B19)	=IF(B19>C18,"Buy!"," ")
1212	347	=MAX(B18:B20)	=IF(B20>C19,"Buy!"," ")
1222	347.5	=MAX(B19:B21)	=IF(B21>C20,"Buy!"," ")
1232	347.6	=MAX(B20:B22)	=IF(B22>C21,"Buy!"," ")
1242	347.55	=MAX(B21:B23)	=IF(B23>C22,"Buy!"," ")
1252	347.4	=MAX(B22:B24)	=IF(B24>C23,"Buy!"," ")
1302	348	=MAX(B23:B25)	=IF(B25>C24,"Buy!"," ")
1312	348.5	=MAX(B24:B26)	=IF(B26>C25,"Buy!"," ")
1322	348.35	=MAX(B25:B27)	=IF(B27>C26,"Buy!"," ")
1332	349	=MAX(B26:B28)	=IF(B28>C27,"Buy!"," ")
1342	349.1	=MAX(B27:B29)	=IF(B29>C28,"Buy!"," ")
1352	348.7	=MAX(B28:B30)	=IF(B30>C29,"Buy!"," ")
1402	348.2	=MAX(B29:B31)	=IF(B31>C30,"Buy!"," ")
1412	348.35	=MAX(B30:B32)	=IF(B32>C31,"Buy!"," ")
1422	349	=MAX(B31:B33)	=IF(B33>C32,"Buy!"," ")
1432	349.1	=MAX(B32:B34)	=IF(B34>C33,"Buy!"," ")
1442	349	=MAX(B33:B35)	=IF(B35>C34,"Buy!"," ")
1452	349.25	=MAX(B34:B36)	=IF(B36>C35,"Buy!"," ")
1502	349.3	=MAX(B35:B37)	=IF(B37>C36,"Buy!"," ")
1512	349.5	=MAX(B36:B38)	=IF(B38>C37,"Buy!"," ")
1522	350	=MAX(B37:B39)	=IF(B39>C38,"Buy!"," ")
1532	351	=MAX(B38:B40)	=IF(B40>C39,"Buy!"," ")
1542	350.25	=MAX(B39:B41)	=IF(B41>C40,"Buy!"," ")
1552	351	=MAX(B40:B42)	=IF(B42>C41,"Buy!"," ")
1602	351.25	=MAX(B41:B43)	=IF(B43>C42,"Buy!"," ")
1612	352	=MAX(B42:B44)	=IF(B44>C43,"Buy!"," ")
1615	351	=MAX(B43:B45)	=IF(B45>C44,"Buy!"," ")

ports come out on Tuesdays that do not come out on other days. The market learns this, and the market data reflect this. This is the way to take day of week data and put it into your own trading systems.

Will recent advances in modern analysis lead to better trading systems? Of course. Use caution here. Remember when I showed you my bond system? It was great in one year, and okay in the next year, and it kept getting worse and worse. It has remained good, but it is not great like it used to be.

This is because the market becomes efficient and learns the system, whether you tell it to or not. You must be careful when you get involved with things you do not understand. This is a basic book. I am not going to try to teach you chaos theory, artificial intelligence, and neural networks.

Rule of thumb: If you cannot put it on a bumper sticker, do not trade it. You should readily understand your own trading system. If the system goes down or the hardware goes down, you should be able to say, "Fine. Call up the broker. Give me the data for the last five days. I can figure it myself." This is the test of a great trading system.

Unusual Systems

The reason I feel these systems work is that everybody is not trading these unconventional systems. Everybody and his brother looks at 30-minute, 5-minute, and hourly S&P charts, so when the hour comes by on the S&P, a lot of traders are doing the same thing. This is why there is a lot of slippage on the hour of the S&P. The systems I try to design are at unusual times. For instance, I will run my bars in three-hour lengths. I will start trading at 2:00 in the afternoon rather than 8:00 in the morning. I will only buy on Friday in a breakout when everyone else is trying to avoid the market. Fewer and fewer people are in the market with me doing the exact same things at the exact same time, which is why my systems sometimes work.

If you notice, I spend a lot of time talking about unusual systems. I think this is the way to "beat the market," if there is such a thing. We have discussed the gap system—the British Pound gap system. We started with a reversal system; then we put a $625 stop, got out on the close; then we decided, let's have a reversal with a $625 stop. That was an unusual time frame. That was the first time we saw a three-hour bar in use.

Paul Revere

The next thing we talked about was Paul Revere. We took a channel breakout, which is pretty much a known system. But we tuned it a little bit. We put a $1,000 stop on it, so when the market gets choppy it takes us out and makes us sit on the sidelines, waiting for big breakouts, rather than just taking every breakout.

One Night Stand

We mentioned One Night Stand in Chapter 4. Now we are going to get into it a little more. It is day of week testing. One Night Stand is brilliant, because nobody will do it. I can teach it forever, and nobody will do this system. They will ooh and they will ah and they will go home and they will not do it. This is the ideal system for a seminar presenter.

One Night Stand/Portana

This is a five-year track record on Portana. (See Figure 6.19.) I have it coded BP1 for British Pound, One Night Stand. I put BM1, SF1, JY1, Crude oil 1, and dollar index 1 together. I needed $21,900 in the account for initial margin. At any one time I have had an average of three contracts trading simultaneously. The most I have ever had trading at the same time was six, one of each. The total drawdown (for all six together) is $5,700.

The gain is $115,000. That means the account goes to $136,900 because we are starting with $21,900. It is right 65 percent of the time. The average winner is $560. The average loser is $310. This is an eight to one ratio. To

Figure 6.19—One Night Stand—Portana

```
ONE NIGHT STAND 01/04/88 to 12/31/92   C:\PA\
BP1(1)    2700  DM1(1)  2700  SF1(1)   2700  JY1(1)   2700  CL1(1)   2700
DX1(1)    2700
==================================================================
Total net profit      115,257.50    <   135,257.50>
Gross profit          163,106.25    Gross loss          -47,848.75

Total # of trades            445    Percent profitable         65%
Number winning trades        291    Number losing trades       154

Largest winning trade   3,095.00    Largest losing trade  -2,267.50
Average winning trade     560.50    Average losing trade    -310.7.
Ratio avg win/avg loss      1.80    Avg trade (win & loss)   259.0.

Max consecutive winners       20    Max consecutive losers       9
Avg # bars in winners          1    Avg # bars in losers         1

Max drawdown            5,700.00    Avg # of contracts held      3
Profit factor             J 18     Max # of contracts held      6
Account size required  21,900.00    Return on account         526%
==================================================================
```

me, this looks like a good system. Look at the daily track record of this put through Portana. This is close to that coveted 45-degree line (see Figure 6.20).

Look at a quarterly report on One Night Stand (Figure 6.21).

Quarterly Reports

Of all the quarterly reports from 1988 through 1992 we have had three losing quarters—one of them lost $1,300, one lost $900. One lost $1,300 again, and yet $20,000 went to $35,000 in five years. Hypothetically. I do not know about you but this looks like a pretty good piece of math. I think we should put this piece of math in our repertoire.

Figure 6.22 shows what this math looks like yearly. There are no losing years; there are three losing quarters.

If you cannot bear risking six of these trades overnight, take one Mid-Am British Pound. You can probably handle that. BP by itself has not done much as of November 1993; on a full size contract you would be up about $380. This is no big deal, but you would be trading the British Pound. This might be a good way for you to "inch" into trading One Night Stand.

I am going to give you the code for One Night Stand, and explain what it is and how I came up with it. (See Figure 6.23.)

One Night Stand

Remember the idea behind Joe's Oil Well? If the 10-day moving average is above the four-day moving average? I took this idea and combined it with the idea behind Paul Revere (the highest high of so many bars), and I used the concept of only taking positions over the weekend. This made up One Night Stand.

In computer terms it is this: "If the 10-day average of yesterday is above the 40-day moving average of yesterday, and day of week is 4 (if it is Thursday), then buy tomorrow the highest high of the last four days on a stop." (If it takes out the week's high and the trend is up, I want to be in.)

Figure 6.20—One Night Stand

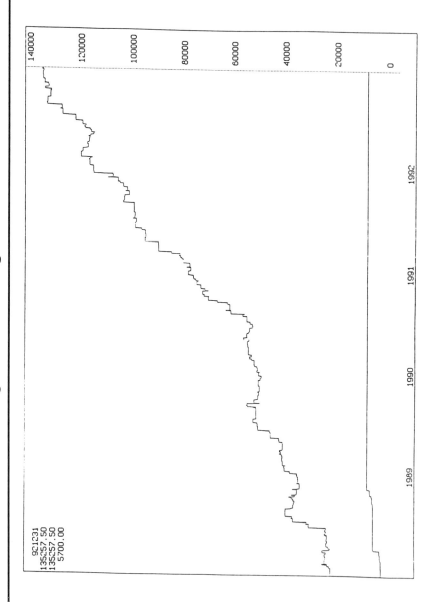

Figure 6.21—Quarterly Report for One Night Stand

PORTFOLIO ANALYZER QUARTLY REPORT for ONE NIGHT STAND

DATE	OPEN EQUITY	CLOSED EQUITY	TOTAL EQUITY	MAX DRAWDOWN	% DD	% CHNG TOT EQ	NUM TRADE
880104	0.00	20000.00	20000.00	0.00	0.0	0.0	0
880331	0.00	23282.50	23282.50	605.00	3.0	16.4	0
880630	0.00	28747.50	28747.50	3153.75	15.8	23.5	0
880930	380.00	34390.00	34770.00	3627.50	18.1	20.9	1
881230	180.00	33297.50	33477.50	5687.50	28.4	-3.7	1
890331	-985.00	40142.50	39157.50	5687.50	28.2	17.0	1
890630	0.00	49230.00	49230.00	5687.50	19.5	25.7	2
890929	-840.00	50507.50	49667.50	5687.50	17.1	0.9	
891229	0.00	48740.00	48740.00	5700.00	17.1	-1.9	
900330	0.00	52860.00	52860.00	5700.00	17.1	8.5	
900629	280.00	51240.00	51520.00	5700.00	16.4	-2.5	
900928	0.00	68965.00	68965.00	5700.00	11.6	33.9	
901231	0.00	77167.50	77167.50	5700.00	10.0	11.9	
910329	0.00	89007.50	89007.50	5700.00	8.3	15.3	
910628	-292.50	98500.00	98207.50	5700.00	7.3	10.3	
910930	0.00	102575.00	102575.00	5700.00	6.8	4.4	
911231	0.00	115022.50	115022.50	5700.00	6.0	12.1	
920331	0.00	117295.00	117295.00	5700.00	5.7	2.0	
920630	0.00	122057.50	122057.50	5700.00	5.6	4.1	
920930	0.00	131992.50	131992.50	5700.00	5.0	8.1	0
921231	0.00	135257.50	135257.50	5700.00	4.9	2.5	0

Figure 6.22—Yearly Report for One Night Stand

PORTFOLIO ANALYZER YEARLY REPORT for ONE NIGHT STAND

DATE	OPEN EQUITY	CLOSED EQUITY	TOTAL EQUITY	MAX DRAWDOWN	% DD	% CHNG TOT EQ	NUM TRADE
880104	0.00	20000.00	20000.00	0.00	0.0	0.0	0
881230	180.00	33297.50	33477.50	5687.50	28.4	67.4	1
891229	0.00	48740.00	48740.00	5700.00	17.1	45.6	0
901231	0.00	77167.50	77167.50	5700.00	10.0	58.3	0
911231	0.00	115022.50	115022.50	5700.00	6.0	49.1	0
921231	0.00	135257.50	135257.50	5700.00	4.9	17.6	0

Figure 6.23—Code for One Night Stand

```
//////////////////////////////////////////////////////////////////

                              SYSTEM

Name      : One Night Stand
Notes :

Last Update : 04/27/93  09:29am
Printed on  : 06/10/93  02:14pm
Verified    : YES

/////////////////////////////// CODE \\\\\\\\\\\\\\\\\\\\\\\\\\\\\\\\\

If Average(C,10)[1] > Average(C,40)[1] and
  DayOfWeek(date)=4 then buy tomorrow at
Highest(H,4) stop;

If Average(C,10)[1] < Average(C,40)[1] and
  DayOfWeek(date)=4 then Sell tomorrow at
Lowest(L,8) stop;

If barssinceentry> 0  then exitlong at market;
If barssinceentry> 0  then exitShort at market;
If DayOfWeek(date)=5 then
ExitShort at market;
If DayOfWeek(date)=5 then
ExitLong at market;
```

The sell side is the reverse with a little exception. "If the 10-day moving average is below the 40-day moving average and the day of the week is 4, then sell at the lowest low of the last eight days on a stop."

Putting in a Bias

I have placed a bias in here. I do not want to be short currencies. I do not know why, but I firmly believe in my bias, and I wanted to put it into this trading system. Consequently, I have told the computer, "I've got to take out the lowest low of the last two weeks." Now I have an exit rule, and I have written it two different ways. If bar since entry greater than 0 then exit long at market; that means if you are in the trade, get out of it.

Someone asks me, why do you not say, "If day of week equals 5, then exit short of market." The problem with this is that if there is not a Friday, then you may be waiting a week to get out on the next Friday. By saying, "If bars since entry greater than 0," it will always get you out on the next trading day.

In recapping unusual systems, let's recall why we think unusual systems tend to work. First of all, most people like to do the same thing. Most funds will trade moving average systems, and they will trade them on the same time frame or the same time bar. Most people and most funds tend to lose market over time. What you must do as a new systems developer is take your trading ideas and put them into your time frame. Remember, there is no right or wrong in system development. The system has to be right for you. Some of us can handle more drawdown than others. Some of us can handle more risk on initial trade than others. Make sure that when you develop your system, you can and will actually be able to trade it.

7

Questions and Answers

Question: *I am just getting into commodities for the third time. I have traded the grains twice with brokers who had systems. I lost both times. Should I trade a broker's idea or my own idea?*

Answer: To obtain the best of both worlds, you might want to combine those two ideas. Here is how you might do it: Study everybody's trading systems. Evaluate them. Decide which ones you can stand, which ones you could do. Evaluate their trading records. Pick one or two markets and trade minis, and get a feel for it. See if this works best for you. If it does, then turn it on, but don't forget about it. Look at it weekly to make sure it's living up to its old track record.

Question: *I'm a bean grower. I currently use the market to hedge my beans, but I'm also interested in developing my own trading strategies. Is there an easy computer program I can buy that will help me develop my own system? Could you please give me the approximate cost?*

Answer: There is cheap, and there is easy, but there is nothing that is both cheap and easy. A fairly inexpensive program is SystemWriter Plus. SystemWriter Plus originally came out with no charting at $3,000. It sold for several years for $2,000 with charting. Now it has charting, and the DOS version is presently being sold (Fall 1993) for $975. But you really do not need system writing software if all you are doing is trying to develop a hedge system. You can go to a programmer and say, "Look, I need a system that only sells. When it gives a buy signal I want to have it say, 'get me out at the market.'" You could do something fairly simple like a channel breakout system. Take a look at Paul Revere—buying at the highest high of the last six, selling at the lowest low of the last six. When it tells you to buy, just change that to exit short. That way you'll only be trading the short side of the market, which is what you should be trading as a hedger, and you will cut your commissions because you will only be doing the short transactions.

Question: *Everybody says what a great system they have. The hypothetical trading looks great. Realtime trades do not do as well. What causes this?*

Answer: Many things. First of all, if there are too many parameters in the system, the system has been overly optimized and has gone back and found the bottom and the top. The chances of it reoccurring in the future are very slim if it is a simple system, but it becomes widely known. For instance, I had a bond system that made very good money. It had over 40 consecutive winning trades, but as the floor got used to my tickets coming in, the size of my orders, and where my stops were placed, the system became less and less profitable.

This is an example of the market becoming efficient. The market is an efficient price-determining mechanism. As systems become known to the floor participants, the system is less likely to perform as in the past. If you have a good system that you have tested and you feel very comfortable with it, do not publish it in *Commodity* magazine. Do not publish it in *Stocks and Commodities*. Most of the systems people publish are systems which have ceased to work.

Question: *Is there an easier book I should read before I read this book?*

Answer: Absolutely. Mark Power's book *Getting Started in Commodities* is an excellent book. Bruce Gold has a good beginning book in commodities, but I guess the one I like the best would have to be Mark Power's book because it is explicitly for beginners. It is available from *Futures* magazine.

Question: *Who would benefit the most from reading this book?*

Answer: A speculator who has tried trading on his or her own, who has tried other people's systems and has a pretty good idea of what he or she would like to do, but just does not know how to make the math work to develop a system. This is a book for someone who wants to learn to become a system developer, not for someone who is an accomplished system developer necessarily.

Question: *What percent of increase per year can you expect to have in a good system?*

Answer: Percent of increase is one parameter, but the main rule of thumb that I look at is: Take a look at the total net profit a system has brought in over a two- or three-year track record and divide that by the total drawdown. If that ratio is 10 to 1 or better, I think you have a great system.

If it is five to one or better, you have a tradeable good system. If it is less than five to one, take another look and find a system you would feel more comfortable with. Although bottom line is nice, and you say, "I want to see a high percent right," to make a lot of money, how much pain will you go through to get to that end?

Will you stay with a system that has a huge drawdown? As far as percent increase, I think you should see at least a 25 to 30 percent yearly increase using futures as a vehicle. If you do not, it probably will not be worth the risk that you are taking as far as drawdown and margin.

Question: *How many times and ways should you test your system?*

Answer: There are several ways. This is the traditional way 90 percent of the systems in the United States are tested: Let's put some money on this and see how it works. When we have three losses let's quit and do something else or change it. This is the way most testing is really done.

A second tier of testing is to go through a program optimizer like a SystemWriter or ProfitTaker 2000 and find the very best parameters that have worked on the data. Crunch and crunch over one piece of data until you have found the "grail" on that piece of data.

The problem with this method is, this was the "grail" on that piece of data, but it may not be the "grail" on that piece of data in the future. The fewer rules that you have down, the better.

A couple of other ways to test is to buy a commercial system. Test it on data it has never seen, and then tune that system to something with which you are more comfortable. This is akin to buying a car and tuning it to racing rather than going to the junkyard and putting parts together or better yet, going to a machine shop and trying to machine a car that will race with world class racers.

You must remember who else is at the table in commodity trading. It is not just people like you and me. First of all, take a look at the floor people. If they are not any good, they do not last very long, because these people are trading with their own money. They are also trading for a very small amount of ticks and a very small amount of commission and overhead. So they are going to be professional.

You also have the commercial interest. These corporations have an awful lot of money to put behind their positions, and most positions are insurance positions against a cash product. They are what you call very strong hands. They are not ones to mess around with.

Then there are the money managers with big amounts of equity. Those guys are not going to get scared out by running a stop or moving around intraday. They are going to look at the closing prices and make decisions maybe on a weekly or monthly basis on how to alter positions.

There are also the individual high level speculators who have the quotation equipment, who have the charting package like TradeStation, and have the analysis packages. They are professional all day long every day. What they do is trade commodities. I am in this category.

Finally, there is the part-time speculator who looks at the prices, collects data at the end of the day, and makes decisions based on news and brokerage ads.

Who do you want to bet your money on? Be very careful when playing this game. It is a game. You can consider that you have a certain stake. You will risk a certain amount of money, and once that amount of money is gone you quit the game or at least sit back from it and reevaluate it.

Ideally, this is how I trade a system: Come up with a system and your idea. If you have 10 years of data, test it over the middle six years of data. For instance, if you have from 1980 to 1990 in data, the middle six years would be 1983 to 1989. Come up with parameters and freeze them.

Test them backwards over the first two years and see what your results are—especially average trade size. Test them forward over two years, so they are tested on unseen data for 40 percent of the time. Now that you have a workable system, if it holds up during those periods or if it gets better towards the end than it was in the beginning, you can either run it through the most current data that is not continuous or run it through real-time money if that is your bent.

Trade it in mini contracts. Get a feel for it. Trade it in very small amounts until you are comfortable.

Question: *Can you overdevelop a system? Have you ever had to back step? How do you keep accurate records of what you have already tried?*

Answer: Those are three really good questions. The answer is: yes, yes, and it is difficult to know. Can you overdevelop a system? Absolutely. The more things you put into an equation, the more chances are it is not going to hold up in the future. This is just a fact of life in commodity trading.

You have to be very careful that you do not say to yourself, "I wouldn't have taken that trade," or "During 1987 I wouldn't have traded a system," or "Since it's never worked in cattle, I'll bet I never would have taken those cattle trades." These kinds of statements can be very dangerous in system writing. System writing has to be mechanical. You have to come up with something that you CAN and WILL actually follow.

For instance, if you come up with a system that works great without a stop, but once you put a stop in, starts getting chopped up, ask yourself,

"Will I really trade without a stop?" "Can I really trade without a stop?" A lot of us do not, so you need to be very careful about overdeveloping a system thinking, "This is the best." It has to be not only the best, but the best that you will actually trade.

Have I ever had to back step? Continually! Lots of times I will come up with a trading system that is great on paper, and I will find out that there has been an error in my methodology. One common error is using a lot of built-in fancy stops that the software will allow for. A lot of times those stops especially for bar of entry will only give you the very best results.

The cleanest test of all is buy on the open, get out on the close because you know what the opening price is and you know what the closing price is, and you know there is volume at the opening and closing because there are people trading at those prices.

Those are legitimate tests, but who knows if you can sell the high tick or buy the low tick of the day? Who knows how many contracts could be done at those values? Those are questions that only realtime trading can tell you.

If I would advise to backstep off anything, it would be to backstep off complication. Make it simple. One key way to keep accurate records of what you have already tried is to take a look at an eighth grade science book. Go to the library and physically look at the scientific method of how to perform experiments. This is the way to test.

I have always kept a diary of each of my trading systems—from the very first idea and why I think it works, and step by step, the tests I have taken. Pretend you are going to be doing a moving average. Here is one test of optimization I performed in 1983 on a silver program I called, "Hi Ho Silver." I was finding the ultimate moving average in my mind. If the price was above it, I would be long. If the price was below it, I would be short. I would always be in the market, and there were no stops, so there was only one trading rule.

Since I only had one trading rule, I allowed myself the luxury of what I call "overoptimizing." I ran every moving average from one day to a hundred in steps of one, every possibility, and found on that piece of data the 32-day moving average was best on silver prices trading the way I had outlined. The trading rule was: If the close was above the 32-day moving average, you were long. If the close was below the 32-day moving average, you were short.

If you look back at it today you will find that this system still is not too bad. Here is a sidebar on this system: Today, if I said, "Look, I don't want to be short silver," I might change the system to say, "If we are above the 32-day moving average, go long. If we are below it, I am on the sidelines." This cuts out half the trades and it makes certain I am never short in a market that I believe fundamentally for one reason or another may have a chance to go up.

One good way to keep accurate records is to put them on your computer. Put up a spreadsheet and at the end of every day about 10 minutes before you are ready to quit, review what you have done for the day—what tests you have done and what results have happened from those tests. I think that you will find that it is time well worth spent.

Question: *Is there a profile on what kind of person makes a good system developer?*

Answer: Usually a good system developer is fairly analytical, often a loner, likes to believe in things that he or she discovers on his or her own rather than taking the word of someone else about it, is fairly successful at what he or she has done in the past (so he or she has the luxury of time to work on system development), and is open to new ideas and new things. You also have to have a certain amount of tenacity. You have to have the ability to keep looking for an answer that does not feel like it is forthcoming.

Thomas Edison looked at 40,000 materials until he found tungsten. I would not have been that tenacious. I probably would have stopped at 30,000. Larry Williams, on the other hand, probably would still be testing it even if he found the tungsten, to find a better tungsten.

Question: *How can I tell if my system is balanced?*

Answer: One way is to look at the pure longs and shorts. Have you made and lost about the same amount of money on both sides of the market? In a big uptrend that usually won't occur, but if you have about the same number of trades in longs and shorts, this will show a degree of balance.

If all your long sides are winners and all your short sides are losers or vice versa, before you discard the system or only trade one side of it, take a look at the failing side. You may have written your code incorrectly. Also, if you show an inordinate number of trades on one side as compared to the other, check that side to see if you have the exact same rules.

One way to do this is to write only the long side of the market, then copy it to the sell side. Now reverse all the symbols—all the greater thans to less thans. Then you will know that you have the exact same verbiage on top and bottom, long and short.

Question: *Who can I trust to see my trading system without stealing it?*

Answer: Hardly anyone. Ultimately, you will have to trust someone, however, if you want to have it checked out. I have had people send me black box systems—systems they have had locked—and asked me to test them. I will not touch them. One of the reasons is, if it is locked up it could have a virus in it and I do not want to put it in my computer. I have too much expensive data to risk it.

With a lock on it you cannot do a virus check. Another reason is, if a trader does not trust me, I do not want to fool with him or her. That person can do business with someone else. Once we have tuned his/her system up, if he/she wants to put a lock on the disk that we both share, that is wonderful. I have done development work with Larry Williams, Wells Wilder, David Wright. If these people have let me see their code and let me help them with their work, I do not see why other people would not. If you cannot trust somebody, do it yourself.

Question: *If a lot of people start trading the same system, can it change the market?*

Answer: Boy, can it! A good example of that is Larry Williams. He is probably the best living commodities trader. The day after one of his seminars, watch the markets he trades. They will get moved around because the people at the seminar who just learned the technique will trade the system. As soon as they have had a losing trade or two they will jump away from that system and do something else, and the markets will go back to where they were.

Keep a schedule of his seminars if you are trading these kinds of systems and keep away from them the day after, because you will have a lot of participants. The market and the people have about a 10-day memory. Ten or 15 days after the market has been exposed, normally the market goes back to where it was.

Question: *What does form-fitting mean?*

Answer: An extreme example of form-fitting would be to take a look at the low date in silver. Let's pretend it is January 25, 1978. Take a System-Writer and say, "If date equals 1-25-78, then buy tomorrow at market." What that would have you do then, is buy one day after the low.

Now take a look at when the high occurred. Maybe it was March 15, 1983. You would have your SystemWriter say, "If day of week equals 3-15-83, sell tomorrow at market." It has you sell one day after the low. Lock it up and black box it. Now you can say that you have a silver system that does not trade very much, but when it does it takes the top and the bottom. This is the extreme, but it is form-fitting.

Another way of doing it is optimizing 5 or 10 or 15 variables to the very "nth" over one piece of data, and then saying, "Here it is. This the system for that market." You will find that it does not hold up.

Question: *Do most people hold trades over the weekend?*

Answer: One of the systems in this book, called One Night Stand, is based on the premise that people hate to carry positions over the weekend. You want to play on that fear. Most people will evaluate their portfolios on a Friday and at least sell down to a sleeping position.

Think about this question, but do not answer it out loud. If you had 10 contracts of silver on and you had been making money and all of a sudden it is Friday afternoon and the market is still making new highs—what would you tend to do? If you are most people, you would get out of half your positions, take your profits, go home and feel comfortable over the weekend in case something happens.

What would you be thinking about on Sunday evening? How do I get my silver back? Of course, you will have to rebuy it. You have to be careful about blindly getting out just because it is the weekend. One Night

Stand analyzes taking positions into the weekend and giving them back on Monday. You will find that 50 to 70 percent of the time holding positions over the weekend is the right thing to do.

Question: *How do you establish the primary trend?*

Answer: A very simple way is to take a look at a 20-day moving average of the closing price. If the price is above the 20-day and the 20-day is rising and it's higher than it was yesterday, you are in a rising market. Your primary trend is up. The opposite is also true. Another one, of course, is a 10-day versus a 40-day crossover. If a 10-day moving average is up and above the 40, if the 40 is rising and the 10 is rising, that primary trend is up.

Question: *Can you overanalyze the market?*

Answer: Constantly. A lot of people will come up with a trading system, test it like mad, put in the orders, then read the news and say, "Oh, my goodness. There's a report next Wednesday. I'd better get out of that trade because I could be caught on the wrong side."

Question: *What is optimizing?*

Answer: Optimizing is finding the exact parameters that work the best. Remember my test in silver—if a test is above a certain point you are long, if it is below a certain point, you are short. I optimized every moving average from 1 to 100. Then I held that tight and asked, did I need a stop?

But I stopped myself and said, "Wait a minute. If I shouldn't be long, I should be short." I'm going to make this an SAR, a stop and reverse system. I'm always either long or short. That way I am looking at only one parameter. When the close is above the 32-day moving average of the close, I'm long. When it's below it, I'm short. This is as unoptimized as I can be.

Question: *What is the different between initial margin and maintenance margin?*

Answer: Initial margin is the amount of money you must have on deposit when you initially put the trade on. Maintenance margin is the money you have to maintain in your account to keep the position on and to keep the firm or exchange from blowing you out. Most people who trade systems should be able to ignore margins by having enough money in their account to trade.

If you take a look at small businesses that have failed, you will find the biggest cause of small businesses failing is under-capitalization. My point is this: Make certain you have enough money to trade commodities if that is what you are going to do.

Question: *How could I determine my comfort level?*

Answer: One easy way is to go through the same systems. Find the one you like the best. Ask yourself, "Why do I like it?" What commodity does it trade? How big is the stop? How often does it trade? How much drawdown is there compared to profit?

I determine my love for a system by taking a look at how much money it makes. I divide this money by its largest drawdown. If I look at a system that has made a hundred grand, and somewhere it had a $10,000 drawdown, my determining ratio for that system is 10 to 1. That to me is a better system than a system that makes $120,000 with a $30,000 drawdown (a ratio of four to one). Even though the second system made more money, it had to take a lot more gas. By trading system number one, you could make $300,000 with a $30,000 drawdown.

I do not like to carry systems overnight. If I have a choice between one system that always has a stop in it and gets out by the end of the day, so I do not have overnight exposure, and one that is always in, I lean toward the one that gets out, because who knows what will happen overnight? You can control your risk better that way.

Question: *What is a "safe" commodity trading system?*

Answer: Commodities is not safe. If I were beginning, looking for a place to start, I would probably take a look at this system: I would take one currency like British Pound or Japanese Yen and trade trends on the MidAm to see how it feels and if I can handle that. Historically, that system has had the best drawdown/profit ratio, and your exposure is limited to one day. Also, it is a very hard system to foul up. You do not need to sit and look at it all week long. You don't need a lot of quote equipment. On Thursday afternoon, you put your order in, and if it fills you get out on Monday's opening.

Question: *There's a lot of talk about bond trading. What should I know about the bond market?*

Answer: The bonds is the biggest pit; it is the grown-ups' game. I think bond systems are more difficult to design because bonds are a 24-hour market. Every tick is $31.25, so it does not take very many ticks to make or lose a lot of money. I would not advise any beginner to start in the bonds. If you really want to trade the financials, take a look at the system in my book called This Is a Ten (see Chapter 4).

This Is a Ten trades the S&P only on Mondays. You might also take a look at my systems called Big Joe, Bigger Joe, or Buy Monday. They all have several things in common. They are all S&P systems. Most of them have $500 stops or a manageable stop, and they get out at the end of the day, but they use different trigger mechanisms to decide when to get in. I think if you have to trade financials, this is the way to go.

Question: *If I love oil and want to start an oil trading system, where should I start?*

Answer: If you are "in love" with a certain commodity, look through my chapter on systems (Chapter 9). Find the one that is comfortable to you even if it is on a different commodity. Pretend you are "in love" with oil, and Paul Revere is a comfortable system to you. Take Paul Revere and run it through oil. See how it trades. Tune it and fix it. There is an oil system in the book called Joe's Oil Well which is a basic moving average cross-over—you are long or short all the time. Take a look at that system and see if you are comfortable with that. These are your starting points.

Question: *What systems are going to give me "fast action"?*

Answer: S&Ps, currencies, and bonds are all good for action-type systems. You hit upon something with this question that hits upon the crux of commodities trading. You did not mention that you wanted to make a lot of money. You want a pinball machine, something happening all the time. What you should do is find one of the systems in the book that you like, and speed it up.

Speeding it up is easy. Go to Paul Revere again (Figures 7.1 and 7.2). Paul Revere is a long-term trend-following system in currencies based on daily bars. Run it one-minute or five-minute or three-minute bars in currencies. You will get a lot of trades, a lot of action, and it will trade with the major trend. Use the systems in this book as models. Find the system you like the best, no matter what commodity it is trading, and apply it to your commodity. It is like looking at a plan book for houses. You find the basic house plan that you like, then make changes in it to make it your house.

Question: *Can you have a trading system without a computer?*

Answer: Absolutely. Until 1983 all systems were done without computers. Candlestick patterns in the rice trade in China were based on, "Where is the opening in relationship to the close and where are all these different patterns in relationship to each other?"

They determined if the close was higher than the opening for two or three successive days and if there was a larger distance between the close and the opening, and if there was a bullish pattern they would buy rice back in the 600s.

Most of the systems I show in this book could be done without the aid of a computer. They have been tested on a computer, so we could see what the tests are, but I write very simple systems. If my computer goes down or I get bad data, I do not want to stop trading. I want to look at the market, use my mind, and make my trades.

You are at a disadvantage as far as testing your system, but as far as implementation without a computer, I am not so sure it is a disadvantage. A TradeStation can watch two hundred systems simultaneously, but who needs to watch two hundred systems simultaneously? This is like asking, "Am I at a disadvantage going into a gunfight without a gun?" You might

Figure 7.1

```
//////////////////////////////////////////////\\\\\\\\\\\\\\\\\\\\\\\\\\\\\\\\\\\
Directory : F:\JKTOOL                          Printed on   : 09/11/93 07:32pm
```

PERFORMANCE SUMMARY

Model Name   : Paul Revere   Developer   : Krutsinger
Test Number   :   1 of   1
Notes : 1000 stop after day of entry

Data   : BRITISH POUND   12/92
Calc Dates   : 03/03/75 - 12/31/92

```
Num. Conv. P. Value Comm  Slippage  Margin  Format  Drive:\Path\FileName
-------------------------------------------------------------------------
 26   2  $   6.250  $ 50   $   0   $ 3,000  Omega   C:\20DATA\F008.DTA
```

```
/////////////////////////// ALL TRADES  - Test 1 \\\\\\\\\\\\\\\\\\\\\\\\\\\\
```

Total net profit	$221,987.50		
Gross profit	$461,762.50	Gross loss	-239,775.00
Total # of trades	423	Percent profitable	38%
Number winning trades	163	Number losing trades	260
Largest winning trade	$14,712.50	Largest losing trade	$-2,387.50
Average winning trade	$2,832.90	Average losing trade	$ -922.21
Ratio avg win/avg loss	3.07	Avg trade (win & loss)	$524.79
Max consecutive winners	6	Max consecutive losers	7
Avg # bars in winners	19	Avg # bars in losers	4
Max closed-out drawdown	$-12,875.00	Max intra-day drawdown	$-13,025.00
Profit factor	1.92	Max # of contracts held	1
Account size required	$16,025.00	Return on account	1,385%

Highlights - All trades

Description	Date	Time	Amount
Largest Winning Trade	08/30/90	-	$ 14,712.50
Largest Losing Trade	09/24/90	-	$ -2,387.50
Largest String of + Trades	09/16/85	-	6
Largest String of - Trades	09/23/82	-	7
Maximum Closed-Out Drawdown	08/07/92	-	$ -12,875.00
Maximum Intra-Day Drawdown	08/14/92	-	$ -13,025.00

```
////////////////////////// LONG TRADES  - Test 1 \\\\\\\\\\\\\\\\\\\\\\\\\\\\\
```

Total net profit	$108,825.00		
Gross profit	$231,437.50	Gross loss	-122,612.50
Total # of trades	213	Percent profitable	39%
Number winning trades	84	Number losing trades	129
Largest winning trade	$14,712.50	Largest losing trade	$-2,300.00
Average winning trade	$2,755.21	Average losing trade	$ -950.48
Ratio avg win/avg loss	2.89	Avg trade (win & loss)	$510.92
Max consecutive winners	7	Max consecutive losers	10
Avg # bars in winners	19	Avg # bars in losers	3

Figure 7.2

```
Max closed-out drawdown  $-17,431.25    Max intra-day drawdown   $-17,681.25
Profit factor                   1.88    Max # of contracts held            1
Account size required     $20,681.25    Return on account                526%

                      Highlights - Long trades
        Description              Date      Time      Amount,
        ------------------------------------------------------------
        Largest Winning Trade    08/30/90    -    $    14,712.50
        Largest Losing Trade     04/22/75    -    $    -2,300.00
        Largest String of + Trades 02/03/78  -              7
        Largest String of - Trades 06/26/89  -             10
        Maximum Closed-Out Drawdown 02/28/85 -    $   -17,431.25
        Maximum Intra-Day Drawdown 03/14/85  -    $   -17,681.25
```

/////////////////////////// SHORT TRADES - Test 1 \\\\\\\\\\\\\\\\\\\\\\\\\\\

```
Total net profit         $113,162.50
Gross profit             $230,325.00    Gross loss                -117,162.50

Total # of trades               210    Percent profitable                37%
Number winning trades            79    Number losing trades             131

Largest winning trade     $13,212.50    Largest losing trade      $-2,387.50
Average winning trade      $2,915.51    Average losing trade      $  -894.37
Ratio avg win/avg loss         3.25     Avg trade (win & loss)      $538.87

Max consecutive winners           5    Max consecutive losers            10
Avg # bars in winners            18    Avg # bars in losers               4

Max closed-out drawdown  $-18,162.50    Max intra-day drawdown   $-18,350.00
Profit factor                   1.96    Max # of contracts held            1
Account size required     $21,350.00    Return on account                530%

                      Highlights - Short trades
        Description              Date      Time      Amount
        ------------------------------------------------------------
        Largest Winning Trade    09/29/92    -    $    13,212.50
        Largest Losing Trade     09/24/90    -    $    -2,387.50
        Largest String of + Trades 02/27/85  -              5
        Largest String of - Trades 08/22/79  -             10
        Maximum Closed-Out Drawdown 09/08/92 -    $   -18,162.50
        Maximum Intra-Day Drawdown 09/10/92  -    $   -18,350.00
```

\\\////////////////////////////////////

Prepared using System Writer Plus Version 2.18 by Omega Research, Inc.

be able to kill your opponent with a rock, but if all the other gunfighters have guns, you had better have a gun too.

Take a blank piece of paper and write down what it is you are trying to accomplish by trading. If all you want is to have entertainment, then you need a system that trades a lot, but does not risk much money. Maybe it wins and maybe it loses, but it is an entertaining vehicle. If you are trying to catch a major trend, you do not want a daytrading system because you might be out when the trend is trending.

Make a want list of what it is you are trying to accomplish. Some traders want to make money, but do not want to risk much money and they do not want to have to watch each tick of the market. There is a way around this. You can put your system on a disk and have a company like Robbins trade your system for you, or you can come up with a system like One Night Stand where you look at the system once a week, put in the order, and forget about it.

Question: *If you could give one "secret" to successful systems trading, what would it be?*

Answer: If I could give anybody a "secret" it would be to look at existing systems; look at the ones in this book because all the rules are disclosed. Find the one which is as much like what you want to do as you can. Copy the math, and use that as your base. Add things and subtract things until it's what you want it to be.

Question: *Which system in this book is the best?*

Answer: The first thing you do when you want to test a system is to write the system. Put it into a piece of testing software like TradeStation or SystemWriter. Put it into computer language.

The basic system of this book is a system called Buy Monday. Here are the rules: If day of week date equals five (if today is Friday) then buy tomorrow at market (Monday), or Tuesday if there is a Monday holiday. That is your entry rule. Now write the exit rule. If market position equals one (if you are long) then exit today on the close.

You need a protective stop so you do not lose too much money. Click the box on the SystemWriter or TradeStation that says, "we'll risk $1,000 on the trade and if it ever hits there during the trade, we want out." Now that we have done that, if it is a TradeStation we take the model and apply it to a chart, push a button, and it gives us our track record. If it is a SystemWriter we can take that model and apply 20 or 30 different commodities to it and see what it does. This is all there is to it.

Question: *What is the key to systems trading?*

Answer: Implementation is the whole key. Most people cannot do it, that is where they blow up. The way to do it is to write your system, then give it to somebody else to implement for you. I know one successful trader who sleeps all day. He has no quotes. At night he pulls up the quotes from the phone line (CSI), looks at the data, runs his systems and gets his orders, then faxes his orders in on a recorder to the brokerage, and goes back to sleep.

He does not want any fills. He calls his broker when he wakes up in the afternoon. He told me this is the only way he could discipline himself to trade his system and not react to the pressure of the market.

If you do not have the luxury of changing your schedule from day to night, the next best thing is to let the clerks implement your trades for you, and train yourself to not look at the market during the day. Tell your people not to bother you with fills.

Question: *How did you come up with Paul Revere's British Pound system?*

Answer: I tested Paul Revere over all the markets. It worked pretty well, but it worked best in the currencies. The best currency was the British Pound. I feel the British Pound is also ignored by most traders, because most of the big funds trade the D-Mark, the Swiss, and the Yen and combinations thereof, but they leave the British Pound alone.

I came up with the concept—I ran a bunch of different indicators on a piece of currency data (let's say it is the British Pound) and found which of the indicators worked best first. Once I found the best indicator which was channel breakout, I tuned that channel for length.

You can choose buy the highest high of the last two days or 20 days or 100 days. You can test and find out what the best length is. Then when I found the length that seemed to be the best, I held that against all the different data to see if it held up, and then applied it to the market that seemed to work with it the best.

Question: *Can you tell me step by step how to develop a system?*

Answer: Number one: Have a trading idea of an indicator that you like. Say that you have four ideas that are similar, and you like moving averages. If the short moving average is above the long one, you want to be long or vice versa, be short. If you like channel breakouts—if it breaks out the high channel, you want to be long. If it breaks out the low channel, you want to be short. Moving averages, channel breakouts, stochastics, and RSI are built into most software packages.

You want to see which of these four will be the best over the commodity you have chosen. Pretend that you have chosen currencies because you think currencies trend, which they do. Once a currency takes off in a certain direction it tends to remain going in that direction. This means you would take a currency and put it on a SystemWriter to study over a five-year period.

Pretend you have a 10-year database from 1982 to 1992. The best time to test it would be the five years in the middle from the middle of 1984 until the middle of 1987. Then you would have two and a half years before you did your testing and two and a half years after you did your testing that you could use as virgin data and run your test over that data to see if your math holds up. This is a lot better technique than running it over the entire database to develop your system.

You have picked your data, which is the British Pound. You have picked your time frame, which is the five years in the middle of your database. You have these four trading indicators, and you can see which indicator works the best. On SystemWriter Plus you can do an ALT run. You attack all four entry techniques in data and let them run each four by themselves—each of them in every possible combination. Since there are four trading systems, the most possibilities there would be would be 16 data runs. You let the machine do its magic, and it will let you know which of these 16 is the best. In this particular case it was channel breakout.

Now you turn the other systems off and test for the length of the channel. Once you have determined which length is the best, you keep your system frozen and test it over 30 commodities to find out which one is best and which one is worst to see if you can handle it. This is the methodology of writing a SystemWriter test.

Question: *Why is Monday an important trading day?*

Answer: The Monday phenomenon is important because people who trade stock indexes tend to lose mostly because they trade too often. By trading too often they pay too many commissions, take unnecessary risks, and end up going away losers. It makes sense to find the very best day to trade and within that day look for the very best times to trade.

The premise I am trying to prove is that Monday is the best day to buy stocks. Let me tell you the methodology of proving this, because it is very simple: Write a little program that says, "If today is _____ then buy tomorrow on the open and get out on the close." There are only five days to use to fill in the blank, so you use five simple tests. You can very easily see Monday jumps out at you in stock indexes.

Hold that piece of information in your mind, and say, "now I'm going to devise buy-only systems for stocks and S&Ps on Mondays. I could write a whole chapter on this because a lot of my systems are based on this.

Question: *The software available confuses me. Can you explain some of the differences between them?*

Answer: I have discussed several software tools in Chapter 4. A very useful one is Portana by Tom Berry Software, which lets you take System-Writer output and lay it on top of each other, up to a hundred different systems simultaneously on top of each other, so you can see how much money it would take to run all of these systems simultaneously.

Question: *What is buy and hold strategy?*

Answer: I have data that goes back to 1962 in IBM stock. Say the first day of my data you purchased 1,000 shares of IBM stock and never sold it. If you did that, as of today you would have $26,000 profit. All the systems I develop in stock I have to compare to the buy and hold strategy. If I have a trading system that does not make as much money as buy and hold does, there is no use in having that trading system.

If you have a problem with trading during market hours you can call me at my voice mail 1-800-767-2508, and I will be glad to help you with your system.

This system never trades overnight, and has a 10- to 11-tick stop in at all times which is like $340. It is a close stop daytrade system. I trade bonds on a daytrade basis. I trade day of the week, which is unusual. I use time of the day, which is unusual. I use a 20-bar length. I use the lowest low and the highest high. I have a close stop, and I get out on the close. This is all I am going to tell you about it.

8

Implementing a Trading System

We cannot become what we need to be
by remaining what we are.
— Max DePreese —

Implementing Your System

The key to profitable trading is to consistently implement your system. Most of the rest of this stuff is talk. The easiest way to overcome your problems and implement your system is to let somebody else do it. It may cost a little more to do this, but this is the optimum because another person is not bamboozled by pride of ownership.

If you develop a system, you might say, "Gee, that may not be a good signal because I thought of it. Maybe it should be a 19-day moving average instead of a 20," and you will tinker around with it until you don't have a system.

Discipline

Discipline is an essential part of implementing a trading system. You must achieve the psychological discipline that you need to constantly and consistently apply your system. Discipline is so hard. If you look at me, you can tell I am not disciplined at the table. I get nervous and I eat.

When I started in commodities I had a full head of hair and weighed 180 pounds. Now I weigh well over 250 pounds. I am almost bald, and I have dark brown circles under my eyes. This is from watching every tick of the market since 1976. You should not do this. I am not doing it anymore. Now I design systems, and let the computers watch the market. When my machines beep at me I say, "Buy bellies and wear diamonds," or whatever I have decided to do.

I sit in my one-room office developing systems. These systems are implemented in a trading room by other people. At the end of the day the trading room employees and I talk, but we try not to talk to each other during the day. I do not want to put my signature on what is going on. I want the machine to beep and do what I want my systems to do.

People say, "Gee, if you know so many systems why are you showing them to me?" First of all, I trade the best and show the rest. As I develop better systems, I show my "old" systems.

Psychological Discipline

An easy way for you to try to learn discipline would be to go to Las Vegas with $300. Take $300 in one dollar bills, go to a roulette wheel, and constantly bet one dollar on red. Keep playing until you use all of the $300.

You should be there for about five days, day and night, because red will keep coming up and you will keep winning your dollar back. However, because the house does win with their 0 and double 0, you eventually will lose your money.

The idea of using this as a discipline step is this: You have to have a systematic approach to the market. To consistently follow that system, you have to get used to winning and losing consistently.

What most people do when they trade, whether discretionarily or with a system, is seek drawdown. Curtis Arnold, a famous trader, says that systems traders often trade a system until it loses three trades in a row. Then they jump to a new system and wait for that one to lose three trades in a row. After jumping through five or six trading systems, they lose half their equity and they stop trading because system trading does not work.

Your objective as a systems developer/trader is to develop a system that you can and will trade, and then follow it religiously. The psychology of discipline is as true in commodities trading as it is in any other business.

Pick Your Favorite Market

Remember how in the first chapter I told you at the beginning of my career I specialized in soybean meal? I learned everything about soybean meal. You should do the same.

Even today I pick a market like the bonds and say, "That's my market." I try everything I know to trade that market the way I want to trade it. I do not like to carry things overnight. I always like to have a stop in, so this is the way I design my systems.

Other People's Systems Performance

Another thing you can look at is other people's systems performance. *Futures* Magazine lists the top 10 trading systems. You can get performance summaries over a period of time from "Futures Truth." Your goal is to beat the performance of other system developers.

Do not think you have to reinvent the wheel. I have only shown you two or three systems so far. I've shown you Joe's Gap and Paul Revere, which were both British Pound systems. I like to emphasize unusual trading systems, my forte. I like to do things that no one else does. I like to use day of week, I like to use time of day, I like to use long bars. I like to buy when other people are selling.

9

$48,000 Worth of Trading Systems?*

Money never starts an idea;
it is the idea that starts the money.
— W.J. Cameran —

Circa 1985—at the then prevalent price of $3,000 per system—16+ trading systems for you to modify, tune, and change.

Well, you've found it! Buried here in the back of the book is the section many TradeStation and SWP users should love. Any questions, call my 24-hour voice mail, 1-800-767-2508, and I'll try to help you.

Some of these systems are written in SystemWriter, some in TradeStation. Some are illustrated with Portana, which is an add-on program that you can put on the SystemWriter Plus, that shows you the daily equities—weekly or monthly—of several systems run on the same money at the same time.

The basic premise of every one of these trading systems is identical: It is to make as much money as possible through that particular commodity with as little drawdown and as large an average trade as possible.

I want to show you the components of these track records and of the tool Portana as an illustration, so you can look through the remainder of the systems very quickly and see which ones suit your needs. Again, the emphasis here is on showing how very simple, short pieces of code can become trading systems, and how you can take this code and add your own biases and come up with a new trading system which you are more comfortable with.

Remember, these are examples in the art of system writing; not pure trading systems for you to trade, but rather, code ready for you to borrow and apply to your own trading system ideas.

I have included the following examples of the art of system writing in no particular order. All performances stated are simulated. The CFTC requires the following disclaimer:

HYPOTHETICAL OR SIMULATED PERFORMANCE RESULTS HAVE CERTAIN INHERENT LIMITATIONS. UNLIKE AN ACTUAL PERFORMANCE RECORD, SIMULATED RESULTS DO NOT REPRESENT ACTUAL TRADING. ALSO, SINCE THE TRADES HAVE NOT ACTUALLY BEEN EXECUTED, THE RESULTS MAY HAVE UNDER-OR-OVER COMPENSATED FOR THE IMPACT, IF ANY, OF CERTAIN MARKET FACTORS, SUCH AS LACK OF LIQUIDITY. SIMULATED TRADING PROGRAMS IN GENERAL ARE ALSO SUBJECT TO THE FACT THAT THEY ARE DESIGNED WITH THE BENEFIT OF HINDSIGHT. NO REPRESENTATION IS BEING MADE THAT ANY ACCOUNT WILL OR IS LIKELY TO ACHIEVE PROFITS OR LOSSES SIMILAR TO THOSE SHOWN. THERE IS A RISK OF LOSS IN FUTURES TRADING.

9.1 Joe's Quarter Pounder

Daily British Pound—one contract only, $55 commission, $2,000 stop, and a five-day trailing stop of $2,000.

Logic

Why do I think this system appears to work?

This system was written in an airport while waiting for a delayed plane. I used the power of SystemWriter Plus to search for the correct VarA and VarB. This is a two-step process. If the setup is true, open-and-close pattern arrangements, then buy a breakout to the upside or sell a breakdown to the downside.

Lesson?

This is a very powerful technique. Use one condition as a setup (like a pattern), and a second condition for an entry trigger. Try this out with different conditions and combinations.

9.2a and 9.2b—Joe's Big Joe

9.2a

Daily S&P 500—one contract only, $55 commission, no stop, exit market on close.

9.2b

Daily S&P 500—one contract only, $55 commission, $2,000 stop, exit market on close.

Logic

Why do I think this system appears to work?

This system is an example of a daily pattern search coupled with some Day-of-Week testing. "A" gets in on the open, out on the close with no stop used. "B" gets in on the open, out on the close with a $2,000 stop used. This is also an example of a biased system. Since the S&P has been in a 30-year uptrend, the system is designed to trigger only buys. This is also a two-step process. If the setup is true, open-and-close pattern arrangements, then we buy a breakout to the upside.

Lesson?

Day-of-Week testing, dual conditions, pattern searches, and a biased system! Big Joe demonstrates many interesting techniques.

9.3a and 9.3b—Joe's Big Joe

9.3a

Daily S&P 500—up to 20 contracts, $55 commission, $2,000 stop, exit market on close.

9.3b

Daily S&P 500—up to 20 contracts, $55 commission, no stop, exit market on close.

Logic

Why do I think this system appears to work?
    This is basically one-contract Big Joe with a twist. I have written a function, MaxMatrix2, which when used in Big Joe will buy a minimum of four contracts up to a maximum of 20 contracts, scaled up and down based on the profitability of the system.

Lesson?

A good one-contract system can be a great pyramid system. Try MaxMatrix2!

9.4 Aztec Real Oil

Daily Crude Oil—one contract only, $55 commission, no stop—always in.

Logic

Why do I think this system appears to work?

 This is a takeoff on Joe's Oil Well and Joe's Paul Revere. This is a simple 20-day channel breakout. Easy. Simple.

Lesson?

Simple ideas can work, can't they? Several intraday 60-minute S&P 500 systems—$500 stop, exit market on close.

9.5 Joe's Alarm Clock
9.6 JK Thunderhead
9.7 Joe's Wakeup Call
9.8 Joe's Bigger Joe
9.9 Joe's Gap
9.10 Joe's Banker (No stop, reversing if need be; holds overnight)

Logic

Why do I think these systems appear to work?

 These are all based on the Big Joe Daily system. This is an example of using daily research to develop intraday systems.

Lesson?

Day-of-Week testing, dual conditions, pattern searches, Time-of-Day testing and a biased system!

9.11 JK OEX Option Buyer

Daily S&P 500—one contract only, $55 commission, no stop, holds longs and shorts a certain number of days, might be ideal for the purchaser of puts and calls.

Logic

Why do I think this system appears to work?

- Low volume and a gap down. Fade that move.

- Low volume and a gap up. Fade that move.

- This is a concept that has been discussed by many stock market technicians; lack of follow-through.

Lesson?

Try volume filters in unusual manners in other systems.

9.12 Fib Catcher

Daily S&P 500—one contract only, $55 commission, no stop, holds longs and shorts a certain number of days, might be ideal for the purchaser of puts and calls.

Logic

Why do I think this system appears to work?

This system was developed as an upwardly biased currency option program. If the market is breaking to new lows and then takes out a short-term high, a cycle low has probably been made and vice versa.

Lesson?

Try surprises in other systems. Examine systems you develop for one market on an entirely different market.

The following are two 180-minute British Pound Systems.

9.13 Joe's Test Pattern

Daily S&P 500—one contract only, $55 commission, no stop, holds longs and shorts a certain number of days, might be ideal for the purchaser of puts and calls.

Logic

Why do I think this system appears to work?

I used the power of SystemWriter Plus to search for the correct VarA, VarB, and VarC on daily data (just as I did in Joe's Quarter Pounder). This is a two-step process. If the setup is true, open-and-close pattern arrangements, then buy a breakout to the upside or sell a breakdown to the downside. It also brings the stop up above breakeven after 180 minutes in the trade.

Lesson?

Daily research, a better-than-breakeven stop, and an unusual bar size. Try these ideas on other systems.

9.14 Joe's Jesse Livermore

Daily Currency System—one contract only, $59 commission, $500 stop, holds longs and shorts a short period of time, might be ideal for the purchaser of puts and calls.

Logic

Why do I think this system appears to work?

This system was developed by reading Jesse Livermore techniques in Perry Kaufman's trading system book. It's our old friend—two steps for an entry with a trailing stop.

Lesson?

Try reading other books and using their ideas for setups to your favorite entry technique.

Note:

The rules below the code in {French brackets} are exit rules and their explanations that, although not used in this system, can be "dropped" into any system you might have. Experiment!

9.15a and 9.15b Joe's Texas Two Step

9.15a

180-minute British Pound—one contract, $55 commission, $5,000 total position stop.

Logic

Why do I think this system appears to work?

This system was developed using my now semifamous two-step formula—an absolute crossover of two moving averages followed by a breakout of a small channel.

Lesson?

This system illustrates the power of SystemWriter. I developed the system for daily data on SystemWriter Plus and then dropped it on different time frames.

9.15b

Daily British Pound—up to 20 contracts, $55 commission, $5,000 total stop.

Logic

Why do I think this system appears to work?

This system was developed using my now semifamous two-step formula—an absolute crossover of two moving averages followed by a breakout of a small channel.

Lesson?

This system illustrates the power of TradeStation. By changing two simple steps, a stop based on total position—not per contract—and box #3 in TradeStation which allows multiple entries in the same direction with a maximum I defined as 20 contracts.

9.16 Yen Again

Daily Yen—one contract only, $55 commission, $1,000 stop.

Logic

Why do I think this system appears to work?
    This system was developed using a traditional channel breakout and was then "biased" by allowing only new sell positions on a Friday.

Lesson?

Try this technique of using an old system and bias the trading. For example, if you are in a very long-term uptrend, make it more difficult, but not impossible, to get a sell signal.

Figure 9.1
Joe's Quarter Pounder

PORTFOLIO ANALYZER QUARTLY REPORT *for* QUARTER POUNDER

DATE	OPEN EQUITY	CLOSED EQUITY	TOTAL EQUITY	MAX DRAWDOWN	% DD	% CHNG TOT EQ	NUM TRADE
750422	0.00	30000.00	30000.00	0.00	0.0	0.0	0
750630	0.00	29622.50	29622.50	2180.00	7.3	-1.3	0
750930	0.00	28132.50	28132.50	4866.25	16.2	-5.0	0
751231	437.50	32006.25	32443.75	4866.25	16.2	15.3	1
760331	62.50	28701.25	28763.75	4866.25	16.2	-11.3	1
760630	743.75	34720.00	35463.75	4866.25	16.2	23.3	1
760930	3468.75	33348.75	36817.50	4866.25	16.2	3.8	1
761231	1500.00	32942.50	34442.50	4866.25	16.2	-6.5	1
770331	6062.50	32942.50	39005.00	4866.25	16.2	13.2	1
770630	-937.50	38808.75	37871.25	4866.25	16.2	-2.9	1
770930	1250.00	36292.50	37542.50	4866.25	16.2	-0.9	1
771230	6187.50	38395.00	44582.50	4866.25	16.2	18.8	1
780331	2343.75	43347.50	45691.25	4866.25	16.2	2.5	1
780630	1500.00	49526.25	51026.25	4866.25	16.2	11.7	1
780929	2806.25	48861.25	51667.50	4866.25	16.2	1.3	1
781229	0.00	52238.75	52238.75	4866.25	16.2	1.1	0
790330	1962.50	51882.50	53845.00	6188.75	20.6	3.1	1
790629	7125.00	52775.00	59900.00	6188.75	20.6	11.2	1
790928	62.50	63198.75	63261.25	6188.75	18.6	5.6	1
791231	0.00	66486.25	66486.25	6188.75	15.7	5.1	0
800331	1531.25	55227.50	56758.75	14782.50	37.6	-14.6	1
800630	1718.75	61140.00	62858.75	14782.50	37.6	10.7	1
800930	250.00	58308.75	58558.75	14782.50	37.6	-6.8	1
801231	2843.75	62158.75	65002.50	14782.50	37.6	11.0	1
810331	0.00	78737.50	78737.50	14782.50	30.3	21.1	0
810630	0.00	76581.25	76581.25	14782.50	29.1	-2.7	0
810930	0.00	74821.25	74821.25	14782.50	29.1	-2.3	0
811231	1556.25	75345.00	76901.25	14782.50	29.1	2.8	1
820331	1562.50	73128.75	74691.25	14782.50	29.1	-2.9	1
820630	-250.00	81185.00	80935.00	14782.50	29.0	8.4	1
820930	900.00	85400.00	86300.00	14782.50	26.5	6.6	1
821231	0.00	82792.50	82792.50	14782.50	26.2	-4.1	0
830331	1562.50	73556.25	75118.75	14782.50	26.2	-9.3	1
830630	-93.75	80736.25	80642.50	14782.50	26.2	7.4	1
830930	1093.75	80321.25	81415.00	14782.50	26.2	1.0	1
831230	2312.50	78841.25	81153.75	14782.50	26.2	-0.3	1
840330	306.25	79902.50	80208.75	14782.50	26.2	-1.2	1
840629	2056.25	82040.00	84096.25	14782.50	26.2	4.8	1
840928	2343.75	84892.50	87236.25	14782.50	26.0	3.7	1
841231	2562.50	88896.25	91458.75	14782.50	25.1	4.8	1
850329	10618.75	90945.00	101563.75	14782.50	24.0	11.0	1
850628	0.00	94707.50	94707.50	14782.50	20.8	-6.8	0
850930	2500.00	96371.25	98871.25	14782.50	20.8	4.4	1
851231	1468.75	103191.25	104660.00	14782.50	20.1	5.9	1
860331	0.00	108841.25	108841.25	14782.50	18.7	4.0	0
860630	0.00	111043.75	111043.75	14782.50	18.2	2.0	0
860930	62.50	104420.00	104482.50	14782.50	18.2	-5.9	1
861231	4462.50	102280.00	106742.50	14782.50	18.2	2.2	1
870331	937.50	107162.50	108100.00	14782.50	18.2	1.3	1
870630	2281.25	112625.00	114906.25	14782.50	17.9	6.3	1
870930	656.25	118275.00	118931.25	14782.50	16.7	3.5	1
871231	3056.25	121667.50	124723.75	14782.50	16.0	4.9	1
880331	0.00	115703.75	115703.75	14782.50	16.0	-7.2	0
880630	0.00	117852.50	117852.50	14782.50	16.0	1.9	0
880930	1212.50	117910.00	119122.50	14782.50	16.0	1.1	1
881230	100.00	126430.00	126530.00	14782.50	15.3	6.2	1

166

Figure 9.1
Joe's Quarter Pounder (continued)

```
/////////////////////////////////////////////\\\\\\\\\\\\\\\\\\\\\\\\\\\\\\\\\\\
Directory : F:\JKTOOL                            Printed on    : 09/10/93 10:31am

                         PERFORMANCE SUMMARY

Model Name       : Joe's Quarter Pound        Developer    : Krutsinger
Test Number      :          1 of    1
Notes : Can be used without quotes

Data             : BRITISH POUND      06/93
Calc Dates       : 04/22/75 - 06/30/93

 Num. Conv. P. Value  Comm  Slippage  Margin  Format  Drive:\Path\FileName
--------------------------------------------------------------------------------
   26    2  $  6.250  $ 55   $   0   $ 3,000  Omega   F:\20DATA06\F008.DTA

////////////////////////// ALL TRADES  - Test 1 \\\\\\\\\\\\\\\\\\\\\\\\\\\\\\\

Total net profit       $164,167.50
Gross profit           $415,498.75    Gross loss                -251,331.25

Total # of trades          349        Percent profitable            45%
Number winning trades      159        Number losing trades          190

Largest winning trade  $14,720.00     Largest losing trade      $-3,305.00
Average winning trade   $2,613.20     Average losing trade      $-1,322.80
Ratio avg win/avg loss       1.97     Avg trade (win & loss)       $470.39

Max consecutive winners      7         Max consecutive losers         7
Avg # bars in winners       16         Avg # bars in losers           5

Max closed-out drawdown $-17,277.50   Max intra-day drawdown    $-17,277.50
Profit factor                1.65     Max # of contracts held         1
Account size required  $20,277.50     Return on account            809%

                    Highlights - All trades
        Description                  Date      Time     Amount
        --------------------------------------------+----------
        Largest Winning Trade       08/30/90    -   $   14,720.00
        Largest Losing Trade        03/08/76    -   $   -3,305.00
        Largest String of + Trades  04/30/91    -        7
        Largest String of - Trades  10/10/80    -        7
        Maximum Closed-Out Drawdown 06/05/92    -   $  -17,277.50
        Maximum Intra-Day Drawdown  06/05/92    -   $  -17,277.50

////////////////////////// LONG TRADES  - Test 1 \\\\\\\\\\\\\\\\\\\\\\\\\\\\\\\

Total net profit        $97,375.00
Gross profit           $241,693.75    Gross loss                -144,318.75

Total # of trades          180        Percent profitable            44%
Number winning trades       80        Number losing trades          100

Largest winning trade  $14,720.00     Largest losing trade      $-3,305.00
Average winning trade   $3,021.17     Average losing trade      $-1,443.19
Ratio avg win/avg loss       2.09     Avg trade (win & loss)       $540.97

Max consecutive winners      4         Max consecutive losers         7
Avg # bars in winners       18         Avg # bars in losers           6
```

Figure 9.1
Joe's Quarter Pounder (continued)

```
Max closed-out drawdown  $-24,455.00   Max intra-day drawdown   $-24,691.25
Profit factor                   1.67   Max # of contracts held            1
Account size required    $27,691.25    Return on account               351%
```

```
                   Highlights - Long trades
        Description                    Date      Time       Amount
        --------------------------------------------------------------
        Largest Winning Trade         08/30/90    -    $    14,720.00
        Largest Losing Trade          03/08/76    -    $    -3,305.00
        Largest String of + Trades    01/03/92    -             4
        Largest String of - Trades    07/29/81    -             7
        Maximum Closed-Out Drawdown   03/21/83    -    $   -24,455.00
        Maximum Intra-Day Drawdown    03/08/85    -    $   -24,691.25
```

///////////////////////////// SHORT TRADES - Test 1 \\\\\\\\\\\\\\\\\\\\\\\\\\\\\\

```
Total net profit        $66,792.50
Gross profit           $173,805.00    Gross loss                -107,012.50

Total # of trades             169     Percent profitable              46%
Number winning trades          79     Number losing trades             90

Largest winning trade   $13,545.00    Largest losing trade      $-2,836.25
Average winning trade    $2,200.06    Average losing trade      $-1,189.03
Ratio avg win/avg loss        1.85    Avg trade (win & loss)       $395.22

Max consecutive winners        11     Max consecutive losers            9
Avg # bars in winners          14     Avg # bars in losers              5

Max closed out drawdown $-21,947.50   Max intra-day drawdown    $-23,228.75
Profit factor                 1.62    Max # of contracts held            1
Account size required   $26,228.75    Return on account               254%
```

```
                   Highlights - Short trades
        Description                    Date      Time       Amount
        --------------------------------------------------------------
        Largest Winning Trade         04/01/91    -    $    13,545.00
        Largest Losing Trade          12/27/79    -    $    -2,836.25
        Largest String of + Trades    11/19/82    -            11
        Largest String of - Trades    10/30/80    -             9
        Maximum Closed-Out Drawdown   10/30/80    -    $   -21,947.50
        Maximum Intra-Day Drawdown    11/03/80    -    $   -23,228.75
```

\\\//////////////////////////////////////

Prepared using System Writer Plus Version 2.18 by Omega Research, Inc.

Figure 9.1
Joe's Quarter Pounder (continued)

```
//////////////////////////////////////////////\\\\\\\\\\\\\\\\\\\\\\\\\\\\\\\\\\\
Directory : F:\JKTOOL                        Printed on   : 09/10/93 10:32am

                             ENTRY SIGNAL

Signal Name       : Delayed              Developer      : Joe
Notes :

Last Update : 02/01/92 03:17am
Long  Entry Verified : YES
Short Entry Verified : YES

///////////////////////////////// LONG ENTRY \\\\\\\\\\\\\\\\\\\\\\\\\\\\\\\\\\

If C(VarA) > O(VarA) and C(VarB) > O(VarB) and C(VarB) > C(VarA)
then buy tomorrow at H(VarB) stop;


///////////////////////////////// SHORT ENTRY \\\\\\\\\\\\\\\\\\\\\\\\\\\\\\\\\\

If C(VarA) < O(VarA) and C(VarB) < O(VarB) and C(VarB) < C(VarA)
then Sell tomorrow at L(VarB) stop;


/////////////////////////// VARIABLE DESCRIPTION \\\\\\\\\\\\\\\\\\\\\\\\\\\\\\\

Name Used Default Notes
-----------------------------------------------------------------------------
VarA  LS      3
VarB  LS      2
VarC          1
VarD          1
VarE          1
VarF          1
VarG          1
VarH          1
VarI          1
VarJ          1

/////////////////////////// MODELS USING SIGNAL \\\\\\\\\\\\\\\\\\\\\\\\\\\\\\\

Model Name                Developer         Last Update
-----------------------------------------------------------------------------
Joe's Quarter Pound       Krutsinger        09/10/93 10:31am

\\\\\\\\\\\\\\\\\\\\\\\\\\\\\\\\\\\\\\\\\\\\\\\//////////////////////////////////

Prepared using System Writer Plus Version 2.18 by Omega Research, Inc.
```

Figure 9.1
Joe's Quarter Pounder (continued)

```
//////////////////////////////////////////////\\\\\\\\\\\\\\\\\\\\\\\\\\\\\\\\\\
Directory : F:\JKTOOL                          Printed on   : 09/10/93 10:32am

                               ENTRY SIGNAL

Signal Name      : Delayed in LA          Developer    : Joe
Notes :

Last Update : 02/02/92 03:32am
Long  Entry Verified : YES
Short Entry Verified : YES

///////////////////////////////// LONG ENTRY \\\\\\\\\\\\\\\\\\\\\\\\\\\\\

If C(VarA) > O(VarA) and C(VarB) > O(VarB) and C(VarB) < C(VarA)
then buy tomorrow at H(VarB) stop;


///////////////////////////////// SHORT ENTRY \\\\\\\\\\\\\\\\\\\\\\\\\\\\\

If C(VarA) < O(VarA) and C(VarB) < O(VarB) and C(VarB) > C(VarA)
then Sell tomorrow at L(VarB) stop;


////////////////////////// VARIABLE DESCRIPTION \\\\\\\\\\\\\\\\\\\\\\\\\\\\\

Name Used Default Notes
-------------------------------------------------------------------------
VarA  LS     3
VarB  LS     2
VarC         1
VarD         1
VarE         1
VarF         1
VarG         1
VarH         1
VarI         1
VarJ         1

//////////////////////////// MODELS USING SIGNAL \\\\\\\\\\\\\\\\\\\\\\\\\\\\

Model Name              Developer          Last Update
-------------------------------------------------------------------------
Joe's Quarter Pound     Krutsinger         09/10/93 10:31am

\\\\\\\\\\\\\\\\\\\\\\\\\\\\\\\\\\\\\\\\\\///////////////////////////////////////

Prepared using System Writer Plus Version 2.18 by Omega Research, Inc.
```

Figure 9.1
Joe's Quarter Pounder (continued)

```
////////////////////////////////////////\\\\\\\\\\\\\\\\\\\\\\\\\\\\\\\\\\\\
Directory : F:\JKTOOL                        Printed on   : 09/10/93 10:32am

                           TRADING MODEL

Model Name     : Joe's Quarter Pound      Developer    : Krutsinger
Last Update    : 09/10/93 10:31am
Tests          :        1                 Data Files   :       1

Notes : Can be used without quotes

///////////////////////////// ENTRY SIGNALS \\\\\\\\\\\\\\\\\\\\\\\\\\\\\\\  .\'

  sTatus   Long   Short   Signal Name              Developer       Tests
------------------------------------------------------------------------------
1) ON      ON     ON      Delayed                  Joe               1
2) ON      ON     ON      Delayed in LA            Joe               1


------------------------------------ 1 ------------------------------------
       VarA   VarB   VarC   VarD   VarE   VarF   VarG   VarH   VarI   VarJ
Start    1      3
End      1      3
Inc      1      1

Notes :

------------------------------------ 2 ------------------------------------
       VarA   VarB   VarC   VarD   VarE   VarF   VarG   VarH   VarI   VarJ
Start    4      1
End      4      1
Inc      1      1

Notes :

///////////////////////////// EXIT SIGNALS \\\\\\\\\\\\\\\\\\\\\\\\\\\\\\\\\\

No exit signals selected

///////////////////////////// STOPS \\\\\\\\\\\\\\\\\\\\\\\\\\\\\\\\\\\\\\\\\

  sTatus   Long   Short   Technique                Amount    Days   Tests
------------------------------------------------------------------------------
1) ON      ON     ON      Money Management Stop    $ 2,000            1
2) ON      ON     ON      N Day $ Trailing Stop    $ 2,000     5      1
3) OFF     OFF    OFF     N Day % Trailing Stop          0%    0      0
4) OFF     OFF    OFF     BreakEven Stop - Floor   $    0             0
5) OFF     OFF    OFF     Profit Target            $    0             0

            Amount                    Days
       Start    End    Inc      Start  End   Inc
------------------------------------------------------------------------------
1)     2000    2000    350
2)     2000    2000    500       5      5     1
3)        0       0      1       0      0     1
4)        0       0      1
5)        0       0      1

///////////////////////////// COMPUTATIONS \\\\\\\\\\\\\\\\\\\\\\\\\\\\\\\\\\\
```

171

Figure 9.1—Joe's Quarter Pounder (continued)

```
QUARTER POUNDER 04/22/75 to 06/30/93        F:\PA\
QBP(1)   3000
==================================================================
Total net profit      164,167.50    <    194,167.50>
Gross profit          415,498.75    Gross loss        -251,331.25

Total # of trades           349     Percent profitable        46%
Number winning trades       159     Number losing trades      190

Largest winning trade  14,720.00    Largest losing trade  -3,305.00
Average winning trade   2,613.20    Average losing trade  -1,322.80
Ratio avg win/avg loss      1.98     Avg trade (win & loss)  470.39

Max consecutive winners       7     Max consecutive losers       7
Avg # bars in winners        17     Avg # bars in losers         7

Max drawdown           17,277.50    Avg # of contracts held      1
Profit factor               0.90    Max # of contracts held      1
Account size required  20,277.50    Return on account         810%
==================================================================
```

Figure 9.1—Joe's Quarter Pounder (continued)

PORTFOLIO ANALYZER YEARLY REPORT for QUARTER POUNDER

DATE	OPEN EQUITY	CLOSED EQUITY	TOTAL EQUITY	MAX DRAWDOWN	% DD	% CHNG TOT EQ	NUM TRADE
750422	0.00	30000.00	30000.00	0.00	0.0	0.0	0
751231	437.50	32006.25	32443.75	4866.25	16.2	8.1	1
761231	1500.00	32942.50	34442.50	4866.25	16.2	6.2	1
771230	6187.50	38395.00	44582.50	4866.25	16.2	29.4	1
781229	0.00	52238.75	52238.75	4866.25	16.2	17.2	0
791231	0.00	66486.25	66486.25	6188.75	15.7	27.3	0
801231	2843.75	62158.75	65002.50	14782.50	37.6	-2.2	
811231	1556.25	75345.00	76901.25	14782.50	29.1	18.3	
821231	0.00	82792.50	82792.50	14782.50	26.2	7.7	
831230	2312.50	78841.25	81153.75	14782.50	26.2	-2.0	1
841231	2562.50	88896.25	91458.75	14782.50	25.1	12.7	1
851231	1468.75	103191.25	104660.00	14782.50	20.1	14.4	1
861231	4462.50	102280.00	106742.50	14782.50	18.2	2.0	1
871231	3056.25	121667.50	124723.75	14782.50	16.0	16.8	1
881230	100.00	126430.00	126530.00	14782.50	15.3	1.4	0
891229	3437.50	144705.00	148142.50	14782.50	12.9	17.1	1
901231	0.00	178887.50	178887.50	14782.50	9.8	20.8	0
911231	3425.00	195187.50	198612.50	14782.50	8.7	11.0	0
921231	0.00	196320.00	196320.00	17277.50	10.1	-1.2	0
930630	0.00	194167.50	194167.50	17277.50	10.1	-1.1	0

Figure 9.1
Joe's Quarter Pounder (continued)

No computations selected.

/////////////////////////////// CYCLES SELECTED \\\\\\\\\\\\\\\\\\\\\\\\\\\\\\\

No cycles selected

/////////////////////////// DATA FILES SELECTED \\\\\\\\\\\\\\\\\\\\\\\\\\\\\\\\

	sTatus	Data name	MM/YY	Calculation Dates	Days	data2	data3
1)	ON	BRITISH POUND	06/93	04/22/75 - 06/30/93	6,644	NO	

------------------------------------ 1 -----------------------------------

Num.	Conv.	P.	Value	Comm	Slippage	Margin	Format	Drive:\Path\FileName
26	2	$	6.25	$ 55	$ 0	$ 3,000	Omega	F:\20DATA06\F008.DTA

\\///////////////////////////////////

Prepared using System Writer Plus Version 2.18 by Omega Research, Inc.

Figure 9.1
Joe's Quarter Pounder (continued)

890331	1775.00	123342.50	125117.50	14782.50	15.3	-1.1	1
890630	2225.00	129530.00	131755.00	14782.50	14.9	5.3	1
890929	4200.00	139492.50	143692.50	14782.50	13.5	9.1	1
891229	3437.50	144705.00	148142.50	14782.50	12.9	3.1	1
900330	0.00	159457.50	159457.50	14782.50	11.4	7.6	0
900629	2937.50	159075.00	162012.50	14782.50	11.2	1.6	1
900928	0.00	178985.00	178985.00	14782.50	9.9	10.5	0
901231	0.00	178887.50	178887.50	14782.50	9.8	-0.1	0
910329	14500.00	183795.00	198295.00	14782.50	9.6	10.8	1
910628	-737.50	199540.00	198802.50	14782.50	8.7	0.3	1
910930	-912.50	197027.50	196115.00	14782.50	8.7	-1.4	1
911231	3425.00	195187.50	198612.50	14782.50	8.7	1.3	1
920331	987.50	190090.00	191077.50	14782.50	8.7	-3.8	1
920630	5000.00	183427.50	188427.50	17277.50	10.1	-1.4	1
920930	425.00	188495.00	188920.00	17277.50	10.1	0.3	1
921231	0.00	196320.00	196320.00	17277.50	10.1	3.9	0
930331	4912.50	193257.50	198170.00	17277.50	10.1	0.9	1
930630	0.00	194167.50	194167.50	17277.50	10.1	-2.0	0

Figure 9.1—Joe's Quarter Pounder (continued)

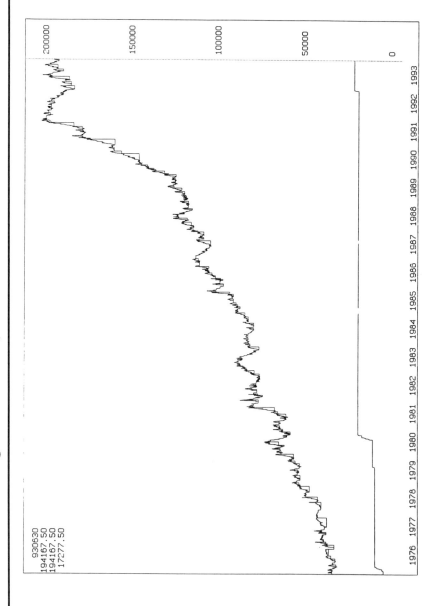

Figures 9.2a and 9.2b
Joe's Big Joe—One Contract Only

```
HISTORICAL RESULTS : Performance Summary       Model : Big Joe with MaxMatrix
Trades   Equity   Chart   Highlights   View-model   Options
Summary, Detailed, Listing
ááááááááááááááááááááááááááááááááááááááááááááááááááááááááááááááááááááááááááá
ëëëëëëëëëëëëëëëëëëëë S&P INDEX      06/93 - All trades ëëëëëëëëëëëëëëëëëëëë£
¤ Test #       1 of    2    No Stop  A         Space bar to toggle display ¤
úáááááááááááááááááááááááááááááááááááááááááááááááááááááááááááááááááááááááááááÑ
¤ Total net profit        $110,760.00                                      ¤
¤ Gross profit            $301,600.00  Gross loss               -190,840.00 ¤
¤
¤ Total # of trades               553  Percent profitable               55%
¤ Number winning trades           305  Number losing trades             248
¤
¤ Largest winning trade     $5,045.00  Largest losing trade       $-5,005.
¤ Average winning trade       $988.85  Average losing trade       $ -769.
¤ Ratio avg win/avg loss         1.29  Avg trade (win & loss)     $200.
¤
¤ Max consecutive winners          15  Max consecutive losers             6
¤ Avg # bars in winners             0  Avg # bars in losers               0
¤
¤ Max closed-out drawdown  $-15,025.00  Max intra-day drawdown   $-15,025.00
¤ Profit factor                  1.58  Max # of contracts held            1
¤ Account size required    $18,025.00  Return on account               614%
àëëëëëëëëëëëëëëëëëëëëëëëëëëëëëëëëëëëëëëëëëëëëëëëëëëëëëëëëëëëëëëëëëëëëëëëëëëëëë
ëë System Writer Plus ëëëëëëëë Omega Research, Inc. ëëëëëëëëë Copyright 1989 ëë

HISTORICAL RESULTS : Performance Summary       Model : Big Joe with MaxMatrix
Trades   Equity   Chart   Highlights   View-model   Options
Summary, Detailed, Listing
ááááááááááááááááááááááááááááááááááááááááááááááááááááááááááááááááááááááááááá
ëëëëëëëëëëëëëëëëëëëë S&P INDEX      06/93 - All trades ëëëëëëëëëëëëëëëëëëëë£
¤ Test #       2 of    2   $2000 Stop  B      Space bar to toggle display ¤
úáááááááááááááááááááááááááááááááááááááááááááááááááááááááááááááááááááááááááááÑ
¤ Total net profit         $99,185.00                                      ¤
¤ Gross profit            $299,320.00  Gross loss               -200,135.00 ¤
¤                                                                          ¤
¤ Total # of trades               553  Percent profitable               54% ¤
¤ Number winning trades           301  Number losing trades             252 ¤
¤                                                                          ¤
¤ Largest winning trade     $5,045.00  Largest losing trade       $-2,055.00 ¤
¤ Average winning trade       $994.42  Average losing trade       $ -794.19 ¤
¤ Ratio avg win/avg loss         1.25  Avg trade (win & loss)       $179.36 ¤
¤                                                                          ¤
¤ Max consecutive winners          15  Max consecutive losers             6 ¤
¤ Avg # bars in winners             0  Avg # bars in losers               0 ¤
¤                                                                          ¤
¤ Max closed-out drawdown  $-12,875.00  Max intra-day drawdown   $-12,875.00 ¤
¤ Profit factor                  1.50  Max # of contracts held            1 ¤
¤ Account size required    $15,875.00  Return on account               624% ¤
àëëëëëëëëëëëëëëëëëëëëëëëëëëëëëëëëëëëëëëëëëëëëëëëëëëëëëëëëëëëëëëëëëëëëëëëëëëëëë¥
ëë System Writer Plus ëëëëëëëë Omega R
```

Figure 9.2a and 9.2b—Joe's Big Joe—One Contract Only (continued)

```
                                ENTRY SIGNAL

Signal Name    : Big Joe 1 Car              Developer    : Krutsinger
Notes : Buy Mon or Wed on open if a certain pattern is present,no equip.need

Last Update : 09/16/93 09:08am
Long  Entry Verified : YES
Short Entry Verified : NO

///////////////////////////////// LONG  ENTRY \\\\\\\\\\\\\\\\\\\\\\\\\\

Condition1=O(1)>O(2);
Condition2=DayOfWeek=5 OR DayOfWeek=2;

If Condition1 and Condition2
then buy tomorrow at Market with
ExitOnCloseOfEntryBar=True;


///////////////////////////////// SHORT ENTRY \\\\\\\\\\\\\\\\\\\\\\\\\\\\\\

No code available.

///////////////////////////// VARIABLE DESCRIPTION \\\\\\\\\\\\\\\\\\\\\\\\\\\

No variables used in entry signal.

////////////////////////// MODELS USING SIGNAL \\\\\\\\\\\\\\\\\\\\\\\\\\\\\

Model Name                  Developer            Last Update
-------------------         ----------           --------------------
Big Joe with MaxMatrix      Krutsinger           09/16/93 09:12am

\\\\\\\\\\\\\\\\\\\\\\\\\\\\\\\\\\\\\\\\\\\\\\\\\\\\\\////////////////////////
```

Figures 9.3a and 9.3b
Joe's Big Joe—Up to 20 Contracts

```
HISTORICAL RESULTS : Performance Summary        Model : Big Joe with MaxMatrix
Trades   Equity   Chart   Highlights   View-model   Options
Summary, Detailed, Listing
áááááááááááááááááááááááááááááááááááááááááááááááááááááááááááááááááááááááá
ëëëëëëëëëëëëëëëëëëëëë S&P INDEX        06/93 - All trades ëëëëëëëëëëëëëëëëëëë£
¤ Test #      1 of    2    $2000 Stop  Ⓐ    Space bar to toggle display ¤
úáááááááááááááááááááááááááááááááááááááááááááaááááááááááááááááááááááááááááááÑ
¤ Total net profit          2091,140.00
¤ Gross profit              5340,480.00  Gross loss            3249,340.00 ¤
¤                                                                .         ¤
¤ Total # of trades             553      Percent profitable         55%    ¤
¤ Number winning trades         305      Number losing trades       248    ¤
¤                                                                          ¤
¤ Largest winning trade   $100,900.00  Largest losing trade  -100,100.00
¤ Average winning trade    $17,509.77  Average losing trade  $-13,102.18
¤ Ratio avg win/avg loss         1.34  Avg trade (win & loss)  $3,781.45
¤
¤ Max consecutive winners        15    Max consecutive losers       6
¤ Avg # bars in winners           0    Avg # bars in losers         0
¤
¤ Max closed-out drawdown  -205,000.00  Max intra-day drawdown -205,000.00
¤ Profit factor                  1.64  Max # of contracts held     20
¤ Account size required   $265,000.00  Return on account          789%
ãëëëëëëëëëëëëëëëëëëëëëëëëëëëëëëëëëëëëëëëëëëëëëëëëëëëëëëëëëëëëëëëëëëëëëëëëëëëë
ëë System Writer Plus ëëëëëëëë Omega Research, Inc. ëëëëëëëëë Copyright 1989 ëë

HISTORICAL RESULTS : Performance Summary        Model : Big Joe with MaxMatrix
Trades   Equity   Chart   Highlights   View-model   Options
Summary, Detailed, Listing
áááááááááááááááááááááááááááááááááááááááááááááááááááááááááááááááááááááááá
ëëëëëëëëëëëëëëëëëëëëë S&P INDEX        06/93 - All trades ëëëëëëëëëëëëëëëëëëë£
¤ Test #      2 of    2    No Stop  Ⓑ      Space bar to toggle display ¤
úáááááááááááááááááááááááááááááááááááááááááááaááááááááááááááááááááááááááááááÑ
¤ Total net profit          1853,820.00
¤ Gross profit              5324,940.00  Gross loss            3471,120.00 ¤
¤                                                                          ¤
¤ Total # of trades             553      Percent profitable         54%    ¤
¤ Number winning trades         301      Number losing trades       252    ¤
¤                                                                          ¤
¤ Largest winning trade   $100,900.00  Largest losing trade  $-41,100.00 ¤
¤ Average winning trade    $17,690.83  Average losing trade  $-13,774.29 ¤
¤ Ratio avg win/avg loss         1.28  Avg trade (win & loss)  $3,352.30 ¤
¤                                                                          ¤
¤ Max consecutive winners        15    Max consecutive losers       6      ¤
¤ Avg # bars in winners           0    Avg # bars in losers         0      ¤
¤                                                                          ¤
¤ Max closed-out drawdown  -201,300.00  Max intra-day drawdown -201,300.00 ¤
¤ Profit factor                  1.53  Max # of contracts held     20      ¤
¤ Account size required   $261,300.00  Return on account          709%     ¤
ãëëëëëëëëëëëëëëëëëëëëëëëëëëëëëëëëëëëëëëëëëëëëëëëëëëëëëëëëëëëëëëëëëëëëëëëëëëëëY
ëë System Writer Plus ëëëëëëëë Omega Research, Inc. ëëëëëëëëë Copyright 1989 ëë
///////////////////////////////////////\\\\\\\\\\\\\\\\\\\\\\\\\\\\\\\\\\
Directory : F:\JKTOOL
```

Figures 9.3a and 9.3b
Joe's Big Joe—Up to 20 Contracts (continued)

```
/////////////////////////////////////////////\\\\\\\\\\\\\\\\\\\\\\\\\\\\\\\\\\\\\\\\
Directory : F:\JKTOOL                          Printed on    : 10/25/93 10:06am

                                  FUNCTION

Function Name    : MaxMatrix2                 Developer  : Krutsinger
Notes :

Last Update : 09/16/93 09:00am
Type        : Numeric
Verified    : YES

///////////////////////////// FUNCTION \\\\\\\\\\\\\\\\\\\\\\\\\\\\\\

@MaxMatrix2=@MaxList#2(0.5,2.5,@IntPortion(@NetProfit/5000 ));


////////////// SIGNALS, COMPUTATIONS AND FUNCTIONS USING FUNCTION \\\\\\\\\\\

Name                     Developer       Type           Last Update
------------------------------------------------------------------------------
BIG JOE TESTER           Krutsinger      Entry signal   09/16/93 09:15am

\\\\\\\\\\\\\\\\\\\\\\\\\\\\\\\\\\\\\\\\\\\\\\\\////////////////////////////////////
```

Prepared using System Writer Plus Version 2.18 by Omega Research, Inc.

Figures 9.3a and 9.3b
Joe's Big Joe—Up to 20 Contracts (continued)

```
//////////////////////////////////////////////\\\\\\\\\\\\\\\\\\\\\\\\\\\\\\\\\\\\\\\\\
Directory : F:\JKTOOL                          Printed on    : 10/25/93 10:08am

                              ENTRY SIGNAL

Signal Name       : BIG JOE TESTER             Developer      : Krutsinger
Notes : Buy Mon or Wed on open if a certain pattern is present,no equip.need

Last Update : 10/25/93 10:08am
Long  Entry Verified : YES
Short Entry Verified : NO

///////////////////////////////// LONG ENTRY \\\\\\\\\\\\\\\\\\\\\\\\\\\\\\\\

Condition1=O(1)>O(2);
Condition2=DayOfWeek=5 OR DayOfWeek=2;

If Condition1 and Condition2
then buy tomorrow (VarA*Maxmatrix2) contracts at Market with
ExitOnCloseOfEntryBar=True;




///////////////////////////////// SHORT ENTRY \\\\\\\\\\\\\\\\\\\\\\\\\\\\\\\\\\

 No code available.


///////////////////////////// VARIABLE DESCRIPTION \\\\\\\\\\\\\\\\\\\\\\\\\\\\\\\

Name Used Default Notes
-------------------------------------------------------------------------------
VarA  L     8    Multiples of Max Matrix2 with 5000 in Base MaxMatrix2
VarB        1
VarC        1
VarD        1
VarE        1
VarF        1
VarG        1
VarH        1
VarI        1
VarJ        1

///////////////////////////// MODELS USING SIGNAL \\\\\\\\\\\\\\\\\\\\\\\\\\\\\\\\\

Model Name                    Developer         Last Update
-------------------------------------------------------------------------------
Big Joe with MaxMatrix        Krutsinger        09/16/93 10:04am

\\\\\\\\\\\\\\\\\\\\\\\\\\\\\\\\\\\\\\\\\\\\\\\\\\///////////////////////////////////

Prepared using System Writer Plus Version 2.18 by Omega Research, Inc.
```

Figures 9.3a and 9.3b—Joe's Big Joe—Up to 20 Contracts (continued)

```
BIG JOE 4 MATIX 06/25/82 to 06/30/93        C:\PA\
BJS(1)   7500
===============================================================
Total net profit       2,091,140.00  <  2,191,140.00>
Gross profit           5,340,480.00     Gross loss          -3,249,340.00

Total # of trades               553     Percent profitable            55%
Number winning trades           305     Number losing trades          248

Largest winning trade    100,900.00     Largest losing trade   -100,100.00
Average winning trade     17,509.77     Average losing trade    -13,102.18
Ratio avg win/avg loss         1.34     Avg trade (win & loss)    3,781.45

Max consecutive winners          15     Max consecutive losers          6
Avg # bars in winners             0     Avg # bars in losers            0

Max drawdown             205,000.00     Avg # of contracts held      -NAN
Profit factor                  0.74     Max # of contracts held         0
Account size required    205,000.00     Return on account           1020%
===============================================================
```

Figures 9.3a and 9.3b—Joe's Big Joe—Up to 20 Contracts (continued)

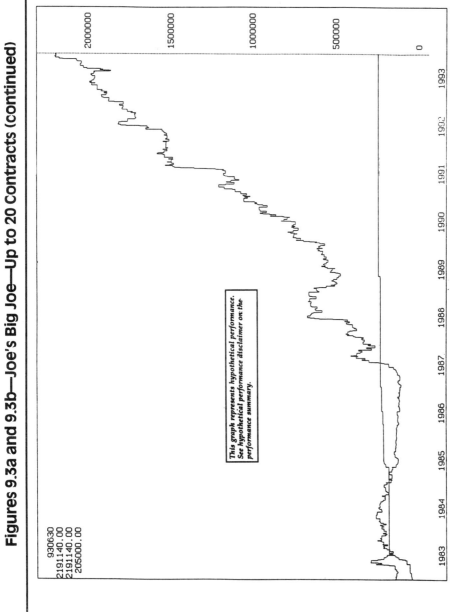

This graph represents hypothetical performance. See hypothetical performance disclaimer on the performance summary.

Figures 9.3a and 9.3b
Joe's Big Joe—Up to 20 Contracts (continued)

PORTFOLIO ANALYZER QUARTLY REPORT for BIG JOE 4 MATIX

DATE	OPEN EQUITY	CLOSED EQUITY	TOTAL EQUITY	MAX DRAWDOWN	% DD	% CHNG TOT EQ	NUM TRADE
820625	0.00	100000.00	100000.00	0.00	0.0	0.0	0
820630	0.00	100260.00	100260.00	3820.00	3.8	0.3	0
820930	0.00	106360.00	106360.00	15740.00	15.7	6.1	0
821231	0.00	156540.00	156540.00	106100.00	66.8	47.2	0
830331	0.00	177440.00	177440.00	142300.00	89.6	13.4	0
830630	0.00	162040.00	162040.00	142300.00	89.6	-8.7	0
830930	0.00	199840.00	199840.00	142300.00	89.6	23.3	0
831230	0.00	208540.00	208540.00	142300.00	89.6	4.4	2
840330	0.00	185440.00	185440.00	142300.00	89.6	-11.1	0
840629	0.00	153340.00	153340.00	142300.00	89.6	-17.3	0
840928	0.00	139540.00	139540.00	142300.00	89.6	-9.0	0
841231	0.00	84560.00	84560.00	174180.00	109.7	-39.4	0
850329	0.00	100960.00	100960.00	174180.00	109.7	19.4	0
850628	0.00	94440.00	94440.00	174180.00	109.7	-6.5	0
850930	0.00	85020.00	85020.00	174180.00	109.7	-10.0	0
851231	0.00	90460.00	90460.00	178340.00	112.3	6.4	0
860331	0.00	75280.00	75280.00	185020.00	116.6	-16.8	0
860630	0.00	72580.00	72580.00	187040.00	117.8	-3.6	0
860930	0.00	72660.00	72660.00	193120.00	121.7	0.1	0
861231	0.00	141340.00	141340.00	193120.00	121.7	94.5	0
870331	0.00	316540.00	316540.00	193120.00	70.0	124.0	0
870630	0.00	291540.00	291540.00	193120.00	70.0	-7.9	0
870930	0.00	353540.00	353540.00	193120.00	63.2	21.3	0
871231	0.00	642640.00	642640.00	193120.00	35.6	81.8	0
880331	0.00	623140.00	623140.00	193120.00	35.6	-3.0	0
880630	0.00	633840.00	633840.00	193120.00	35.6	1.7	0
880930	0.00	490640.00	490640.00	193120.00	35.6	-22.6	0
881230	0.00	485940.00	485940.00	205000.00	37.8	-1.0	0
890331	0.00	524440.00	524440.00	205000.00	37.8	7.9	0
890630	0.00	533740.00	533740.00	205000.00	37.8	1.8	0
890929	0.00	722840.00	722840.00	205000.00	32.6	35.4	0
891229	0.00	741440.00	741440.00	205000.00	31.0	2.6	0
900330	0.00	936340.00	936340.00	205000.00	24.5	26.3	0
900629	0.00	1007940.00	1007940.00	205000.00	22.0	7.6	0
900928	0.00	1187840.00	1187840.00	205000.00	18.8	17.8	0
901231	0.00	1144440.00	1144440.00	205000.00	18.8	-3.7	0
910329	0.00	1484940.00	1484940.00	205000.00	14.4	29.8	0
910628	0.00	1509340.00	1509340.00	205000.00	13.9	1.6	0
910930	0.00	1509240.00	1509240.00	205000.00	13.9	-0.0	0
911231	0.00	1766040.00	1766040.00	205000.00	12.3	17.0	0
920331	0.00	1704040.00	1704040.00	205000.00	12.0	-3.5	0
920630	0.00	1835940.00	1835940.00	205000.00	11.8	7.7	0
920930	0.00	1942040.00	1942040.00	205000.00	11.1	5.8	0
921231	0.00	1956040.00	1956040.00	205000.00	10.8	0.7	0
930331	0.00	2045640.00	2045640.00	205000.00	10.5	4.6	0
930630	0.00	2191140.00	2191140.00	205000.00	9.8	7.1	0

Figures 9.3a and 9.3b—Joe's Big Joe—Up to 20 Contracts (continued)

PORTFOLIO ANALYZER YEARLY REPORT for BIG JOE 4 MATIX

DATE	OPEN EQUITY	CLOSED EQUITY	TOTAL EQUITY	MAX DRAWDOWN	% DD	% CHNG TOT EQ	NUM TRADE
820625	0.00	100000.00	100000.00	0.00	0.0	0.0	0
821231	0.00	156540.00	156540.00	106100.00	66.8	56.5	0
831230	0.00	208540.00	208540.00	142300.00	89.6	33.2	0
841231	0.00	84560.00	84560.00	174180.00	109.7	-59.5	0
851231	0.00	90460.00	90460.00	178340.00	112.3	7.0	0
861231	0.00	141340.00	141340.00	193120.00	121.7	56.2	0
871231	0.00	642640.00	642640.00	193120.00	35.6	354.7	0
881230	0.00	485940.00	485940.00	205000.00	37.8	-24.4	0
891229	0.00	741440.00	741440.00	205000.00	31.0	52.6	0
901231	0.00	1144440.00	1144440.00	205000.00	18.8	54.4	0
911231	0.00	1766040.00	1766040.00	205000.00	12.3	54.3	0
921231	0.00	1956040.00	1956040.00	205000.00	10.8	10.8	0
930630	0.00	2191140.00	2191140.00	205000.00	9.8	12.0	0

Figure 9.4
Aztec Real Oil

Aztec Real Oil   NY LIGHT CRUDE OIL 06/93-Daily   03/30/83 - 06/30/93

Performance Summary: All Trades

Total net profit	$	48965.00	Open position P/L	$ 1790.00
Gross profit	$	77465.00	Gross loss	$ -28500.00
Total # of trades		61	Percent profitable	51%
Number winning trades		31	Number losing trades	30
Largest winning trade	$	13905.00	Largest losing trade	$ -5425.00
Average winning trade	$	2498.87	Average losing trade	$ -950.00
Ratio avg win/avg loss		2.63	Avg trade(win & loss)	$ 802.70
Max consec. winners		3	Max consec. losers	3
Avg # bars in winners		62	Avg # bars in losers	19
Max intraday drawdown	$	-8290.00		
Profit factor		2.72	Max # contracts held	1
Account size required	$	11290.00	Return on account	434%

Performance Summary: Long Trades

Total net profit	$	31235.00	Open position P/L	$ 0.00
Gross profit	$	46270.00	Gross loss	$ -15035.00
Total # of trades		31	Percent profitable	58%
Number winning trades		18	Number losing trades	13
Largest winning trade	$	13435.00	Largest losing trade	$ -5425.00
Average winning trade	$	2570.56	Average losing trade	$ -1156.54
Ratio avg win/avg loss		2.22	Avg trade(win & loss)	$ 1007.58
Max consec. winners		4	Max consec. losers	2
Avg # bars in winners		61	Avg # bars in losers	18
Max intraday drawdown	$	-6715.00		
Profit factor		3.08	Max # contracts held	1
Account size required	$	9715.00	Return on account	322%

Performance Summary: Short Trades

Total net profit	$	17730.00	Open position P/L	$ 1790.00
Gross profit	$	31195.00	Gross loss	$ -13465.00
Total # of trades		30	Percent profitable	43%
Number winning trades		13	Number losing trades	17
Largest winning trade	$	13905.00	Largest losing trade	$ -1975.00
Average winning trade	$	2399.62	Average losing trade	$ -792.06
Ratio avg win/avg loss		3.03	Avg trade(win & loss)	$ 591.00
Max consec. winners		3	Max consec. losers	4
Avg # bars in winners		64	Avg # bars in losers	19
Max intraday drawdown	$	-7200.00		
Profit factor		2.32	Max # contracts held	1
Account size required	$	10200.00	Return on account	174%

186

Figure 9.4
Aztec Real Oil (continued)

```
/////////////////////////////////////////////\\\\\\\\\\\\\\\\\\\\\\\\\\\\\\\\\\\\\\
                                    SYSTEM

Name        : Aztec Real Oil
Notes :

Last Update : 09/10/93 05:26pm
Printed on  : 09/10/93 05:27pm
Verified    : YES

///////////////////////////////// CODE \\\\\\\\\\\\\\\\\\\\\\\\\\\\\\\\\\\\\
{System:  Aztec Real Oil-Daily Crude Oil- always in the market- 1 car


WARNING !- I am not advising anyone to trade or use these systems.
They arewritten only as educational examples of the art of system
writing and development that I want to share with you.

FUTURES TRADING IS A RISKY BUSINESS.
FUTURES TRADERS CAN AND DO LOSE MONEY.

 These materials copyright Joe Krutsinger, 1993.
  All rights reserved.  1-800-767-2508}

{ Crude Oil  Daily , No stop }


Input : Length(20);

Buy at Highest(High,Length) + 1 point stop;

Sell at Lowest(Low,Length) - 1 point stop;
```

Figure 9.5
Joe's Alarm Clock

```
Joe's Alarm Clock   SP E92-60 min    01/02/92 - 12/31/92
                     Performance Summary:  All Trades
```

Total net profit	$ 12635.00	Open position P/L	$ 0.00
Gross profit	$ 38800.00	Gross loss	$ -26165.00
Total # of trades	138	Percent profitable	47%
Number winning trades	65	Number losing trades	73
Largest winning trade	$ 3995.00	Largest losing trade	$ -555.00
Average winning trade	$ 596.92	Average losing trade	$ -358.42
Ratio avg win/avg loss	1.67	Avg trade(win & loss)	$ 91.56
Max consec. winners	4	Max consec. losers	6
Avg # bars in winners	3	Avg # bars in losers	1
Max intraday drawdown	$ -5590.00		
Profit factor	1.48	Max # contracts held	1
Account size required	$ 8590.00	Return on account	147%

```
                     Performance Summary:  Long Trades
```

Total net profit	$ 12225.00	Open position P/L	$ 0.00
Gross profit	$ 33660.00	Gross loss	$ -21435.00
Total # of trades	115	Percent profitable	50%
Number winning trades	58	Number losing trades	57
Largest winning trade	$ 3995.00	Largest losing trade	$ -555.00
Average winning trade	$ 580.34	Average losing trade	$ -376.05
Ratio avg win/avg loss	1.54	Avg trade(win & loss)	$ 106.30
Max consec. winners	4	Max consec. losers	5
Avg # bars in winners	3	Avg # bars in losers	1
Max intraday drawdown	$ -4575.00		
Profit factor	1.57	Max # contracts held	1
Account size required	$ 7575.00	Return on account	161%

```
                     Performance Summary:  Short Trades
```

Total net profit	$ 410.00	Open position P/L	$ 0.00
Gross profit	$ 5140.00	Gross loss	$ -4730.00
Total # of trades	23	Percent profitable	30%
Number winning trades	7	Number losing trades	16
Largest winning trade	$ 2120.00	Largest losing trade	$ -555.00
Average winning trade	$ 734.29	Average losing trade	$ -295.63
Ratio avg win/avg loss	2.48	Avg trade(win & loss)	$ 17.83
Max consec. winners	2	Max consec. losers	7
Avg # bars in winners	2	Avg # bars in losers	1
Max intraday drawdown	$ -3580.00		
Profit factor	1.09	Max # contracts held	1
Account size required	$ 6580.00	Return on account	6%

Figure 9.5
Joe's Alarm Clock (continued)

```
//////////////////////////////////////////////\\\\\\\\\\\\\\\\\\\\\\\\\\\\\\\\\\\\\\\\
                                    SYSTEM

Name      : Joe's Alarm Clock
Notes : Hourly SP with $500 stop-after 1 hr BTBE

Last Update : 07/17/92 10:54am
Printed on  : 09/15/93 07:31pm
Verified    : YES

////////////////////////////////////// CODE \\\\\\\\\\\\\\\\\\\\\\\\\\\\\\\\\\\\\\\\\\

If (Time=1430 and DayOfWeek(date)=1 )
and LosersToday(0) =0 then buy at market;

If (Time=1030 and DayOfWeek(date)=1)
then buy tomorrow at H[2] stop;

If (Time=1030 and DayOfWeek(date)=3)
then buy tomorrow  at h[2] stop;

If (Time=1030 and DayOfWeek(date)=5)
then buy tomorrow  at h[2] stop;

If BarsSinceEntry>=1 then
 ExitLong at EntryPrice + 15 points Stop;


If ( H > H[1] and L < L[1] and C < C[1] and DayOfWeek(date)=2)
then sell  tomorrow  at L[1] stop;

If ( H > H[1] and L > L[1] and C > C[1] and DayOfWeek(date)=1)
and LosersToday(0) =0  then sell  tomorrow  at L[1] stop;
If BarsSinceEntry>=1 then
 ExitShort at EntryPrice - 15 points Stop;
```

Figure 9.6
J.K. Thunderhead

```
JK Thunderhead   SP E92-60 min   01/02/92 - 12/31/92
                 Performance Summary:  All Trades

Total net profit      $  18915.00   Open position P/L     $      0.00
Gross profit          $  44930.00   Gross loss            $ -26015.00

Total # of trades           147     Percent profitable          47%
Number winning trades        69     Number losing trades         78

Largest winning trade $   3995.00   Largest losing trade  $   -555.00
Average winning trade $    651.16   Average losing trade  $   -333.53
Ratio avg win/avg loss       1.95   Avg trade(win & loss) $    128.67

Max consec. winners           5     Max consec. losers            6
Avg # bars in winners         2     Avg # bars in losers          1

Max intraday drawdown $  -2990.00
Profit factor                1.73   Max # contracts held          1
Account size required $   5990.00   Return on account          316%
```

```
                 Performance Summary:  Long Trades

Total net profit      $  17475.00   Open position P/L     $      0.00
Gross profit          $  37460.00   Gross loss            $ -19985.00

Total # of trades           120     Percent profitable          48%
Number winning trades        58     Number losing trades         62

Largest winning trade $   3995.00   Largest losing trade  $   -555.00
Average winning trade $    645.86   Average losing trade  $   -322.34
Ratio avg win/avg loss       2.00   Avg trade(win & loss) $    145.63

Max consec. winners           4     Max consec. losers            6
Avg # bars in winners         2     Avg # bars in losers          1

Max intraday drawdown $  -1800.00
Profit factor                1.87   Max # contracts held          1
Account size required $   4800.00   Return on account          364%
```

```
                 Performance Summary:  Short Trades

Total net profit      $   1440.00   Open position P/L     $      0.00
Gross profit          $   7470.00   Gross loss            $  -6030.00

Total # of trades            27     Percent profitable          41%
Number winning trades        11     Number losing trades         16

Largest winning trade $   1845.00   Largest losing trade  $   -555.00
Average winning trade $    679.09   Average losing trade  $   -376.88
Ratio avg win/avg loss       1.80   Avg trade(win & loss) $     53.33

Max consec. winners           3     Max consec. losers            5
Avg # bars in winners         2     Avg # bars in losers          1

Max intraday drawdown $  -1975.00
Profit factor                1.24   Max # contracts held          1
Account size required $   4975.00   Return on account           29%
```

Figure 9.6
J.K. Thunderhead (continued)

```
////////////////////////////////////////////////////\\\\\\\\\\\\\\\\\\\\\\\\\\\\\\\\\\\\\\\\
                                  SYSTEM

Name      : JK Thunderhead
Notes : Trades Sp500 Everyday

Last Update : 11/25/92 10:37am
Printed on  : 09/15/93 07:34pm
Verified    : YES

/////////////////////////////////////// CODE \\\\\\\\\\\\\\\\\\\\\\\\\\\\\\\\\\\\\\\\\\\\\!

{
System: JK-Thunderhead-1 hour S&P 500 Bars- up to 2 car
Notes :Everyday Trader


[ 3] MaxBarsBack
  [ ] Generate Realtime Orders
Entry Options :
  [*] Do not allow multiple entries in same direction
  [ ] Allow multiple entries in same direction
      by different entry signals
  [*] Allow multiple entries in same direction
      by same and different entry signals

  [*] Money Management Stop
      Amount: ($) [500]
  [*] Close all trades at end of day

These materials copyright Joe Krutsinger, 1992
All rights reserved. 1-800-767-2508.}

If DayOfWeek(date)=1 and time=1430 and O[1] > O[2]  then buy("Mon1B")  at market;
If DayOfWeek(date)=1 and time=1130 then buy("Mon2B")   at H[1] stop;
If DayOfWeek(date)=2 and time=1430  and O[1] < O[2] then buy("Tue1B")   at market;
If DayOfWeek(date)=3 and time=1130 and O[1] > O[2] then buy("Wed1B")   at market;
If DayOfWeek(date)=4 and time=1130  and O[1] > O[2] then buy("Thur1B")   at market;
If DayOfWeek(date)=4 and time=1330  and O[1] > O[2] and TradesToday(0)=0 then buy("Thur2B")
at ma rket;
If DayOfWeek(date)=5 and time=1330  and O[1] < O[2] then Sell("Fri1S")  at market;
If DayOfWeek(date)=5 and time=1430  and TradesToday(0)=0 then Sell("Fri2S")  at market;

If BarsSinceEntry>=1 then
 ExitLong("XL+")  at EntryPrice + 15 points Stop;
If BarsSinceEntry>=1 then
 ExitShort ("XS-")at EntryPrice - 15 points Stop;



/////////////////////////////////////////////////////\\\\\\\\\\\\\\\\\\\\\\\\\\\\\\\\\\\\\\\\\\\\\
Prepared using Omega TradeStation Version 3.01 by Omega Research, Inc.
```

Figure 9.7
Joe's Wakeup Call

```
Joe's WakeUp Call  SP E92-60 min   01/02/92 - 12/31/92
                    Performance Summary:  All Trades

Total net profit.     $  14260.00  Open position P/L    $       0.00
Gross profit          $  23150.00  Gross loss           $   -8890.00

Total # of trades            49    Percent profitable           53%
Number winning trades        26    Number losing trades         23

Largest winning trade $   7495.00  Largest losing trade $    -690.00
Average winning trade $    890.38  Average losing trade $    -386.52
Ratio avg win/avg loss      2.30   Avg trade(win & loss) $    291.02

Max consec. winners           4    Max consec. losers             4
Avg # bars in winners         3    Avg # bars in losers           1

Max intraday drawdown $  -2370.00
Profit factor               2.60   Max # contracts held           3
Account size required $  10215.00  Return on account           140%
- - .. - - - - - - - . - - - - - - - - - - - -
                    Performance Summary:  Long Trades

Total net profit      $  14260.00  Open position P/L    $       0.00
Gross profit          $  23150.00  Gross loss           $   -8890.00

Total # of trades            49    Percent profitable           53%
Number winning trades        26    Number losing trades         23

Largest winning trade $   7495.00  Largest losing trade $    -690.00
Average winning trade $    890.38  Average losing trade $    -386.52
Ratio avg win/avg loss      2.30   Avg trade(win & loss) $    291.02

Max consec. winners           4    Max consec. losers             4
Avg # bars in winners         3    Avg # bars in losers           1

Max intraday drawdown $  -2370.00
Profit factor               2.60   Max # contracts held           3
Account size required $  10215.00  Return on account           140%
- .. - - .. - - - - - - - - - - - - - - - - -
                    Performance Summary:  Short Trades

Total net profit      $      0.00  Open position P/L    $       0.00
Gross profit          $      0.00  Gross loss           $       0.00

Total # of trades             0    Percent profitable            0%
Number winning trades         0    Number losing trades          0

Largest winning trade $      0.00  Largest losing trade $       0.00
Average winning trade $      0.00  Average losing trade $       0.00
Ratio avg win/avg loss    100.00   Avg trade(win & loss) $       0.00

Max consec. winners           0    Max consec. losers             0
Avg # bars in winners         0    Avg # bars in losers           0

Max intraday drawdown $      0.00
Profit factor             100.00   Max # contracts held           0
Account size required $      0.00  Return on account            0%
```

192

Figure 9.7
Joe's Wakeup Call (continued)

```
/////////////////////////////////////////////////////\\\\\\\\\\\\\\\\\\\\\\\\\\\\\\\\\\\\\\\\
                                    SYSTEM

Name      : Joe's WakeUp Call
Notes : Buy S&P at 230pm EDT-$500 stp-x moc

Last Update : 07/11/92 11:19am
Printed on  : 09/15/93 07:34pm
Verified    : YES

///////////////////////////////////////////// CODE \\\\\\\\\\\\\\\\\\\\\\\\\\\\\\\\\\\\\\\\\

If (Time=1130 and DayOfWeek(date)=1 ) then buy matrix contracts
at market ;
{
If (Time=1430 and DayOfWeek(date)=1 )
and LosersToday(0) =0 then buy  matrix contracts at market;}


If BarsSinceEntry>=1 then
 ExitLong at EntryPrice + 15 points Stop;

{Uses EDT , buy at Market on Monday's one
half hour prior to the Currency and US Bond futures
close- use a $500 money management stop,
exit Market on close- shown with a $59 commission
already deducted from each trade. No quotes,
computers or software needed, one call once per week
on Monday to your broker at 2:30 pm EDT- You say:
"Buy one SP 500 at market,
 place a stop loss $500 below the current price
 One cancels the Other
Sell one contract Market on Close."

Written By Joe Krutsinger-1-800-267-2508 }
```

```
//////////////////////////////////////////////////////\\\\\\\\\\\\\\\\\\\\\\\\\\\\\\\\\\\\\\\\
Prepared using Omega TradeStation Version 3.01 by Omega Research, Inc.
```

Figure 9.8
Joe's Bigger Joe

```
Bigger Joe  SP E92-60 min   01/02/92 - 12/31/92
                 Performance Summary:  All Trades

Total net profit       $  12400.00   Open position P/L     $       0.00
Gross profit           $  34605.00   Gross loss            $  -22205.00

Total # of trades             95     Percent profitable            52%
Number winning trades         49     Number losing trades          46

Largest winning trade  $   2845.00   Largest losing trade  $    -555.00
Average winning trade  $    706.22   Average losing trade  $    -482.72
Ratio avg win/avg loss        1.46   Avg trade(win & loss) $     130.53

Max consec. winners            5     Max consec. losers             4
Avg # bars in winners          3     Avg # bars in losers           2

Max intraday drawdown  $  -3495.00
Profit factor                 1.56   Max # contracts held           1
Account size required  $   3495.00   Return on account            355%
- - - - - - - - - - - - - - - - - - - - - - - - - - - - - - - - - - - - -
                 Performance Summary:  Long Trades

Total net profit       $  12400.00   Open position P/L     $       0.00
Gross profit           $  34605.00   Gross loss            $  -22205.00

Total # of trades             95     Percent profitable            52%
Number winning trades         49     Number losing trades          46

Largest winning trade  $   2845.00   Largest losing trade  $    -555.00
Average winning trade  $    706.22   Average losing trade  $    -482.72
Ratio avg win/avg loss        1.46   Avg trade(win & loss) $     130.53

Max consec. winners            5     Max consec. losers             4
Avg # bars in winners          3     Avg # bars in losers           2

Max intraday drawdown  $  -3495.00
Profit factor                 1.56   Max # contracts held           1
Account size required  $   3495.00   Return on account            355%
- - - - - - - - - - - - - - - - - - - - - - - - - - - - - - - - - - - - -
                 Performance Summary:  Short Trades

Total net profit       $      0.00   Open position P/L     $       0.00
Gross profit           $      0.00   Gross loss            $       0.00

Total # of trades              0     Percent profitable             0%
Number winning trades          0     Number losing trades           0

Largest winning trade  $      0.00   Largest losing trade  $       0.00
Average winning trade  $      0.00   Average losing trade  $       0.00
Ratio avg win/avg loss      100.00   Avg trade(win & loss) $       0.00

Max consec. winners            0     Max consec. losers             0
Avg # bars in winners          0     Avg # bars in losers           0

Max intraday drawdown  $      0.00
Profit factor               100.00   Max # contracts held           0
Account size required  $      0.00   Return on account             0%
```

194

Figure 9.8
Joe's Bigger Joe (continued)

```
Bigger Joe  SP60.TXT-60 min   12/09/86 - 02/20/92
                    Performance Summary:  All Trades

Total net profit       $   41040.00   Open position P/L      $       0.00
Gross profit           $  180660.00   Gross loss             $-139620.00

Total # of trades            457      Percent profitable            40%
Number winning trades        183      Number losing trades          274

Largest winning trade  $    4570.00   Largest losing trade   $    -555.00
Average winning trade  $     987.21   Average losing trade   $    -509.56
Ratio avg win/avg loss         1.94   Avg trade(win & loss)  $      89.80

Max consec. winners           10      Max consec. losers             14
Avg # bars in winners          3      Avg # bars in losers            1

Max intraday drawdown  $  -13940.00
Profit factor                  1.29   Max # contracts held            1
Account size required  $   16940.00   Return on account            242%
```

```
                    Performance Summary:  Long Trades

Total net profit       $   41040.00   Open position P/L      $       0.00
Gross profit           $  180660.00   Gross loss             $-139620.00

Total # of trades            457      Percent profitable            40%
Number winning trades        183      Number losing trades          274

Largest winning trade  $    4570.00   Largest losing trade   $    -555.00
Average winning trade  $     987.21   Average losing trade   $    -509.56
Ratio avg win/avg loss         1.94   Avg trade(win & loss)  $      89.80

Max consec. winners           10      Max consec. losers             14
Avg # bars in winners          3      Avg # bars in losers            1

Max intraday drawdown  $  -13940.00
Profit factor                  1.29   Max # contracts held            1
Account size required  $   16940.00   Return on account            242%
```

```
                    Performance Summary:  Short Trades

Total net profit       $       0.00   Open position P/L      $       0.00
Gross profit           $       0.00   Gross loss             $       0.00

Total # of trades              0      Percent profitable             0%
Number winning trades          0      Number losing trades            0

Largest winning trade  $       0.00   Largest losing trade   $       0.00
Average winning trade  $       0.00   Average losing trade   $       0.00
Ratio avg win/avg loss       100.00   Avg trade(win & loss)  $       0.00

Max consec. winners            0      Max consec. losers              0
Avg # bars in winners          0      Avg # bars in losers            0

Max intraday drawdown  $       0.00
Profit factor                100.00   Max # contracts held            0
Account size required  $       0.00   Return on account             0%
```

Figure 9.8
Joe's Bigger Joe (continued)

```
////////////////////////////////////////////////\\\\\\\\\\\\\\\\\\\\\\\\\\\\\\\\\\\\\\\\\\\\\\
                                        SYSTEM

Name      : Bigger Joe
Notes : 1 contract Version

Last Update : 08/19/93 05:17pm
Printed on  : 08/19/93 05:21pm
Verified    : YES

///////////////////////////////////////// CODE \\\\\\\\\\\\\\\\\\\\\\\\\\\\\\\\\\\\\\\\\\\\\'
{
System: Bigger Joe-60 min. S&P 500 Bars- 1 car
Notes : Short term system with one contract only-never
more than one contract with a $500 stop, $55 comm.

[ 5] MaxBarsBack
   [ ] Generate Realtime Orders
Entry Options :
   [*] Do not allow multiple entries in same direction
   [ ] Allow multiple entries in same direction
       by different entry signals
   [ ] Allow multiple entries in same direction
       by same and different entry signals

   [*] Money Management Stop
       Amount: ($) [500]
   [*] Close all trades at end of day

These materials copyright Joe Krutsinger, 1992
All rights reserved. 1-800-767-2508.}


Condition1=O[1] > O[2];
Condition2=DayOfWeek(date)=1 or DayOfWeek(date)=3 ;
If Condition1 and Condition2
and (time=1130 or  time =1230 or time =1330) and LosersToday(date)=0
 then buy tomorrow at market;
```

```
//////////////////////////////////////////////////\\\\\\\\\\\\\\\\\\\\\\\\\\\\\\\\\\\\\\\\\\\\
```
Prepared using Omega TradeStation Version 3.01 by Omega Research, Inc.

Figure 9.9
Joe's Gap

```
Joe's Gap   SP60.TXT-60 min    12/09/86 - 02/20/92
                    Performance Summary:  All Trades

Total net profit    $  35340.00   Open position P/L     $       0.00
Gross profit        $ 142810.00   Gross loss            $-107470.00

Total # of trades         312     Percent profitable           35%
Number winning trades     108     Number losing trades         204

Largest winning trade $  13095.00  Largest losing trade  $   -555.00
Average winning trade $   1322.31  Average losing trade  $   -526.81
Ratio avg win/avg loss      2.51   Avg trade(win & loss) $    113.27

Max consec. winners         5      Max consec. losers            15
Avg # bars in winners       5      Avg # bars in losers           1

Max intraday drawdown $ -12325.00
Profit factor               1.33   Max # contracts held           1
Account size required $  15325.00  Return on account           231%
```
```
                    Performance Summary:  Long Trades

Total net profit    $  31295.00   Open position P/L     $       0.00
Gross profit        $  87730.00   Gross loss            $ -56435.00

Total # of trades         176     Percent profitable           39%
Number winning trades      69     Number losing trades         107

Largest winning trade $   4320.00  Largest losing trade  $   -555.00
Average winning trade $   1271.45  Average losing trade  $   -527.43
Ratio avg win/avg loss      2.41   Avg trade(win & loss) $    177.81

Max consec. winners         4      Max consec. losers            11
Avg # bars in winners       5      Avg # bars in losers           2

Max intraday drawdown $  -7450.00
Profit factor               1.55   Max # contracts held           1
Account size required $  10450.00  Return on account           299%
```
```
                    Performance Summary:  Short Trades

Total net profit    $   4045.00   Open position P/L     $       0.00
Gross profit        $  55080.00   Gross loss            $ -51035.00

Total # of trades         136     Percent profitable           29%
Number winning trades      39     Number losing trades          97

Largest winning trade $  13095.00  Largest losing trade  $   -555.00
Average winning trade $   1412.31  Average losing trade  $   -526.13
Ratio avg win/avg loss      2.68   Avg trade(win & loss) $     29.74

Max consec. winners         4      Max consec. losers            24
Avg # bars in winners       5      Avg # bars in losers           1

Max intraday drawdown $ -13930.00
Profit factor               1.08   Max # contracts held           1
Account size required $  16930.00  Return on account            24%
```

Figure 9.9
Joe's Gap (continued)

```
Joe's Gap   SP E92-60 min    02/21/92 - 06/30/92
                    Performance Summary:  All Trades

Total net profit       $     7510.00   Open position P/L        $        0.00
Gross profit           $    12660.00   Gross loss               $    -5150.00

Total # of trades               23     Percent profitable              57%
Number winning trades           13     Number losing trades            10

Largest winning trade  $     2920.00   Largest losing trade     $     -555.00
Average winning trade  $      973.85   Average losing trade     $     -515.00
Ratio avg win/avg loss          1.89   Avg trade(win & loss)    $      326.52

Max consec. winners              7     Max consec. losers               4
Avg # bars in winners            5     Avg # bars in losers             3

Max intraday drawdown  $    -2345.00
Profit factor                   2.46   Max # contracts held             1
Account size required  $     5345.00   Return on account              141%
```

```
                    Performance Summary:  Long Trades

Total net profit       $     3665.00   Open position P/L        $        0.00
Gross profit           $     6670.00   Gross loss               $    -3005.00

Total # of trades               12     Percent profitable              50%
Number winning trades            6     Number losing trades             6

Largest winning trade  $     2495.00   Largest losing trade     $     -555.00
Average winning trade  $     1111.67   Average losing trade     $     -500.83
Ratio avg win/avg loss          2.22   Avg trade(win & loss)    $      305.42

Max consec. winners              3     Max consec. losers               2
Avg # bars in winners            5     Avg # bars in losers             3

Max intraday drawdown  $     -960.00
Profit factor                   2.22   Max # contracts held             1
Account size required  $     3960.00   Return on account               93%
```

```
                    Performance Summary:  Short Trades

Total net profit       $     3845.00   Open position P/L        $        0.00
Gross profit           $     5990.00   Gross loss               $    -2145.00

Total # of trades               11     Percent profitable              64%
Number winning trades            7     Number losing trades             4

Largest winning trade  $     2920.00   Largest losing trade     $     -555.00
Average winning trade  $      855.71   Average losing trade     $     -536.25
Ratio avg win/avg loss          1.60   Avg trade(win & loss)    $      349.55

Max consec. winners              4     Max consec. losers               3
Avg # bars in winners            5     Avg # bars in losers             2

Max intraday drawdown  $    -1790.00
Profit factor                   2.79   Max # contracts held             1
Account size required  $     4790.00   Return on account               80%
```

Figure 9.9
Joe's Gap (continued)

```
Joe's Gap   SP E93-60 min    07/01/92 - 06/30/93
                   Performance Summary:  All Trades

Total net profit       $   17395.00   Open position P/L     $       0.00
Gross profit           $   27385.00   Gross loss            $   -9990.00

Total # of trades             46      Percent profitable            61%
Number winning trades         28      Number losing trades          18

Largest winning trade  $    4120.00   Largest losing trade  $    -555.00
Average winning trade  $     978.04   Average losing trade  $    -555.00
Ratio avg win/avg loss        1.76    Avg trade(win & loss) $     378.15

Max consec. winners            4      Max consec. losers             4
Avg # bars in winners          5      Avg # bars in losers           1

Max intraday drawdown  $   -2220.00
Profit factor                 2.74    Max # contracts held           1
Account size required  $    5220.00   Return on account            333%
```

- -

```
                   Performance Summary:  Long Trades

Total net profit       $   11100.00   Open position P/L     $       0.00
Gross profit           $   16095.00   Gross loss            $   -4995.00

Total # of trades             25      Percent profitable            64%
Number winning trades         16      Number losing trades           9

Largest winning trade  $    4120.00   Largest losing trade  $    -555.00
Average winning trade  $    1005.94   Average losing trade  $    -555.00
Ratio avg win/avg loss        1.81    Avg trade(win & loss) $     444.00

Max consec. winners            4      Max consec. losers             3
Avg # bars in winners          5      Avg # bars in losers           2

Max intraday drawdown  $   -1665.00
Profit factor                 3.22    Max # contracts held           1
Account size required  $    4665.00   Return on account            238%
```

- -

```
                   Performance Summary:  Short Trades

Total net profit       $    6295.00   Open position P/L     $       0.00
Gross profit           $   11290.00   Gross loss            $   -4995.00

Total # of trades             21      Percent profitable            57%
Number winning trades         12      Number losing trades           9

Largest winning trade  $    2745.00   Largest losing trade  $    -555.00
Average winning trade  $     940.83   Average losing trade  $    -555.00
Ratio avg win/avg loss        1.70    Avg trade(win & loss) $     299.76

Max consec. winners            3      Max consec. losers             2
Avg # bars in winners          5      Avg # bars in losers           1

Max intraday drawdown  $   -1485.00
Profit factor                 2.26    Max # contracts held           1
Account size required  $    4485.00   Return on account            140%
```

Figure 9.9
Joe's Gap (continued)

```
//////////////////////////////////////////////\\\\\\\\\\\\\\\\\\\\\\\\\\\\\\\\\\\\\\\\\\
                                        SYSTEM

Name      : Joe's Gap
Notes :

Last Update : 08/28/93 11:24am
Printed on  : 09/15/93 07:36pm
Verified    : YES

/////////////////////////////////////////// CODE \\\\\\\\\\\\\\\\\\\\\\\\\\\\\\\\\\\\\\\\

{System: Joe's Gap
Notes : Written as a 60 min. daytrade system in 1991

[ 2] MaxBarsBack
  [*] Generate Realtime Orders
Entry Options :
  [ ] Do not allow multiple entries in same direction
  [ ] Allow multiple entries in same direction
      by different entry signals
  [*] Allow multiple entries in same direction
      by same and different entry signals( up to 20 contracts)

  [ ] Money Management Stop
      Amount: ($) [0000.00]
  [ ] Close all trades at end of day

 Copyright 1993, Krutsinger & Krutsinger, Inc. 1-800-767-2508,
 PO Box 822, Centerville, Iowa 52544

Provided as an educational example in the art of system writing
}

If H < L[1] then Sell tomorrow at market;
If L > H[1] then Buy  tomorrow at market;


{ Here's a currency model that's simple enough to execute without a computer,
The thinking behind this model is that most currency trading happens while US
traders sleep. If a gap occurs and is not filled, there is a tendency to trend in the
direction of the gap. The model adds positions on additional gaps in the same
direction and is always in the market. A $55 commission per contract has been
deducted.

Prepared using Omega Tick Data and Omega TradeStation
Version 3.01 by Omega Research,Inc.}



//////////////////////////////////////////////\\\\\\\\\\\\\\\\\\\\\\\\\\\\\\\\\\\\\\\\\\
Prepared using Omega TradeStation Version 3.01 by Omega Research, Inc.
```

Figure 9.10
Joe's Banker

```
Joe's Banker  SP E92-60 min    01/02/92 - 12/31/92
                    Performance Summary:  All Trades

Total net profit       $   32240.00   Open position P/L      $   1000.00
Gross profit           $   97820.00   Gross loss             $ -65580.00

Total # of trades            107      Percent profitable           57%
Number winning trades         61      Number losing trades          46

Largest winning trade  $   11495.00   Largest losing trade   $  -2955.00
Average winning trade  $    1603.61   Average losing trade   $  -1425.65
Ratio avg win/avg loss        1.12    Avg trade(win & loss)  $    301.31

Max consec. winners            6      Max consec. losers             5
Avg # bars in winners         17      Avg # bars in losers          14

Max intraday drawdown  $  -14545.00
Profit factor                 1.49    Max # contracts held           1
Account size required  $   17545.00   Return on account           184%
- - . . - - . . - - . . - - . . - - . . - - . . - - . . - - . . - - . .
                    Performance Summary:  Long Trades

Total net profit       $   18990.00   Open position P/L      $      0.00
Gross profit           $   54920.00   Gross loss             $ -35930.00

Total # of trades             57      Percent profitable           63%
Number winning trades         36      Number losing trades          21

Largest winning trade  $    5970.00   Largest losing trade   $  -2705.00
Average winning trade  $    1525.56   Average losing trade   $  -1710.95
Ratio avg win/avg loss        0.89    Avg trade(win & loss)  $    333.16

Max consec. winners            6      Max consec. losers             3
Avg # bars in winners         18      Avg # bars in losers          15

Max intraday drawdown  $   -8955.00
Profit factor                 1.53    Max # contracts held           1
Account size required  $   11955.00   Return on account           159%
- - . . - - . . - - . . - - →. . - . . - - . . - - . . - - . . - - . .
                    Performance Summary:  Short Trades

Total net profit       $   13250.00   Open position P/L      $   1000.00
Gross profit           $   42900.00   Gross loss             $ -29650.00

Total # of trades             50      Percent profitable           50%
Number winning trades         25      Number losing trades          25

Largest winning trade  $   11495.00   Largest losing trade   $  -2955.00
Average winning trade  $    1716.00   Average losing trade   $  -1186.00
Ratio avg win/avg loss        1.45    Avg trade(win & loss)  $    265.00

Max consec. winners            4      Max consec. losers             4
Avg # bars in winners         14      Avg # bars in losers          14

Max intraday drawdown  $  -10275.00
Profit factor                 1.45    Max # contracts held           1
Account size required  $   13275.00   Return on account           100%
```

Figure 9.10
Joe's Banker (continued)

```
//////////////////////////////////////////////////////\\\\\\\\\\\\\\\\\\\\\\\\\\\\\\\\\\\
                                    SYSTEM

Name       : Joe's Banker
Notes : Buys SP after a time lag

Last Update : 11/24/92 03:32pm
Printed on  : 09/15/93 07:32pm
Verified    : YES

////////////////////////////////////////// CODE \\\\\\\\\\\\\\\\\\\\\\\\\\\\\\\\\\\\\\\\\\


If Time=1130
and DayofWeek(date)=1
Then buy at market;

If Time=1430
and DayofWeek(date)=2
Then buy at market;

If Time=1230
and DayofWeek(date)=3
Then buy at market;

If Time=1030
and DayofWeek(date)=4
Then sell at market;

{60 minute S&P, $50 commission,
written as an educational example by Joe Krutsinger.  Copyright 1992, allrights reserved.
1-800-767-2508}
```

```
////////////////////////////////////////////////////////\\\\\\\\\\\\\\\\\\\\\\\\\\\\\\\\\\\\\
Prepared using Omega TradeStation Version 3.01 by Omega Research, Inc.
```

$48,000 WORTH OF TRADING SYSTEMS

Figure 9.11
JK OEX Option Buyer

```
//////////////////////////////////////////\\\\\\\\\\\\\\\\\\\\\\\\\\\\\\\\
Directory : F:\JKTOOL                    Printed on   : 09/10/93 09:48am
                        PERFORMANCE SUMMARY

Model Name      : JK OEX Option Buyer      Developer    : Krutsinger
Test Number     :        1 of      1
Notes : Buys Options

Data            : S&P INDEX        06/93
Calc Dates      : 06/25/82 - 06/30/93

 Num. Conv. P. Value  Comm Slippage  Margin  Format  Drive:\Path\FileName
 -------------------------------------------------------------------------
  149   2  $  5.000  $ 55   $  0   $ 22,000  Omega   F:\20DATA06\F002.DTA

//////////////////////////// ALL TRADES  - Test 1 \\\\\\\\\\\\\\\\\\\\\\\\\\\\

Total net profit        $54,975.00
Gross profit            $82,840.00   Gross loss             $-27,865.00

Total # of trades             55     Percent profitable           58%
Number winning trades         32     Number losing trades          23

Largest winning trade   $6,795.00    Largest losing trade    $-6,455.00
Average winning trade   $2,588.75    Average losing trade    $-1,211.52
Ratio avg win/avg loss        2.13   Avg trade (win & loss)     $999.55

Max consecutive winners        6     Max consecutive losers         3
Avg # bars in winners          7     Avg # bars in losers           3

Max closed-out drawdown $-7,365.00   Max intra-day drawdown  $-8,905.00
Profit factor                 2.97   Max # of contracts held        1
Account size required   $30,905.00   Return on account            177%

                    Highlights - All trades
        Description                 Date      Time     Amount
        -------------------------------------------------------------
        Largest Winning Trade       12/16/87   -    $   6,795.00
        Largest Losing Trade        12/24/91   -    $  -6,455.00
        Largest String of + Trades  01/19/88   -        6
        Largest String of - Trades  06/11/85   -        3
        Maximum Closed-Out Drawdown 04/08/93   -    $  -7,365.00
        Maximum Intra-Day Drawdown  02/18/93   -    $  -8,905.00

//////////////////////////// LONG TRADES  - Test 1 \\\\\\\\\\\\\\\\\\\\\\\\\\\\

Total net profit        $43,575.00
Gross profit            $55,255.00   Gross loss             $-11,680.00

Total # of trades             25     Percent profitable           76%
Number winning trades         19     Number losing trades           6

Largest winning trade   $6,795.00    Largest losing trade    $-3,455.00
Average winning trade   $2,908.16    Average losing trade    $-1,946.67
Ratio avg win/avg loss        1.49   Avg trade (win & loss)   $1,743.00

Max consecutive winners       10     Max consecutive losers         2
Avg # bars in winners         11     Avg # bars in losers          12
```

203

Figure 9.11
JK OEX Option Buyer (continued)

```
Max closed-out drawdown    $-5,385.00    Max intra-day drawdown    $-6,925.00
Profit factor                    4.73    Max # of contracts held            1
Account size required     $28,925.00     Return on account               150%
```

Highlights - Long trades

Description	Date	Time	Amount
Largest Winning Trade	12/16/87	-	$ 6,795.00
Largest Losing Trade	04/08/93	-	$ -3,455.00
Largest String of + Trades	11/13/90	-	10
Largest String of - Trades	04/08/93	-	2
Maximum Closed-Out Drawdown	04/08/93	-	$ -5,385.00
Maximum Intra-Day Drawdown	02/18/93	-	$ -6,925.00

```
////////////////////////// SHORT TRADES  - Test 1 \\\\\\\\\\\\\\\\\\\\\\\\\
```

```
Total net profit          $11,400.00
Gross profit              $27,585.00    Gross loss               $-16,185.00

Total # of trades                 30    Percent profitable               43%
Number winning trades             13    Number losing trades              17

Largest winning trade      $5,820.00    Largest losing trade      $-6,455.00
Average winning trade      $2,121.92    Average losing trade       $ -952.06
Ratio avg win/avg loss          2.22    Avg trade (win & loss)      $380.00

Max consecutive winners            4    Max consecutive losers             4
Avg # bars in winners              1    Avg # bars in losers               1

Max closed-out drawdown   $-7,535.00    Max intra-day drawdown    $-7,535.00
Profit factor                   1.70    Max # of contracts held            1
Account size required     $29,535.00    Return on account                38%
```

Highlights - Short trades

Description	Date	Time	Amount
Largest Winning Trade	01/23/90	-	$ 5,820.00
Largest Losing Trade	12/24/91	-	$ -6,455.00
Largest String of + Trades	01/19/88	-	4
Largest String of - Trades	06/06/84	-	4
Maximum Closed-Out Drawdown	03/19/92	-	$ -7,535.00
Maximum Intra-Day Drawdown	03/19/92	-	$ -7,535.00

```
\\\\\\\\\\\\\\\\\\\\\\\\\\\\\\\\\\\\\\\\\\\\\\//////////////////////////////////
```

Prepared using System Writer Plus Version 2.18 by Omega Research, Inc.

Figure 9.11—JK OEX Option Buyer (continued)

```
OEX OPTION BUY   06/25/82 to 06/30/93        F:\PA\
OSP(1)   22000
=================================================================
Total net profit          54,975.00   <    84,975.00>   -27,865.00
Gross profit              82,840.00        Gross loss

Total # of trades                55        Percent profitable        58%
Number winning trades            32        Number losing trades       23

Largest winning trade      6,795.00        Largest losing trade   -6,455.00
Average winning trade      2,588.75        Average losing trade   -1,211.52
Ratio avg win/avg loss         2.14        Avg trade (win & loss)   999.55

Max consecutive winners           6        Max consecutive losers       3
Avg # bars in winners             7        Avg # bars in losers         4

Max drawdown               8,905.00        Avg # of contracts held      1
Profit factor                  1.24        Max # of contracts held      1
Account size required     30,905.00        Return on account         178%
=================================================================
```

Figure 9.11
JK OEX Option Buyer (continued)

PORTFOLIO ANALYZER QUARTLY REPORT for OEX OPTION BUY

DATE	OPEN EQUITY	CLOSED EQUITY	TOTAL EQUITY	MAX DRAWDOWN	% DD	% CHNG TOT EQ	NUM TRADE
820625	0.00	30000.00	30000.00	0.00	0.0	0.0	0
820630	0.00	30000.00	30000.00	0.00	0.0	0.0	0
820930	0.00	32520.00	32520.00	0.00	0.0	'8.4	0
821231	0.00	38785.00	38785.00	1875.00	6.2	19.3	0
830331	0.00	40075.00	40075.00	1875.00	6.2	3.3	0
830630	0.00	40245.00	40245.00	1875.00	6.2	0.4	0
830930	0.00	40660.00	40660.00	1875.00	6.2	1.0	0
831230	0.00	42650.00	42650.00	1875.00	6.2	4.9	0
840330	125.00	42650.00	42775.00	1875.00	6.2	0.3	1
840629	0.00	39865.00	39865.00	2815.00	9.4	-6.8	0
840928	0.00	41105.00	41105.00	3970.00	13.2	3.1	0
841231	0.00	39820.00	39820.00	4225.00	14.1	-3.1	0
850329	0.00	39820.00	39820.00	4225.00	14.1	0.0	0
850628	0.00	39790.00	39790.00	4225.00	14.1	-0.1	0
850930	0.00	39790.00	39790.00	4225.00	14.1	0.0	0
851231	0.00	45055.00	45055.00	4225.00	14.1	13.2	0
860331	0.00	45055.00	45055.00	4225.00	14.1	0.0	0
860630	0.00	46350.00	46350.00	4225.00	14.1	2.9	0
860930	0.00	46350.00	46350.00	4225.00	14.1	0.0	0
861231	0.00	51245.00	51245.00	4225.00	14.1	10.6	0
870331	625.00	51245.00	51870.00	4225.00	14.1	1.2	1
870630	0.00	51900.00	51900.00	4225.00	14.1	0.1	0
870930	0.00	51900.00	51900.00	4225.00	14.1	0.0	0
871231	-325.00	65360.00	65035.00	5200.00	14.7	25.3	1
880331	0.00	68945.00	68945.00	5200.00	13.3	6.0	0
880630	2400.00	70490.00	72890.00	5200.00	12.8	5.7	1
880930	0.00	71535.00	71535.00	5200.00	12.5	-1.9	0
881230	0.00	75030.00	75030.00	5200.00	11.5	4.9	0
890331	1375.00	75050.00	76425.00	5200.00	11.5	1.9	1
890630	0.00	76720.00	76720.00	5200.00	11.1	0.4	0
890929	0.00	76720.00	76720.00	5200.00	11.1	0.0	0
891229	0.00	76040.00	76040.00	5200.00	11.1	-0.9	0
900330	0.00	81860.00	81860.00	5200.00	10.0	7.7	0
900629	0.00	85630.00	85630.00	5200.00	9.3	4.6	0
900928	0.00	84050.00	84050.00	5200.00	9.3	-1.8	0
901231	0.00	89360.00	89360.00	5200.00	8.6	6.3	0
910329	0.00	89360.00	89360.00	5200.00	8.6	0.0	0
910628	0.00	87875.00	87875.00	6055.00	10.0	-1.7	0
910930	0.00	91620.00	91620.00	6055.00	9.8	4.3	0
911231	0.00	85885.00	85885.00	6455.00	10.4	-6.3	0
920331	0.00	85480.00	85480.00	6860.00	11.0	-0.5	0
920630	0.00	90770.00	90770.00	6860.00	11.0	6.2	0
920930	0.00	90770.00	90770.00	6860.00	11.0	0.0	0
921231	0.00	90215.00	90215.00	6860.00	11.0	-0.6	0
930331	1600.00	88430.00	90030.00	8905.00	14.3	-0.2	1
930630	0.00	84975.00	84975.00	8905.00	14.3	-5.6	0

Figure 9.11—JK OEX Option Buyer (continued)

PORTFOLIO ANALYZER YEARLY REPORT for OEX OPTION BUY

DATE	OPEN EQUITY	CLOSED EQUITY	TOTAL EQUITY	MAX DRAWDOWN	% DD	% CHNG TOT EQ	NUM TRADE
820625	0.00	30000.00	30000.00	0.00	0.0	0.0	0
821231	0.00	38785.00	38785.00	1875.00	6.2	29.3	0
831230	0.00	42650.00	42650.00	1875.00	6.2	10.0	0
841231	0.00	39820.00	39820.00	4225.00	14.1	-6.6	0
851231	0.00	45055.00	45055.00	4225.00	14.1	13.1	0
861231	0.00	51245.00	51245.00	4225.00	14.1	13.7	0
871231	-325.00	65360.00	65035.00	5200.00	14.7	26.9	
881230	0.00	75030.00	75030.00	5200.00	11.5	15.4	
891229	0.00	76040.00	76040.00	5200.00	11.1	1.3	
901231	0.00	89360.00	89360.00	5200.00	8.6	17.5	
911231	0.00	85885.00	85885.00	6455.00	10.4	-3.9	
921231	0.00	90215.00	90215.00	6860.00	11.0	5.0	0
930630	0.00	84975.00	84975.00	8905.00	14.3	-5.8	0

Figure 9.11—JK OEX Option Buyer (continued)

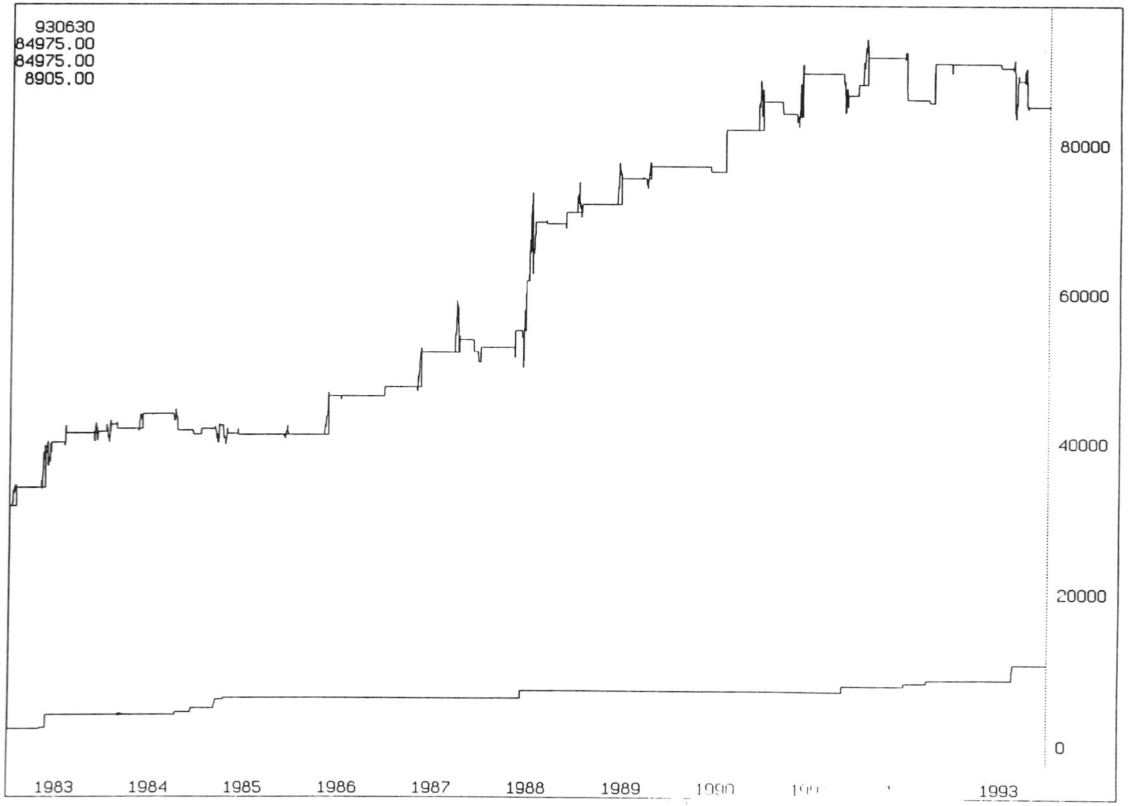

Figure 9.11
JK OEX Option Buyer (continued)

```
///////////////////////////////////////////\\\\\\\\\\\\\\\\\\\\\\\\\\\\\\\\\\\
Directory : F:\JKTOOL                    |  Printed on    : 10/25/93 09:55am
                              ENTRY SIGNAL

Signal Name    : OEX Option Buyer        Developer    : Krutsinger
Notes :

Last Update : 08/19/92 02:55pm
Long  Entry Verified : YES
Short Entry Verified : YES

//////////////////////////////// LONG ENTRY \\\\\\\\\\\\\\\\\\\\\\\\\\\\\\\\\\

If V < @Average(V,5) and H < L(1) then Buy Tomorrow at Market;


//////////////////////////////// SHORT ENTRY \\\\\\\\\\\\\\\\\\\\\\\\\\\\\\\\\

If V < @Average(V,5) and L > H(1) then Sell Tomorrow at Market;


//////////////////////////// VARIABLE DESCRIPTION \\\\\\\\\\\\\\\\\\\\\\\\\\\\\

No variables used in entry signal.

//////////////////////////// MODELS USING SIGNAL \\\\\\\\\\\\\\\\\\\\\\\\\\\\\

Model Name                 Developer         Last Update
-----------------------------------------------------------------------------
JK OEX Option Buyer        Krutsinger        09/10/93 09:48am
OEX Tester                 Krutsinger        09/15/93 09:11pm

\\\\\\\\\\\\\\\\\\\\\\\\\\\\\\\\\\\\\\\\\\\\\\/////////////////////////////////

Prepared using System Writer Plus Version 2.18 by Omega Research, Inc.
```

Figure 9.11
JK OEX Option Buyer (continued)

```
//////////////////////////////////////////////\\\\\\\\\\\\\\\\\\\\\\\\\\\\\\\\\\\\\
Directory : F:\JKTOOL                        Printed on   : 10/25/93 09:56am

                              EXIT SIGNAL

Signal Name      : Exit On Close Variety       Developer  : Krutsinger
Notes : Exit all open positions on close of nth day in trade.

Last Update : 08/19/92 03:14pm
Long  Exit  Verified : YES
Short Exit  Verified : YES

///////////////////////////////// LONG EXIT \\\\\\\\\\\\\\\\\\\\\\\\\\\\\\\\

{ Exit on close of nth day }

If BarsSinceEntry = VarA - 1 then exit long tomorrow on the close;



///////////////////////////////// SHORT EXIT \\\\\\\\\\\\\\\\\\\\\\\\\\\\\\\\\

{ Exit on close of nth day }

If BarsSinceEntry = VarB - 1 then exit short tomorrow on the close;


////////////////////////// VARIABLE DESCRIPTION \\\\\\\\\\\\\\\\\\\\\\\\\\\\\\

Name Used Default Notes
--------------------------------------------------------------   -------------
VarA   L    7   4    Day number after entry on which to exit.
VarB   S    3   1
VarC            1
VarD            1
VarE            1
VarF            1
VarG            1
VarH            1
VarI            1
VarJ            1

/////////////////////////// MODELS USING SIGNAL \\\\\\\\\\\\\\\\\\\\\\\\\\\\\\

Model Name                 Developer          Last Update
-----------------------------------------------------------------------------
JK OEX Option Buyer        Krutsinger         09/10/93 09:48am

\\\\\\\\\\\\\\\\\\\\\\\\\\\\\\\\\\\\\\\\\//////////////////////////////////////
```

Prepared using System Writer Plus Version 2.18 by Omega Research, Inc.

Figure 9.12
Fib Catcher

```
////////////////////////////////////////////\\\\\\\\\\\\\\\\\\\\\\\\\\\\\\\\\\\\\
Directory : F:\JKTOOL                          Printed on    : 09/10/93 10:07am
                          PERFORMANCE SUMMARY

Model Name      : Fib Catcher             Developer      : Krutsinger
Test Number     :       1 of      1
Notes : Try on Call Options-holds 21 days and exits-no stops on futures

Data            : S&P INDEX        06/93
Calc Dates      : 06/25/82 - 06/30/93

 Num. Conv. P. Value  Comm  Slippage  Margin  Format  Drive:\Path\FileName
 ------------------------------------------------------------------------
  149    2  $   5.000  $ 55  $  0    $ 22,000  Omega   F:\20DATA06\F002.DTA

/////////////////////////// ALL TRADES  - Test 1 \\\\\\\\\\\\\\\\\\\\\\\\\\\\\\\

Total net profit        $80,605.00
Gross profit            $103,635.00    Gross loss              $-23,030.00

Total # of trades            39        Percent profitable           71%
Number winning trades        28        Number losing trades         11

Largest winning trade   $18,570.00     Largest losing trade     $-5,580.00
Average winning trade    $3,701.25     Average losing trade     $-2,093.64
Ratio avg win/avg loss        1.76     Avg trade (win & loss)    $2,066.79

Max consecutive winners       6        Max consecutive losers        2
Avg # bars in winners        17        Avg # bars in losers         17

Max closed-out drawdown $-5,580.00     Max intra-day drawdown   $-8,005.00
Profit factor                 4.50     Max # of contracts held       1
Account size required   $30,005.00     Return on account           268%

                    Highlights - All trades
        Description                Date      Time     Amount
        ---------------------------------------------------------
        Largest Winning Trade     01/03/92    -   $   18,570.00,
        Largest Losing Trade      05/03/83    -   $   -5,580.00
        Largest String of + Trades 05/06/92   -           6
        Largest String of - Trades 01/29/93   -           2
        Maximum Closed-Out Drawdown 05/03/83  -   $   -5,580.00
        Maximum Intra-Day Drawdown 06/08/83   -   $   -8,005.00

/////////////////////////// LONG TRADES  - Test 1 \\\\\\\\\\\\\\\\\\\\\\\\\\\\\\\

Total net profit        $50,305.00
Gross profit            $54,970.00     Gross loss               $-4,665.00

Total # of trades            14        Percent profitable           78%
Number winning trades        11        Number losing trades          3

Largest winning trade   $18,570.00     Largest losing trade     $-2,805.00
Average winning trade    $4,997.27     Average losing trade     $-1,555.00
Ratio avg win/avg loss        3.21     Avg trade (win & loss)    $3,593.21

Max consecutive winners       7        Max consecutive losers        1
Avg # bars in winners        17        Avg # bars in losers         21
```

Figure 9.12—Fib Catcher (continued)

```
FIB CATCHER      06/25/82 to 06/30/93        F:\PA\
SPF(1)  22000
=================================================================
Total net profit      80,605.00    < 110,605.00>
Gross profit'        103,635.00      Gross loss         -23,030.00

Total # of trades           39      Percent profitable        72%
Number winning trades       28      Number losing trades       11

Largest winning trade   18,570.00   Largest losing trade   -5,580.00
Average winning trade    3,701.25   Average losing trade   -2,093.64
Ratio avg win/avg loss       1.77   Avg trade (win & loss)  2,066.75

Max consecutive winners      6      Max consecutive losers      2
Avg # bars in winners       17      Avg # bars in losers       18

Max drawdown             8,005.C0   Avg # of contracts held     1
Profit factor                1.27   Max # of contracts held     1
Account size required   30,005.00   Return on account         269%
=================================================================
```

Figure 9.12
Fib Catcher (continued)

```
////////////////////////////////////////\\\\\\\\\\\\\\\\\\\\\\\\\\\\\\\\\\\\\\\
Directory : F:\JKTOOL                         Printed on    : 09/10/93 10:08am

                              ENTRY SIGNAL

Signal Name      : JK Fib Cycles           Developer     : Krutsinger
Notes : Currency daily long side only

Last Update : 09/10/93 09:58am
Long  Entry Verified : YES
Short Entry Verified : YES

/////////////////////////////// LONG ENTRY \\\\\\\\\\\\\\\\\\\\\\\\\\\\\\.

If Low of Today < @Lowest(L,13,1) then buy tomorrow at @Highest(H,3,1) stop

/////////////////////////////// SHORT ENTRY \\\\\\\\\\\\\\\\\\\\\\\\\\\\\\\

If High of Today > @Highest(H,13,1) then Sell tomorrow at @Lowest(L,3,1) stop

/////////////////////////// VARIABLE DESCRIPTION \\\\\\\\\\\\\\\\\\\\\\\\\\\

No variables used in entry signal.

/////////////////////////// MODELS USING SIGNAL \\\\\\\\\\\\\\\\\\\\\\\\\\\\

Model Name                  Developer          Last Update
------------------------------------------------------------------------
Fib Catcher                 Krutsinger         09/10/93 10:06am

\\\\\\\\\\\\\\\\\\\\\\\\\\\\\\\\\\\\\\\\\\//////////////////////////////////////

Prepared using System Writer Plus Version 2.18 by Omega Research, Inc.
```

Figure 9.12
Fib Catcher (continued)

```
//////////////////////////////////////////////////\\\\\\\\\\\\\\\\\\\\\\\\\\\\\\\\\\\\\\\
Directory : F:\JKTOOL                          Printed on   : 09/10/93 10:08am

                              EXIT SIGNAL

Signal Name      : Exit on close of nth day     Developer  : Omega
Notes : Exit all open positions on close of nth day in trade.

Last Update : 03/16/89 08:24am
Long  Exit  Verified : YES
Short Exit  Verified : YES

//////////////////////////////// LONG EXIT \\\\\\\\\\\\\\\\\\\\\\\\\\\\\\\\\\\

{ Exit on close of nth day }

If BarsSinceEntry = VarA - 1 then exit long tomorrow on the close;


//////////////////////////////// SHORT EXIT \\\\\\\\\\\\\\\\\\\\\\\\\\\\\\\\\\\

{ Exit on close of nth day }

If BarsSinceEntry = VarA - 1 then exit short tomorrow on the close;


/////////////////////////// VARIABLE DESCRIPTION \\\\\\\\\\\\\\\\\\\\\\\\\\\\\\

Name Used Default Notes
-----------------------------------------------------------------------------
VarA   LS    4    Day number after entry on which to exit.   (16)
VarB         1
VarC         1
VarD         1
VarE         1
VarF         1
VarG         1
VarH         1
VarI         1
VarJ         1

/////////////////////////// MODELS USING SIGNAL \\\\\\\\\\\\\\\\\\\\\\\\\\\\\\

Model Name                 Developer           Last Update
-----------------------------------------------------------------------------
Fib Catcher                Krutsinger          09/10/93 10:06am

\\\\\\\\\\\\\\\\\\\\\\\\\\\\\\\\\\\\\\\\\\\\\\\//////////////////////////////////////////

Prepared using System Writer Plus Version 2.18 by Omega Research, Inc.
```

Figure 9.12
Fib Catcher (continued)

```
Max closed-out drawdown   $-2,805.00   Max intra-day drawdown      $-7,175.00
Profit factor                  11.78   Max # of contracts held               1
Account size required     $29,175.00   Return on account                  172%
```

```
                        Highlights - Long trades
         Description                Date      Time      Amount
         ----------------------------------------------------------------
         Largest Winning Trade      01/03/92    -    $   18,570.00
         Largest Losing Trade       10/30/90    -    $   -2,805.00
         Largest String of + Trades 10/11/89    -             7
         Largest String of - Trades 06/21/93    -             1
         Maximum Closed-Out Drawdown 10/30/90   -    $   -2,805.00
         Maximum Intra-Day Drawdown 10/11/90    -    $   -7,175.00
```

//////////////////////////// SHORT TRADES - Test 1 \\\\\\\\\\\\\\\\\\\\\\\\\\\\\

```
Total net profit         $30,300.00
Gross profit             $48,665.00   Gross loss             $-18,365.00

Total # of trades                25   Percent profitable             68%
Number winning trades            17   Number losing trades             8

Largest winning trade    $10,870.00   Largest losing trade    $-5,580.00
Average winning trade     $2,862.65   Average losing trade    $-2,295.62
Ratio avg win/avg loss         1.24   Avg trade (win & loss)   $1,212.00

Max consecutive winners           5   Max consecutive losers            2
Avg # bars in winners            17   Avg # bars in losers             16

Max closed-out drawdown  $-5,580.00   Max intra-day drawdown  $-7,380.00
Profit factor                  2.64   Max # of contracts held           1
Account size required    $29,380.00   Return on account              103%
```

```
                        Highlights - Short trades
         Description                Date      Time      Amount
         ----------------------------------------------------------------
         Largest Winning Trade      11/09/89    -    $   10,870.00
         Largest Losing Trade       05/03/83    -    $   -5,580.00
         Largest String of + Trades 04/06/92    -             5
         Largest String of - Trades 01/29/93    -             2
         Maximum Closed-Out Drawdown 05/03/83   -    $   -5,580.00
         Maximum Intra-Day Drawdown 03/17/88    -    $   -7,380.00
```

\\\//////////////////////////////////////

Prepared using System Writer Plus Version 2.18 by Omega Research, Inc.

Figure 9.12—Fib Catcher (continued)

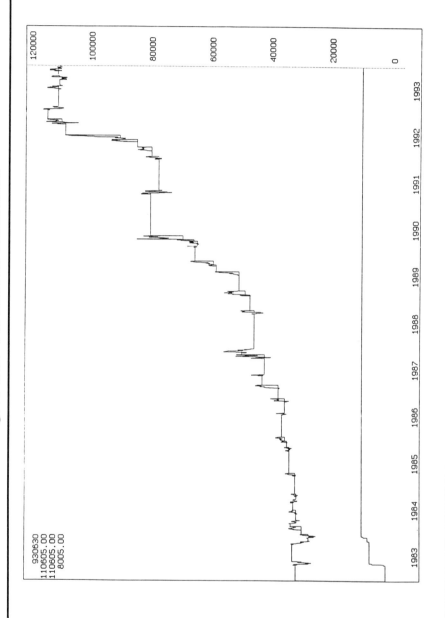

Figure 9.12
Fib Catcher (continued)

PORTFOLIO ANALYZER QUARTERLY REPORT for FIB CATCHER

DATE	OPEN EQUITY	CLOSED EQUITY	TOTAL EQUITY	MAX DRAWDOWN	% DD	% CHNG TOT EQ	NUM TRADE
820625	0.00	30000.00	30000.00	0.00	0.0	0.0	0
820630	0.00	30000.00	30000.00	0.00	0.0	0.0	0
820930	0.00	30000.00	30000.00	0.00	0.0	0.0	0
821231	0.00	31220.00	31220.00	5350.00	17.8	4.1	0
830331	0.00	31220.00	31220.00	5350.00	17.8	0.0	0
830630	0.00	27985.00	27985.00	8005.00	26.7	-10.4	
830930	-425.00	31805.00	31380.00	8005.00	26.7	12.1	
831230	0.00	30895.00	30895.00	8005.00	26.7	-1.5	
840330	0.00	29815.00	29815.00	8005.00	26.7	-3.5	
840629	0.00	30260.00	30260.00	8005.00	26.7	1.5	
840928	525.00	30260.00	30785.00	8005.00	26.7	1.7	
841231	0.00	32280.00	32280.00	8005.00	26.7	4.9	
850329	0.00	32280.00	32280.00	8005.00	26.7	0.0	
850628	1125.00	33820.00	34945.00	8005.00	26.7	8.3	
850930	0.00	34840.00	34840.00	8005.00	26.7	-0.3	
851231	0.00	34840.00	34840.00	8005.00	26.7	0.0	
860331	0.00	33910.00	33910.00	8005.00	26.7	-2.7	
860630	0.00	36055.00	36055.00	8005.00	26.7	6.3	
860930	0.00	41625.00	41625.00	8005.00	26.7	15.4	
861231	0.00	40895.00	40895.00	8005.00	26.7	-1.8	0
870331	4175.00	40895.00	45070.00	8005.00	26.7	10.2	1
870630	0.00	44485.00	44485.00	8005.00	26.7	-1.3	0
870930	0.00	44485.00	44485.00	8005.00	26.7	0.0	0
871231	0.00	44485.00	44485.00	8005.00	26.7	0.0	0
880331	3500.00	44485.00	47985.00	8005.00	26.7	7.9	1
880630	0.00	45955.00	45955.00	8005.00	26.7	-4.2	0
880930	0.00	49695.00	49695.00	8005.00	26.7	8.1	0
881230	0.00	49695.00	49695.00	8005.00	26.7	0.0	0
890331	975.00	58385.00	59360.00	8005.00	26.7	19.4	1
890630	0.00	64805.00	64805.00	8005.00	23.0	9.2	0
890929	150.00	65120.00	65270.00	8005.00	22.8	0.7	1
891229	0.00	79760.00	79760.00	8005.00	16.1	22.2	0
900330	0.00	79760.00	79760.00	8005.00	16.1	0.0	0
900629	0.00	79760.00	79760.00	8005.00	16.1	0.0	0
900928	0.00	79760.00	79760.00	8005.00	16.1	0.0	0
901231	0.00	76955.00	76955.00	8005.00	16.1	-3.5	0
910329	0.00	76955.00	76955.00	8005.00	16.1	0.0	0
910628	0.00	76955.00	76955.00	8005.00	16.1	0.0	0
910930	2725.00	79375.00	82100.00	8005.00	16.1	6.7	1
911231	17600.00	90090.00	107690.00	8005.00	13.3	31.2	1
920331	2500.00	108660.00	111160.00	8005.00	10.2	3.2	1
920630	0.00	114950.00	114950.00	8005.00	9.4	3.4	0
920930	0.00	111245.00	111245.00	8005.00	9.4	-3.2	0
921231	-25.00	111245.00	111220.00	8005.00	9.4	-0.0	1
930331	-2475.00	110865.00	108390.00	8005.00	9.4	-2.5	1
930630	0.00	110605.00	110605.00	8005.00	9.4	2.0	0

Figure 9.12—Fib Catcher (continued)

PORTFOLIO ANALYZER YEARLY REPORT for FIB CATCHER

DATE	OPEN EQUITY	CLOSED EQUITY	TOTAL EQUITY	MAX DRAWDOWN	% DD	% CHNG TOT EQ	NUM TRADE
820625	0.00	30000.00	30000.00	0.00	0.0	0.0	0
821231	0.00	31220.00	31220.00	5350.00	17.8	4.1	0
831230	0.00	30895.00	30895.00	8005.00	26.7	-1.0	0
841231	0.00	32280.00	32280.00	8005.00	26.7	4.5	0
851231	0.00	34840.00	34840.00	8005.00	26.7	7.9	0
861231	0.00	40895.00	40895.00	8005.00	26.7	17.4	0
871231	0.00	44485.00	44485.00	8005.00	26.7	8.8	0
881230	0.00	49695.00	49695.00	8005.00	26.7	11.7	0
891229	0.00	79760.00	79760.00	8005.00	16.1	60.5	0
901231	0.00	76955.00	76955.00	8005.00	16.1	-3.5	0
911231	17600.00	90090.00	107690.00	8005.00	13.3	39.9	1
921231	-25.00	111245.00	111220.00	8005.00	9.4	3.3	1
930630	0.00	110605.00	110605.00	8005.00	9.4	-0.6	0

Figure 9.13
Joe's Test Pattern

```
Joe's Test Pattern  BP E92-180 min    01/02/92 - 12/31/92
                       Performance Summary:  All Trades

Total net profit      $  24803.75   Open position P/L    $      0.00
Gross profit          $  39102.50   Gross loss           $ -14298.75

Total # of trades           88      Percent profitable         42%
Number winning trades       37      Number losing trades       51

Largest winning trade $   8945.00   Largest losing trade $  -2005.00
Average winning trade $   1056.82   Average losing trade $   -280.37
Ratio avg win/avg loss      3.77    Avg trade(win & loss)$    281.86

Max consec. winners          4      Max consec. losers          6
Avg # bars in winners       10      Avg # bars in losers        1

Max intraday drawdown $  -3155.00
Profit factor               2.73    Max # contracts held        1
Account size required $   6155.00   Return on account         403%
```

```
                       Performance Summary:  Long Trades

Total net profit      $   5860.00   Open position P/L    $      0.00
Gross profit          $  14513.75   Gross loss           $  -8653.75

Total # of trades           48      Percent profitable         44%
Number winning trades       21      Number losing trades       27

Largest winning trade $   4370.00   Largest losing trade $  -2005.00
Average winning trade $    691.13   Average losing trade $   -320.51
Ratio avg win/avg loss      2.16    Avg trade(win & loss)$    122.08

Max consec. winners          4      Max consec. losers          6
Avg # bars in winners       10      Avg # bars in losers        2

Max intraday drawdown $  -3822.50
Profit factor               1.68    Max # contracts held        1
Account size required $   6822.50   Return on account          86%
```

```
                       Performance Summary:  Short Trades

Total net profit      $  18943.75   Open position P/L    $      0.00
Gross profit          $  24588.75   Gross loss           $  -5645.00

Total # of trades           40      Percent profitable         40%
Number winning trades       16      Number losing trades       24

Largest winning trade $   8945.00   Largest losing trade $   -767.50
Average winning trade $   1536.80   Average losing trade $   -235.21
Ratio avg win/avg loss      6.53    Avg trade(win & loss)$    473.59

Max consec. winners          2      Max consec. losers          6
Avg # bars in winners       10      Avg # bars in losers        1

Max intraday drawdown $  -4151.25
Profit factor               4.36    Max # contracts held        1
Account size required $   7151.25   Return on account         265%
```

Figure 9.13
Joe's Test Pattern (continued)

```
//////////////////////////////////////////////\\\\\\\\\\\\\\\\\\\\\\\\\\\\\\\\\\\\\\\\\\\
                                    SYSTEM

Name      : Joe's Test Pattern
Notes : 180 min BP

Last Update : 09/22/92 08:47pm
Printed on  : 09/15/93 07:31pm
Verified    : YES

/////////////////////////////////////////// CODE \\\\\\\\\\\\\\\\\\\\\\\\\\\\\\\\\\\\\\\\

Condition1= C[2] < O[2] and C[4] > O[4] and C[4] > C[2];
Condition2= C[5] > O[2] and C[2] > O[2] and C[2] < C[5];
IF CONDITION1 OR CONDITION2 THEN sell AT LowEST(l,2) STOP;

Condition3= C[2] > O[2] and C[4] < O[4] and C[4] < C[2];
Condition4= C[5] < O[2] and C[2] < O[2] and C[2] > C[5];
IF CONDITION3 OR CONDITION4 THEN buy AT highEST(h,2) STOP;


If BarsSinceEntry>=1 then ExitLong at
EntryPrice + 15 points Stop;

If BarsSinceEntry>=1 then ExitShort at
EntryPrice - 15 points Stop;
```

```
//////////////////////////////////////////////\\\\\\\\\\\\\\\\\\\\\\\\\\\\\\\\\\\\\\\\\\\
Prepared using Omega TradeStation Version 3.01 by Omega Research, Inc.
```

Figure 9.14
Joe's Jesse Livermore

```
Joe-Jesse Livermore  BP E92-180 min   01/02/92 - 12/31/92
                      Performance Summary:  All Trades

Total net profit      $  26220.00   Open position P/L    $      0.00
Gross profit          $  47455.00   Gross loss           $ -21235.00

Total # of trades            51     Percent profitable          37%
Number winning trades        19     Number losing trades         32

Largest winning trade $  15120.00   Largest losing trade $  -1492.50
Average winning trade $   2497.63   Average losing trade $   -663.59
Ratio avg win/avg loss     3.76     Avg trade(win & loss)$    514.12

Max consec. winners           5     Max consec. losers            5
Avg # bars in winners        19     Avg # bars in losers          5

Max intraday drawdown $  -6200.00
Profit factor              2.23     Max # contracts held          1
Account size required $   9200.00   Return on account          285%
```
--- --- --- --- --- --- --- --- --- --- --- --- --- --- ---
```
                      Performance Summary:  Long Trades

Total net profit      $   5822.50   Open position P/L    $      0.00
Gross profit          $  17165.00   Gross loss           $ -11342.50

Total # of trades            28     Percent profitable          43%
Number winning trades        12     Number losing trades         16

Largest winning trade $   4007.50   Largest losing trade $  -1492.50
Average winning trade $   1430.42   Average losing trade $   -708.91
Ratio avg win/avg loss     2.02     Avg trade(win & loss)$    207.95

Max consec. winners           3     Max consec. losers            6
Avg # bars in winners        17     Avg # bars in losers          5

Max intraday drawdown $  -5140.00
Profit factor              1.51     Max # contracts held          1
Account size required $   8140.00   Return on account           72%
```
--- --- --- --- --- --- --- --- --- --- --- --- --- --- ---
```
                      Performance Summary:  Short Trades

Total net profit      $  20397.50   Open position P/L    $      0.00
Gross profit          $  30290.00   Gross loss           $  -9892.50

Total # of trades            23     Percent profitable          30%
Number winning trades         7     Number losing trades         16

Largest winning trade $  15120.00   Largest losing trade $  -1392.50
Average winning trade $   4327.14   Average losing trade $   -618.28
Ratio avg win/avg loss     7.00     Avg trade(win & loss)$    886.85

Max consec. winners           3     Max consec. losers           12
Avg # bars in winners        23     Avg # bars in losers          5

Max intraday drawdown $  -6110.00
Profit factor              3.06     Max # contracts held          1
Account size required $   9110.00   Return on account          224%
```

Figure 9.14
Joe's Jesse Livermore (continued)

```
//////////////////////////////////////////////\\\\\\\\\\\\\\\\\\\\\\\\\\\\\\\\\\\\\\\\\\\\
                                  SYSTEM

Name      : Joe-Jesse Livermore
Notes : Kaufman's CTSM

Last Update : 08/14/92 12:16pm
Printed on  : 09/15/93 07:29pm
Verified    : YES

///////////////////////////////////////// CODE \\\\\\\\\\\\\\\\\\\\\\\\\\\\\\\\\\\\\\\\\\\

If (L < Low[1] and H > H[1]) then Sell at Lowest(1,2)[1] stop;
ExitShort at Highest(h,8)[1] stop;

If (L < Low[1] and H > H[1]) then Buy at Highest(h,2)[1] stop;
ExitLong at Lowest(1,8)[1] stop;

{2,8}
{3,5 DT}
{H<H(1)}
{Pg.208 Kaufman- with tune by Joe-Use on daily currency,
$500 stop-$59 rate- about 25 trades per year, over $600 per avg.
trade, great for options-holds losers short time}
{
{Rule 1
If time = (Sess1EndTime-40) and
OpenPositionProfit < 150 then exitlong at market;
If time = (Sess1EndTime-40) and
OpenPositionProfit < 150 then exitShort at market;

{Rule2}
If barssinceentry> 12 then exitlong at market;
If barssinceentry> 12 then exitShort at market;
}

{Rule3}
If BarsSinceEntry>=1 then ExitLong at
EntryPrice + 15 points Stop;

If BarsSinceEntry>=1 then ExitShort at
EntryPrice - 15 points Stop;

{Rule1- use as your 'should I hold another day or get out rule'-
45 minutes before close, and your profit is less than $150 exit,
otherwise hold on . Change 45 min. and 150 as you choose.}

{Rule2- Use with indicators, once they "lose their gas". Length
should be at least half of base indicator-e.g. 20 ma= 10 barssincentry}

Rule3- This rule is a great risk reducer for Day trading systems,
in that it reduces to a riskless trade after a short time}




//////////////////////////////////////////////\\\\\\\\\\\\\\\\\\\\\\\\\\\\\\\\\\\\\\\\\\\\
Prepared using Omega TradeStation Version 3.01 by Omega Research, Inc.
```

Figures 9.15a and 9.15b
Joe's Texas Two Step

```
Joe's Texas Two Step  BP E92-180 min   01/02/92 - 12/31/92
```

Performance Summary: All Trades

Total net profit	$ 30302.50	Open position P/L	$ 25.00
Gross profit	$ 45585.00	Gross loss	$ -15282.50
Total # of trades	22	Percent profitable	36%
Number winning trades	8	Number losing trades	14
Largest winning trade	$ 14782.50	Largest losing trade	$ -1605.00
Average winning trade	$ 5698.13	Average losing trade	$ -1091.61
Ratio avg win/avg loss	5.22	Avg trade(win & loss)	$ 1377.39
Max consec. winners	4	Max consec. losers	5
Avg # bars in winners	54	Avg # bars in losers	11
Max intraday drawdown	$ -6050.00		
Profit factor	2.98	Max # contracts held	1
Account size required	$ 9050.00	Return on account	335%

Performance Summary: Long Trades

Total net profit	$ 8470.00	Open position P/L	$ 0.00
Gross profit	$ 15867.50	Gross loss	$ -7397.50
Total # of trades	11	Percent profitable	36%
Number winning trades	4	Number losing trades	7
Largest winning trade	$ 7170.00	Largest losing trade	$ -1605.00
Average winning trade	$ 3966.88	Average losing trade	$ -1056.79
Ratio avg win/avg loss	3.75	Avg trade(win & loss)	$ 770.00
Max consec. winners	2	Max consec. losers	3
Avg # bars in winners	60	Avg # bars in losers	14
Max intraday drawdown	$ -3915.00		
Profit factor	2.14	Max # contracts held	1
Account size required	$ 6915.00	Return on account	122%

Performance Summary: Short Trades

Total net profit	$ 21832.50	Open position P/L	$ 25.00
Gross profit	$ 29717.50	Gross loss	$ -7885.00
Total # of trades	11	Percent profitable	36%
Number winning trades	4	Number losing trades	7
Largest winning trade	$ 14782.50	Largest losing trade	$ -1330.00
Average winning trade	$ 7429.38	Average losing trade	$ -1126.43
Ratio avg win/avg loss	6.60	Avg trade(win & loss)	$ 1984.77
Max consec. winners	2	Max consec. losers	5
Avg # bars in winners	48	Avg # bars in losers	8
Max intraday drawdown	$ -5575.00		
Profit factor	3.77	Max # contracts held	1
Account size required	$ 8575.00	Return on account	255%

Figure 9.15a
Joe's Texas Two Step

```
////////////////////////////////////////////////\\\\\\\\\\\\\\\\\\\\\\\\\\\\\\\\\\\
                                 SYSTEM

Name       : Joe's Texas Two Step
Notes :

Last Update : 09/01/93 10:23pm
Printed on  : 09/15/93 07:27pm
Verified    : YES

//////////////////////////////////////// CODE \\\\\\\\\\\\\\\\\\\\\\\\\\\\\\\\\\\\\\

{System:  Joe's Texas Two Step-Daily or 180 min. B. Pound 1 car
 Notes:   Intermediate term system with one contract only,$1000 stop

WARNING !- I am not advising anyone to trade or use these systems. They are
written only as educational examples of the art of system writing and development
that I want to share with you.

FUTURES TRADING IS A RISKY BUSINESS.
FUTURES TRADERS CAN AND DO LOSE MONEY.

 These materials copyright Joe Krutsinger, 1993.
  All rights reserved.  1-800-767-2508}

{ 180 min. BP or Daily , $5000 Position stop }
{Allow Multiple Entries, Max 20, $5000 stop on total position,
this system illustrates the power of TradeStation by 2 simple
steps with multiple entries checked and a common dollar stop,
regardless of number of contracts in position}


{Note: When used on 180 min. chart, use $5000 Position trailing stop,
TradeStation will signal when to exit}

If  Average(C,8) > xAverage(C,8) and
Average(C,8)[1] < xAverage(C,8)[1]
then  Buy tomorrow at Highest(h,6) stop;


If Average(C,8) < xAverage(C,8) and
Average(C,8)[1] > xAverage(C,8)[1]
then  Sell tomorrow at Lowest(L,6) stop;




////////////////////////////////////////////////\\\\\\\\\\\\\\\\\\\\\\\\\\\\\\\\\\\
Prepared using Omega TradeStation Version 3.01 by Omega Research, Inc.
```

Figure 9.15b
Joe's Texas Two Step

```
Joe's Texas Two Step   BRITISH POUND 06/93-Daily    02/13/75 - 06/30/93

                    Performance Summary:  All Trades

Total net profit      $ 760093.75  Open position P/L    $       0.00
Gross profit          $ 867070.00  Gross loss           $-106976.25

Total # of trades            90    Percent profitable          68%
Number winning trades        61    Number losing trades         29

Largest winning trade $  60601.25  Largest losing trade $  -8405.00
Average winning trade $  14214.26  Average losing trade $  -3688.84
Ratio avg win/avg loss      3.85   Avg trade(win & loss) $  8445.49

Max consec. winners          28    Max consec. losers            5
Avg # bars in winners       203    Avg # bars in losers         38

Max intraday drawdown $ -37498.75
Profit factor                8.11  Max # contracts held         13
Account size required $  46171.25  Return on account         1646%
```

```
                    Performance Summary:   Long Trades

Total net profit      $ 386816.25  Open position P/L    $       0.00
Gross profit          $ 440791.25  Gross loss           $ -53975.00

Total # of trades            48    Percent profitable          69%
Number winning trades        33    Number losing trades         15

Largest winning trade $  44820.00  Largest losing trade $  -6711.25
Average winning trade $  13357.31  Average losing trade $  -3598.33
Ratio avg win/avg loss      3.71   Avg trade(win & loss) $  8058.67

Max consec. winners          14    Max consec. losers            4
Avg # bars in winners       193    Avg # bars in losers         29

Max intraday drawdown $ -21196.25
Profit factor                8.17  Max # contracts held         13
Account size required $  24196.25  Return on account         1599%
```

```
                    Performance Summary:  Short Trades

Total net profit      $ 373277.50  Open position P/L     $       0.00
Gross profit          $ 426278.75  Gross loss            $ -53001.25

Total # of trades            42    Percent profitable          67%
Number winning trades        28    Number losing trades         14

Largest winning trade $  60601.25  Largest losing trade $  -8405.00
Average winning trade $  15224.24  Average losing trade $  -3785.80
Ratio avg win/avg loss      4.02   Avg trade(win & loss) $  8887.56

Max consec. winners          17    Max consec. losers            5
Avg # bars in winners       216    Avg # bars in losers         46

Max intraday drawdown $ -27131.25
Profit factor                8.04  Max # contracts held         10
Account size required $  35566.25  Return on account         1050%
```

Figure 9.16
Yen Again

```
/////////////////////////////////////////////\\\\\\\\\\\\\\\\\\\\\\\\\\\\\\\\\\\
Directory : F:\JKTOOL                          Printed on   : 09/10/93 12:25pm
                          PERFORMANCE SUMMARY

Model Name      : Yen Again              Developer   : Joe
Test Number     :      1 of      1
Notes :

Data            : JAPANESE YEN      06/93
Calc Dates      : 01/11/77 - 06/30/93

 Num. Conv. P. Value  Comm Slippage Margin  Format  Drive:\Path\FileName
 --------------------------------------------------------------------------
  65   2  $ 12.500  $ 55  $  0  $ 3,000  Omega  F:\20DATA06\F011.DTA

/////////////////////////// ALL TRADES  - Test 1 \\\\\\\\\\\\\\\\\\\\\\\\\\\\\

Total net profit        $96,780.00
Gross profit           $130,422.50    Gross loss              $-33,642.50

Total # of trades             54      Percent profitable            42%
Number winning trades         23      Number losing trades           31

Largest winning trade   $20,857.50    Largest losing trade    $-2,630.00
Average winning trade    $5,670.54    Average losing trade    $-1,085.24
Ratio avg win/avg loss        5.22    Avg trade (win & loss)   $1,792.22

Max consecutive winners        4      Max consecutive losers          4
Avg # bars in winners        137      Avg # bars in losers           12

Max closed-out drawdown  $-4,220.00   Max intra-day drawdown  $-4,375.00
Profit factor                 3.87    Max # of contracts held         1
Account size required    $7,375.00    Return on account          1,312%

                     Highlights - All trades
         Description                   Date      Time      Amount
         ----------------------------------------------------------
         Largest Winning Trade       10/24/86    -   '$   20,857.50
         Largest Losing Trade        09/23/85    -    $   -2,630.00
         Largest String of + Trades  07/31/89    -               4
         Largest String of - Trades  01/25/93    -               4
         Maximum Closed-Out Drawdown 12/28/89    -    $   -4,220.00
         Maximum Intra-Day Drawdown  09/11/91    -    $   -4,375.00

/////////////////////////// LONG TRADES  - Test 1 \\\\\\\\\\\\\\\\\\\\\\\\\\\\\

Total net profit        $70,925.00
Gross profit            $88,122.50    Gross loss              $-17,197.50

Total # of trades             30      Percent profitable            43%
Number winning trades         13      Number losing trades           17

Largest winning trade   $20,857.50    Largest losing trade    $-1,230.00
Average winning trade    $6,778.65    Average losing trade    $-1,011.62
Ratio avg win/avg loss        6.70    Avg trade (win & loss)   $2,364.17

Max consecutive winners        5      Max consecutive losers          6
Avg # bars in winners        160      Avg # bars in losers           11
```

Figure 9.16
Yen Again (continued)

```
Max closed-out drawdown   $-6,330.00   Max intra-day drawdown   $-6,342.50
Profit factor                   5.12   Max # of contracts held           1
Account size required     $9,342.50    Return on account              759%
```

```
                     Highlights - Long trades
     Description                  Date      Time      Amount
     -------------------------------------------------------------
     Largest Winning Trade       10/24/86   -    $   20,857.50
     Largest Losing Trade        02/19/91   -    $   -1,230.00
     Largest String of + Trades  01/06/89   -             5
     Largest String of - Trades  08/01/90   -             6
     Maximum Closed-Out Drawdown 08/01/90   -    $   -6,330.00
     Maximum Intra-Day Drawdown  08/30/90   -    $   -6,342.50
```

///////////////////////////// SHORT TRADES - Test 1 \\\\\\\\\\\\\\\\\\\\\\\\\\\\\\

```
Total net profit      $25,855.00
Gross profit          $42,300.00    Gross loss             $-16,445.00

Total # of trades             24    Percent profitable            41%
Number winning trades         10    Number losing trades          14

Largest winning trade  $9,982.50    Largest losing trade   $-2,630.00
Average winning trade  $4,230.00    Average losing trade   $-1,174.64
Ratio avg win/avg loss      3.60    Avg trade (win & loss)  $1,077.29

Max consecutive winners        2    Max consecutive losers          4
Avg # bars in winners        107    Avg # bars in losers           14

Max closed-out drawdown $-5,882.50  Max intra-day drawdown  $-5,882.50
Profit factor                2.57   Max # of contracts held          1
Account size required   $8,882.50   Return on account             291%
```

```
                     Highlights - Short trades
     Description                  Date      Time      Amount
     -------------------------------------------------------------
     Largest Winning Trade       07/31/89   -    $    9,982.50
     Largest Losing Trade        09/23/85   -    $   -2,630.00
     Largest String of + Trades  07/31/89   -             2
     Largest String of - Trades  08/18/87   -             4
     Maximum Closed-Out Drawdown 08/18/87   -    $   -5,882.50
     Maximum Intra-Day Drawdown  08/18/87   -    $   -5,882.50
```

\\//////////////////////////////////////

Prepared using System Writer Plus Version 2.18 by Omega Research, Inc.

Figure 9.16
Yen Again (continued)

```
/////////////////////////////////////////////\\\\\\\\\\\\\\\\\\\\\\\\\\\\\\\\\\\\\
Directory : F:\JKTOOL                          Printed on   : 10/25/93 10:16am

                            TRADING MODEL

Model Name      : Yen Again            Developer    : Joe
Last Update     : 09/10/93 12:25pm
Tests           :        1             Data Files   :         1

Notes :

///////////////////////////// ENTRY SIGNALS \\\\\\\\\\\\\\\\\\\\\\\\\\\\\  \\
```

sTatus	Long	Short	Signal Name	Developer	Tests
1) ON	ON	ON	CBO Yen Again-Fri.Sell	Krutsinger	1

```
--------------------------------- 1 --------------------------------------
        VarA   VarB   VarC   VarD   VarE   VarF   VarG   VarH   VarI   VarJ
Start    30     2
End      30     2
Inc       1     1
```

Notes : Enters market after channel breakout on a closing basis.

```
///////////////////////////// EXIT SIGNALS \\\\\\\\\\\\\\\\\\\\\\\\\\\\\\\\\\\
```

No exit signals selected

```
///////////////////////////// STOPS \\\\\\\\\\\\\\\\\\\\\\\\\\\\\\\\\\\\\\\\
```

	sTatus	Long	Short	Technique	Amount	Days	Tests
1)	ON	ON	ON	Money Management Stop	$ 1,000		1
2)	OFF	OFF	OFF	N Day $ Trailing Stop	$ 0	0	0
3)	OFF	OFF	OFF	N Day % Trailing Stop	0%	0	0
4)	OFF	OFF	OFF	BreakEven Stop - Floor	$ 0		0
5)	OFF	OFF	OFF	Profit Target	$ 0		0

		Amount			Days		
	Start	End	Inc	Start	End	Inc	
1)	1000	1000	500				
2)	0	0	1	0	0	1	
3)	0	0	1	0	0	1	
4)	0	0	1				
5)	0	0	1				

```
///////////////////////////// COMPUTATIONS \\\\\\\\\\\\\\\\\\\\\\\\\\\\\\\\\\\
```

No computations selected.

```
///////////////////////////// CYCLES SELECTED \\\\\\\\\\\\\\\\\\\\\\\\\\\\\\\
```

No cycles selected

```
///////////////////////////// DATA FILES SELECTED \\\\\\\\\\\\\\\\\\\\\\\\\\\\
```

Figure 9.16
Yen Again (continued)

sTatus	Data name	MM/YY	Calculation Dates	Days	data2	data3
1) ON	JAPANESE YEN	06/93	01/11/77 - 06/30/93	6,014	NO	NO

------------------------------------ 1 ------------------------------------

Num.	Conv.	P.	Value	Comm	Slippage	Margin	Format	Drive:\Path\FileName
65	2	$	12.5	$ 55	$ 0	$ 3,000	Omega	F:\20DATA06\F011.DTA

\\///////////////////////////////////////

Prepared using System Writer Plus Version 2.18 by Omega Research, Inc.

CHAPTER 9

Figure 9.16
Yen Again (continued)

```
//////////////////////////////////////////////\\\\\\\\\\\\\\\\\\\\\\\\\\\\\\\\\\\\\\\
Directory : F:\JKTOOL                      Printed on    : 10/25/93 10:16am

                              ENTRY SIGNAL

Signal Name      : CBO Yen Again-Fri.Sell      Developer    : Krutsinger
Notes : Enters market after channel breakout on a closing basis.

Last Update : 11/09/91 03:56am
Long  Entry Verified : YES
Short Entry Verified : YES

////////////////////////////// LONG ENTRY \\\\\\\\\\\\\\\\\\\\\\\\\\\\\\

{ Channel Breakout on Close }

Buy tomorrow at @Highest(High,VarA) + VarB points stop close only;


////////////////////////////// SHORT ENTRY \\\\\\\\\\\\\\\\\\\\\\\\\\\\\\

{ Channel Breakout on Close }
If DayofWeek=4 then
Sell tomorrow at @Lowest(Low,VarA) - VarB points stop close only;


////////////////////////// VARIABLE DESCRIPTION \\\\\\\\\\\\\\\\\\\\\\\\\\

Name Used Default Notes
------------------------------------------------------------------------
VarA  LS     6    Length in price channel in bars for both LEntry and SEntry.
VarB  LS     0    Number of points needed for breakout for both LEntry & SEntry
VarC         1
VarD         1
VarE         1
VarF         1
VarG         1
VarH         1
VarI         1
VarJ         1

/////////////////////////// MODELS USING SIGNAL \\\\\\\\\\\\\\\\\\\\\\\\\\\

Model Name              Developer       Last Update
------------------------------------------------------------------------
Yen Again               Joe             09/10/93 12:25pm

\\\\\\\\\\\\\\\\\\\\\\\\\\\\\\\\\\\\\\\\\\\//////////////////////////////////////

Prepared using System Writer Plus Version 2.18 by Omega Research, Inc.
```

230

Figure 9.16—Yen Again (continued)

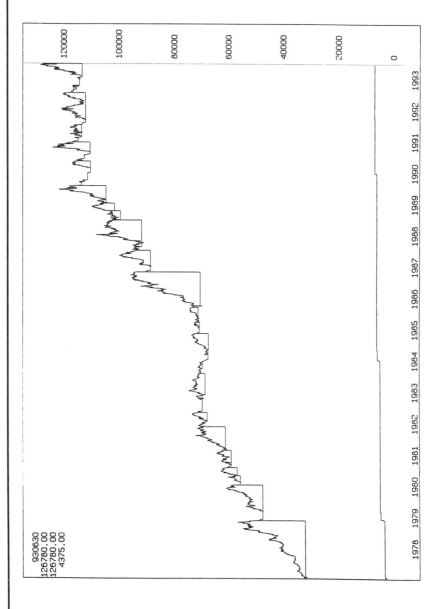

Figure 9.16—Yen Again (continued)

```
YEN AGAIN        01/11/77 to 06/30/93        F:\PA\
JYA(1)   3000
===================================================================
Total net profit      96,780.00    <   126,780.00>    -33,642.50
Gross profit         130,422.50    Gross loss

Total # of trades             54    Percent profitable           43%
Number winning trades         23    Number losing trades          31

Largest winning trade  20,857.50    Largest losing trade   -2,630.00
Average winning trade   5,670.54    Average losing trade   -1,085.24
Ratio avg win/avg loss      5.23    Avg trade (win & loss)  1,792.22

Max consecutive winners        4    Max consecutive losers         4
Avg # bars in winners        138    Avg # bars in losers          13

Max drawdown            4,375.00    Avg # of contracts held        1
Profit factor               2.23    Max # of contracts held        1
Account size required   7,375.00    Return on account          1312%
===================================================================
```

Figure 9.16—Yen Again (continued)

PORTFOLIO ANALYZER YEARLY REPORT for YEN AGAIN

DATE	OPEN EQUITY	CLOSED EQUITY	TOTAL EQUITY	MAX DRAWDOWN	% DD	% CHNG TOT EQ	NUM TRADE
770111	0.00	30000.00	30000.00	0.00	0.0	0.0	0
771230	9287.50	30000.00	39287.50	625.00	2.1	31.0	1
781229	0.00	46010.00	46010.00	2110.00	7.0	17.1	0
791231	11850.00	46010.00	57860.00	2297.50	7.7	25.8	1
801231	4512.50	57785.00	62297.50	2297.50	7.7	7.7	1
811231	700.00	67775.00	68475.00	2297.50	6.1	9.9	1
821231	4850.00	67480.00	72330.00	2297.50	5.8	5.6	1
831230	0.00	67410.00	67410.00	2297.50	5.8	-6.8	1
841231	0.00	69665.00	69665.00	3477.50	8.5	3.3	1
851231	7087.50	69312.50	76400.00	3477.50	8.3	9.7	0
861231	662.50	87972.50	88635.00	3477.50	5.8	16.0	1
871231	16650.00	91237.50	107887.50	3477.50	5.6	21.7	1
881230	4475.00	101240.00	105715.00	3477.50	4.9	-2.0	1
891229	0.00	110147.50	110147.50	4220.00	5.0	4.2	0
901231	87.50	116060.00	116147.50	4220.00	4.9	5.4	1
911231	7587.50	111947.50	119535.00	4375.00	5.1	2.9	1
921231	-150.00	114240.00	114090.00	4375.00	5.0	-4.6	1
930630	0.00	126780.00	126780.00	4375.00	4.5	11.1	0

Figure 9.16—Yen Again (continued)

901231	87.50	116060.00	116147.50	4220.00	4.9	2.0	1
910329	4312.50	113450.00	117762.50	4220.00	4.9	1.4	1
910628	1600.00	113450.00	115050.00	4220.00	4.9	-2.3	1
910930	1300.00	111947.50	113247.50	4375.00	5.1	-1.6	1
911231	7587.50	111947.50	119535.00	4375.00	5.1	5.6	1
920331	1950.00	111947.50	113897.50	4375.00	5.1	-4.7	1
920630	7300.00	111947.50	119247.50	4375.00	5.1	4.7	1
920930	925.00	115295.00	116220.00	4375.00	5.0	-2.5	1
921231	-150.00	114240.00	114090.00	4375.00	5.0	-1.8	1
930331	5625.00	113185.00	118810.00	4375.00	5.0	4.1	1
930630	0.00	126780.00	126780.00	4375.00	4.5	6.7	0

10

The Future of Trading Systems

Today's opportunities erase yesterday's failures.
— Gene Brown —

In this short book we have just touched on a few technical indicators. We have just touched on a few of the traditional ways of trading commodities. The reason we have not spent a lot of time on these factors is that most of the time they do not work. Also, when you are designing a trading system, it really does not make a lot of difference whether you use a 9-day RSI or a 20-day moving average or a 10-day channel breakout. The real key to systems trading in my belief is: Follow the scientific method. Use an entry technique, an exit technique with loss, and an exit technique with profit, and design a system you will really follow in realtime, in the heat of battle.

As we look to the future of trading systems you will hear more and more about the chaos theory, artificial intelligence, neural networks, candlestick charting, and whatever new advance comes around the corner. Let's look at these one at a time. The chaos theory boiled down, in my estimation, is nothing more than a validation of a channel breakout. It is the fact that the markets, although they look like they are unorganized, and they look like they are in chaos, they really are not. You can prove this to yourself if you like, looking back at my Paul Revere system. If the market was a random walk, how could Paul Revere make over $220,000 since the inception of the British Pound contract? You shouldn't be able to do it. The chaos theory is a validation that systems do tend to work.

Artificial intelligence has gotten a lot of play in the last few years. Many people are spending hundreds of thousands of dollars to try to teach their computer to learn over the last 10 or 15 days. My feeling is, I have over 17 years experience in commodities watching every tick of the market. I would rather use my real intelligence than artificial intelligence. Rather than form-fitting a system that worked over the last 10 days, I would rather use my ideas and my observations of different markets to come up with trade ideas and trade them. As artificial intelligence grows, I may change my mind. One of the reasons I may change my mind is that the cost of technology has changed so dramatically. Just three years ago a computer like the one I have on my desk would have cost over $35,000. Now it sells for less than $1,500. The software I have on my desk was not available three years ago at any price. Now, thousands of traders have this software for less than $3,000 apiece. As technological advancements occur, artificial intelligence might become the next wave of the future.

Neural networks are basically an outgrowth of the artificial intelligence movement of 1987 on. Neural networks show a learning curve of a system, having a system learn from its mistakes. To me that is very similar to optimizing every day, finding an indicator that works, and keep optimizing it day after day. Maybe that is the way of the future, but I really do not think so.

If you look back at the systems I introduced in this book, these systems have not been reoptimized and reoptimized and reoptimized after every turn of the market. These systems should and could hold up because of their low degree of optimization.

I believe the real future of systems is the systems you have in your head, the systems you can do with your observations. By using the tools I have given you in this toolkit, your systems will be unique because they are not being done by everybody and his brother, everybody who has a computer. A system you develop yourself is a system that you can actually follow day in, day out. That in itself is a very unusual trading system.

Ready, Set, Go!

I have tried to show you three major areas: (1) The background of trading systems, how I got started, and how I think you should get started with trading systems. (2) Trading systems which I have written, exposing the code, showing you what they are to do. (3) The third part is up to you. I suggest that you steal my code, take some of my trading ideas, combine them with your own, and come up with your own trading system.

An example would be: If you like the idea behind Joe's Gap, but you only want to buy if the moving average is up and the RSI is up and the stochastic is up, then write a trading system that says: "If the moving averages are up and the RSI is up and the stochastic is up, and the language of Joe's Gap is true, then buy." Obviously, the more restrictions you put on trading systems the fewer trades you have.

If you want more trades, another way to use my code is to take some of my systems and put them together and put them all in the same system and link them with the word OR. "If this is true or this is true or this is true, then trade." If you want fewer trades, you can link them with the word AND. "If the moving averages are up and we do a six-day breakout, then buy."

Let me leave you with this final thought. No one likes your money better than you do. No one knows how much risk-taking ability you have more than you do. Ultimately, no one can design a system that you will actually follow that applies to your personality better than you can. If you need some help writing the code, give me a call. I have a 24-hour voice mail number: 800-767-2508. I will be glad to help you as much as I can. Good luck and good trading.

As for the Future, your task is not to foresee,
but to enable it.
—Antoine De Saint-Exupery—

Index

239

INDEX

About the Author

Joe Krutsinger began his futures and options career over 16 years ago with ContiCommodity. He has worked in every facet of the industry and continues to be a prolific developer of trading systems. He develops proprietary trading programs for Robbins and works directly with clients designing custom systems. Joe is an independent consultant to Omega Research, Inc. and teaches traders how to develop systems using Omega's SystemWriter Plus™ and TradeStation™.

He was recognized as the Outstanding Senior in Food Systems, Economics, and Management at Michigan State University in 1973 and is a member of the faculty of the CEI Futures & Options School.

A featured speaker at seminars and meetings worldwide, Joe coauthored the introductory futures textbook *The Commodity Cookbook: Recipes for Success,* and is a contributing author to *High Performance Futures Trading, Lessons from the Master.* (1990 Book of the Year, The 1990 Supertrader's Almanac-Calendar edition).

Joe is president of Krutsinger and Krutsinger, Inc. in Centerville, Iowa, a consulting firm. You can call his 24 hour voice mail at 1-800-767-2508.